Jews and Shoes

Jews and Shoes

Edna Nahshon

Oxford • New York

English edition
First published in 2008 by
Berg
Editorial offices:
First Floor, Angel Court, 81 St Clements Street, Oxford OX4 1AW, UK
175 Fifth Avenue, New York, NY 10010, USA

Berg is the imprint of Oxford International Publishers Ltd.

Library of Congress Cataloging-in-Publication Data

Jews and shoes / [edited by] Edna Nahshon.—English ed.
p. cm.
Includes bibliographical references and index.
ISBN 978-1-84788-049-9 (cloth)
ISBN 978-1-84788-050-5 (pbk.)
1. Shoes—Social aspects.   2. Shoes—Psychological aspects.
3. Clothing and dress—Religious aspects—Judaism.
4. Jews—Material culture.
5. Jews—Folklore.   I. Nahshon, Edna.
GT2130.J49 2008
391.4'13—dc22
2008010698

British Library Cataloguing-in-Publication Data

A catalogue record for this book is available from the British Library.

ISBN 978 1 84788 049 9 (Cloth)
978 1 84788 050 5 (Paper)

Typeset by Apex CoVantage.
Printed in the United Kingdom by Biddles Ltd, King's Lynn

www.bergpublishers.com

To Gadi

CONTENTS

LIST OF ILLUSTRATIONS

ACKNOWLEDGMENTS

It is a pleasure to acknowledge the people and institutions that have helped make this book a reality.

First I wish to thank the contributors to this volume for putting their trust in me and signing on to what seemed at first a madcap scholarly enterprise. I am greatly indebted to Israeli artists Nechama Golan, whose fascinating artwork appears the book cover, and Yosl Bergner, who generously allowed me to reproduce images from his unique "Shoes" series. Many thanks to Hungarian artists Gyula Pauer and Can Togay for sharing images of their Budapest Holocaust shoe memorial and offering a detailed description of its genesis.

I am beholden to the institutions that have financially supported this publication: The American Academy for Jewish Research (AAJR), The Jewish Theological Seminary (JTS), and the Lucius N. Littauer Foundation. I hope that the people representing them in this matter—Professor Michael A. Mayer, Professor Alan Cooper, and Mr. William Lee Frost—are not disappointed with the results.

My colleagues at JTS responded graciously to queries pertaining to their specialized fields. I am particularly indebted to professors Vivian Mann (Jewish art), Joel Roth and David Kraemer (Talmud and Rabbinics), and David Marcus and Sharon Keller (Bible). I also wish to thank Professors Menahem Schmelzer, David Roskies, Eitan Fishbane, and Burton Visotsky for their helpful suggestions. Dr. Rebecca Joseph deserves special kudos for her informed assistance. I always appreciated the helping hand provided by Jeanette Bland, administrative assistant at the JTS faculty office.

Professor Hasia Diner of New York University, Professor Sander L. Gilman of Emory University, and Rickie Burman, Director of the Jewish Museum in London lent their names and publicly endorsed this book. I cherish their vote of confidence.

I am grateful to all the individuals and institutions who granted us permission to use the images included in this volume. I am particularly indebted to two: the YIVO Institute for Jewish Research and the Library of the Jewish Theological Seminary. At YIVO I wish to acknowledge Krysia Fisher, senior photo and film archivist, and Jesse Aaron Cohen, assistant photo and film archivist; at the JTS Library I thank Sharon Lieberman Mintz, curator of Jewish art, and Naomi Steinberger, executive librarian.

Szilvia Dittel of the Holocaust Memorial Center in Budapest, Hungary, Dr. Arno Parik, exhibition curator, the Jewish Museum in Prague, and Efraim Rosenfeld of Yeshivat Mercaz Harav in Jerusalem, went out of their way to respond to my requests and queries. Thank you so much.

I am grateful to Orna Goldman for astute comments. I will always be indebted to Tim Oliver, friend and editor par excellence, and to Irit Sivan, my dear friend since time immemorial.

I wish to recognize the extraordinary professionalism of Hannah Shakespeare, my first editor at Berg Publishers, and of Julia Rosen, project manager at Apex CoVantage. Hannah directed me with caring attentiveness at the proposal stage of this book. Julia oversaw its production with phenomenal patience and goodwill.

Last, but not least, the genesis of this book was the direct outcome of an accidental visit to the Bata Shoe Museum in Toronto. This volume is a tribute to the inspiring and catalyzing power of museums.

Edna Nahshon

1   JEWS AND SHOES

EDNA NAHSHON

Often regarded as no more than humble articles of clothing, shoes, as well as their makers, occupy a special niche in the Jewish closet of memories. They are evoked in tandem with experiences of exile and immigration, and with nostalgia for a lost world of craftsmen and artisans (see Figure 1.1). Above all, shoes have become a metonym for the victims of the Holocaust, their footwear and other personal effects collected by the Nazi killing machine in a gruesome attempt to profit from every last aspect of genocide.

Jewish law, which regulates the life of the individual, including certain specifics of attire, played an important role in the inclusion of shoes in the repertoire of Jewish culture, as did several well-known shoe references in the Bible. And we may add a more poetic reason. Since the day of Abraham, the first of the patriarchs, Jewish history has been punctuated by voluntary and imposed migrations. There is hardly a better metaphor for wandering than the shoe, the most basic external facilitator of human locomotion. It is indeed in this capacity that shoes appear early on in the saga of the ancient Israelites, when on the eve of their mythic journey out of Egypt they are instructed to be prepared with "your shoes on your feet, and your staff in your hand" (Ex. 12:11).[1] These shoes, we are told, did not wear out during the forty years spent in the desert (Deut. 29:5). The existential link between shoes and locomotion was synopsized by Primo Levi, author and Auschwitz survivor, who wrote, "When war is raging, one has to think of two things before all others: in the first place of one's shoes, in the second place of food to eat; and not vice versa, as the common herd

Figure 1.1   Old World Polish Jewish shoemaker. Zdunska Wola, Poland, ca. 2000. Wood. 30 × 12.5 cm. Photographer: Rina Benari, Courtesy of Rivka Parciack, Jerusalem. Wooden statuettes depicting traditional Jewish craftsmen are produced as souvenirs intended for Jewish tourists, many of them visiting Poland on heritage tours. Before World War II Poland had more than three million Jews (10 percent of the total population), many of them of the artisan class.

believes, because he who has shoes can search for food, but the inverse is not true" (Levi 1979, 215).

The association of shoes and corporeal travel reappears in the Bible in the context of the Israelites' conquest of the land of Canaan. The Gibeonites, native inhabitants of the land, deliberately disguise themselves as travelers from a distant land in order to trick the conquering Joshua into signing a binding treaty that would guarantee their future. They point to their shabby appearance as certificates of authenticity for their false identity, explaining, "And these our garments and our shoes are worn by reason of the very long journey" (Josh. 9:13). Although shoes appear some twenty times in the Hebrew Bible, notably in several of its most foundational stories, we have no surviving artifacts or descriptions that offer specific information about their design and materiality. Dictionaries of the Bible inform us that *na'al*, Hebrew for shoe, is used generically as footgear, and there is no way to distinguish different types of shoes from such generalized terminology. Only once does footwear appear under an appellation other than *na'al*, when *se'on*, which refers to the laced boot worn by Assyrian soldiers, is used by the prophet Isaiah (Isa. 9:4) (Ringgren 1977, 465–67). Most scholars agree that the biblical shoe was essentially a sandal with leather or wooden sole, to which leather straps were attached, perhaps threaded through a latchet and then strapped to the foot.

It is noteworthy that while Hebrew employs *na'al* as a general term, in Arabic *na'l* usually indicates the sole of the shoe (Stillman 2000, 21).[2] This meaning emphasizes footwear's primary function of assisting mobility by shielding and separating the foot from the ground. This detachment from direct tactile contact with the earth has led to a whole range of metaphors, from our dominion of the natural world to our estrangement from nature and the promotion of barefootedness as morally uplifting. The romanticism of the latter, hardly shared by the genuinely shoeless denizens of our world, is typically expressed in *The Complete Idiot's Guide to Meditation,* which recommends, "If appropriate…walk barefoot outside. The closer your foot comes to making contact with the earth, the more vivid will be your experience and the earth energy you utilize" (Budilovsky 2003, 183). The primordial connection of the naked or semi-naked foot to the land was an important element in Israel's Zionist pioneer culture.

We can assume that footwear did not remain the same for the well over a millennium during which the events described in the Bible unfolded, that is to say from the time of the patriarchs until the construction of the Second Temple in Jerusalem circa 515 B.C.E. Not only did skills and materials change and improve over this long period, we must also assume that footwear, like garments, was used to advertise status, authority, and wealth. The "Black Obelisk" of Shalmaneser III (858–824 B.C.E.), which offers the oldest available representation of ancient Israelites, includes a scene showing King Jehu of Israel (or possibly his representative) paying homage to the Assyrian king. Jehu and his thirteen Israelite porters are wearing upturned pointed shoes (Pritchard 1969, 291). It may be that the king and courtiers are depicted, as was often the case, in their national garb. This would suggest that a bare-bones sandal may not have been the one and only typical Israelite shoe of the period. The question also arises whether Jehu and his entourage, when engaged in ceremonial and diplomatic duties, wore the same standard footwear used by persons of lower social rank and resources. The dearth of concrete information proved problematic for costume designers such as Salvatore Ferragamo, who in 1923 was commissioned by Cecil B. DeMille to provide 12,000 pairs of sandals for the first film rendition of *The Ten Commandments*. Ferragamo ended up using some Victorian illustrations and his own imagination. This Hollywood work inspired him to create high-heeled sandals that quickly proved popular evening gear in balmy California (Turim 2001, 88 n10).[3]

The Talmud exhorts Jews to wear shoes, so much so that it proclaims that one should even sell the roof beams of his house in order to avoid barefootedness (Shabbat 129a).[4] It is especially demanding when it comes to the appearance of scholars, who, it insists, should always present themselves in clean and proper clothes and avoid worn-out and patched shoes (Berakhot 43b). Judaism even offers a special blessing for putting on shoes that is part of *Birkot Hashachar* (Dawn Blessings), a series of blessings—now incorporated into synagogue morning service—in which people, upon waking in the morning, thank God for their physical bodies and various routine elements of daily life such as walking, dressing, and studying. The blessings were originally meant to be recited as one actually performed the activity for the first time that day: "Blessed be He who has supplied all my needs" was recited as a person was putting on and tying his shoes.

Jewish law even prescribes the order in which one ought to do this: first you put on the right shoe, then the left, you tie the left shoe, and only then, the right, with the order reversed when taking them off. This order was prescribed in the *Shulchan Aruch* (Orach Chayim 2:4), a codification of Jewish law composed by Joseph Karo in the sixteenth century, and considered to this day as a most authoritative source. *Kitzur Shulchan Aruch*, written in 1864, and widely popular as an abridged version of the original, explains:

> …when dressing and in all other actions, we must always give preference to the right (hand or foot) over the left; but when removing shoes and other clothes, one removes that of the left first (for the honour of the right). With regard to (lace) tying, the left is more important, because the *tefillin* [phylacteries: two boxes with Biblical verses and the leather straps attached to them used in prayer] are tied on the left hand. Therefore, when one needs to tie, one ties that on the left first. For example, shoes with laces, we first put on the right (shoe) without lacing it, then we put on the left and lace it, and afterward we lace the right one. (Kitzur Shulchan Aruch I 3:4)

Symbolic meaning has been attached to this prescribed procedure, with one explanation making the case that the priests of the Temple in Jerusalem performed the sacrificial service with their right hand, and thus even the most mundane activities should follow the sacred paradigm. Others equated the two sides of the body with the two aspects of the soul, commenting that because tying represents binding and restraint, and as the right side stands for mercy and kindness, it is the one in particular need of strength and protection and hence should be tied last. Some scholars consider it nothing more than a reflection of the Roman superstition of putting on the right shoe first when dressing (Kolatch 1985, 113).

This prescribed order is also reflected in Islam, where one is to put on the right shoe first and take it off last. Be that as it may, the intriguing correspondence between the upper and lower extremities and between shoes and the leather straps attached to *tefillin* [phylacteries] suggests a deeper significance regarding the human form and its correspondence to the animal world. Noted Israeli poet Yehuda Amichai (1924–2000) draws on this theme in his poem "Sandals":

> Sandals are the skeleton of a whole shoe,
> the skeleton, and its only true spirit.
> Sandals are the reins of my galloping feet
> and the *tefillin* straps
> of a tired foot, praying. (Amichai 1986, 68)

Shoes are mentioned for the first time in the Bible when Abraham, following his victory over the four kings, refuses the booty offered to him by the king of Sodom, exclaiming, "I will not take a thread nor a shoe-latchet nor aught that is thine, lest thou shouldest say: I have made Abram rich" (Gen. 14:23). The text suggests that the straps of the biblical sandal were objects of minimal value, mentioned here for purposes of hyperbole. The Talmud, in turn, connects the thread and latchet mentioned in the story to the imperatives to wear the thread of the *tzitzit* (tassels worn by observant Jews on the corners of four-cornered garments) and the strap of the *tefillin*, suggesting they are a blessing bestowed on Abraham's descendants by virtue of their ancestor's righteousness (Hulin 89a).

The well-known biblical story of the marriage of Ruth, a widowed Moabite, to Boaz, a wealthy Israelite farmer, involves the use of a shoe as formal legal instrument for the acquisition of rights and property:

> Now this was the custom in former time in Israel concerning redeeming and concerning exchanging, to confirm all things: a man drew off his shoe, and gave it to his neighbour; and this was the attestation in Israel. So the near kinsman said unto Boaz: "Buy it for thyself." And he drew off his shoe. And Boaz said unto the elders, and unto all the people: "Ye are witnesses this day, that I have bought all that was Elimelech's, and all that was Chilion's and Mahlon's, of the hand of Naomi. Moreover Ruth the Moabitess, the wife of Mahlon, have I acquired to be my wife, to raise up the name of the dead upon his inheritance, that the name of the dead be not cut off from among his brethren, and from the gate of his place; ye are witnesses this day." And all the people that were in the gate, and the elders, said: "We are witnesses. The Lord make the woman that is come into thy house like Rachel and like Leah, which two did build the house of Israel; and do thou worthily in Ephrath, and be famous in Bethlehem." (Ruth 4:7–11)

Despite the detailed nature of the text it is not clear who removed the shoe; was it the kinsman who then gave it to Boaz or was it Boaz himself? Still, the ceremonial nature of the transaction makes it clear that the shoe was not used as barter in a quid pro quo exchange but in a legal/symbolic capacity. Some scholars, in an effort to better understand the Ruth story, link the shoe scene with an Arab form of divorce in which the male removes his shoe and declares "She [the wife] was my slipper; I have cast her off," and to the Arabic use of *na'l* (shoe) in the sense of "wife of the husband" (Carmichael 1977, 323). The verse "Over Edom I shall throw My shoe" (Ps. 60:8) is explained as possibly reflective of the shoe ritual in taking possession of property.

In an effort to contextualize the woman/ownership/shoe nexus, Jacob Nacht, writing in 1915, cites a shoe ceremony practiced among some of the Jews then living in Palestine where it was customary for the bridegroom to send a shoemaker to the bride's house to prepare shoes for the bride and female family members, this indicating that a date for the wedding had been set (Nacht 1915, 16). The custom also existed among the Jews of Baghdad where it survived into the late nineteenth century. (Goitein 1983, 164). Nacht emphasizes the symbolic nature of this tradition by explaining that little importance was attached to the actual fitting (Nacht 1915, 16). In an attempt to offer Western equivalency to the association of shoes with material acquisition, he cites the decidedly non-Jewish custom, practiced into the nineteenth century, of throwing good luck shoes behind a bridal pair, the shoe representing a wish for material good fortune, a custom later modified to the use of rice (Crombie 1895, 258).

One should not overlook the fact that, regardless of the aforementioned wedding custom, hurling footwear at other persons or their representatives is commonly regarded as an insult. Hitting someone with a shoe is considered one of the most demeaning acts in Arab culture to this day. Hence, it is not surprising that shoes feature in the carnivalesque celebration of Purim, where Haman is the ultimate arch-villain whose name should be obliterated from memory—at least until next year's celebration. Not only are feet stomped so shoes generate noise whenever Haman's name is mentioned during the reading of the story, but some follow the custom of writing his name on the soles of their shoes so that it can literally be wiped out (Rubenstein 1992, 258).

Shoes as commodity are conjured by the prophet Amos, who railed against social transgressors who "sell the righteous for silver, and the needy for a pair of shoes" (Amos 2:6). Robert Gordis dubbed the traditional explication of the verse as the callous willingness of the rich to trade human lives for worthless artifacts "substantially difficult and textually dubious," noting that the idea that the rich would sell the poor for a pair of shoes is excessive and that silver and shoes are not even remotely parallel (Gordis 1979–1980, 213). He suggests instead that the verse alludes to the role played by the biblical shoe as either object or instrument in economic transactions, as is the case in the levirate rite, where a shoe serves in a legal capacity during the *halitzah* ceremony when a man relinquishes his rights over his dead brother's widow. Yet the metaphor of the shoe in exchange for human life was too good to pass up, and so we find rabbinic tales that link the verse with the story of the sale of Joseph by his brothers. Summarizing the story Louis Ginzburg wrote in his *Legends of the Jews,*

> The brethren of Joseph bought shoes for the money [from the sale of Joseph], for they said: "We will not eat it, for it is the price for the blood of our brother, but we will tread

upon him, for that he spake, he would have dominion over us, and we will see what will become of his dreams." (Ginzburg 1956, 18)

Another rabbinic legend tied the brothers' treason to the mythologized death of the ten martyrs murdered by the Roman rulers of Palestine (Stern and Mirsky 1990, 143–46). The fantastic tale involves a Torah-reading Roman emperor who, after acquainting himself with the Joseph brother-for-shoe transaction, plasters his walls with shoes and, in line with a biblical command—"And he that stealeth a man, and selleth him, or if he be found in his hand, he shall surely be put to death" (Ex. 21:16)—executes the ten sages as surrogates for Joseph's brothers, the original perpetrators.

The most famous mention of footwear in the Bible occurs during the scene of the burning bush, when Moses is commanded to "Draw not nigh hither; put off thy shoes from off thy feet, for the place whereon thou standest is holy ground" (Ex. 3:5), a scene discussed elsewhere in this volume. A similar command is issued to Joshua at Gilgal, after the Exodus has come to its official close when the entire nation has been circumcised and has celebrated Passover, eating the fruit of the land, no longer needing the manna that had sustained them in the desert. Faced with a divine messenger, Joshua falls on his face to the ground and asks, "What saith my lord unto his servant?" and is told, "Put off thy shoe from off thy foot; for the place whereon thou standest is holy" (Josh. 5:14–5).

The association of sacred space with barefootedness was reflected in the ministry of the Temple priests (see Figure 1.2). The absence of shoes from the detailed list of priestly vestments leads many scholars to assume that the priests administered with their feet bare, a practice deemed imperative after the destruction of the Temple, when the rabbis pronounced the dictum "wherever the *shechinah* [divine presence] appears one must not go about with shoes on" (Exodus Rabbah 2:6). This custom is reflected in the ceremony of the priestly blessing that is practiced to this date in all Orthodox synagogues. The core ritual consists of the *Kohanim,* that is, men of priestly descent, who, after having washed their hands and removed their shoes, stand on the *bimah,* the synagogue's platform, their heads covered with their prayer shawls, and in dialogic exchange with the cantor recite the three verses of the biblical blessing: "The Lord bless thee, and keep thee; The Lord make His face to shine upon thee, and be gracious unto thee; The Lord lift up His countenance upon thee, and give thee peace" (Num 6:24–26).

There is a strong indication that Jews worshiped with bare feet in the early Palestinian synagogues of late antiquity. In his discussion of the mosaic floor of the ancient synagogue in Sepphoris, located in northern Palestine, Lee I. Levine notes that many of its features can be explained by "positing a significant degree of priestly influence" (Levine 2003, 121). One of his arguments for priestly impact is the frequent barefootedness of the characters depicted in the mosaic. The association of sacredness and shoelessness is particularly striking in the scene of the binding of Isaac, which displays two pairs of shoes left by Abraham and Isaac before going up the mountain, although the biblical text includes no mention of footwear. Levine notes that, although the rabbis of the period disapproved of shoeless

Figure 1.2 Illustration of the High Priest in his ceremonial garb. Source: *De Repulyk der Hebreen* (Amsterdam, 1700). Courtesy of the Library of the Jewish Theological Seminary, New York.

worship, it was a well-known practice (Levine 2003, 124). Shoelessness during worship has been until recently the practice of several Eastern Jewish communities. In the late twelfth century Ptaxja of Regensburg reported that the "Babylonian" (Iraqi) Jews prayed barefoot (Kister 1989, 364, cited in Wexler 1996, 181), and more recent accounts come from Cochin, India (Katz 2000, 71–72).

A contemporary description is offered by Saul Bellow in his 1976 *To Jerusalem and Back,* in which he tells of a Friday visit to a Yemenite synagogue in Jerusalem: "The early arrivals have left their shoes at the door, Arab style. Bearded, dark-faced, they sit along the wall. You see their stockinged feet on the footrests of their lecterns" (Bellow 1976, 105). He associates the custom with Muslim culture; however, scholars make the case that it was in fact Muslims who adopted the custom of shoelessness in devotional spaces from Jews (Wexler 1996, 367). There are a number of traditions according to which Muhammad allowed his followers to have their feet covered during worship, saying, "Act the reverse of Jews in your prayers, for they do not pray in boots or shoes" (Patrick-Hughes 1995, 580–81). Muhammad would change the custom, regarding shoes as impure, which in turn led most Jews to give up barefootedness in prayer. It is possible that later on, under the influence of Islam, Jews in certain Muslim and Eastern territories adopted the custom, as well as that of removing footwear upon entering a home (see Figure 1.3). Internalizing their Muslim host society's view of shoes as polluted objects, they adopted some of its superstitions, such as the prohibition against leaving shoes with the soles pointing heavenward (Stillman 2000, 27). S. D. Goitein, in his monumental study of Jewish life as reflected in the documents of the Cairo Geniza (a repository of discarded writings attached to one of the synagogues in old Cairo), explains that shoes were regarded as a debased "'unmentionable," and that the word "shoe" was politely circumvented and referred to with the Hebrew phrase "that which is beneath your honor [to be mentioned in your presence]" (Goitein 1983, 162). He cites a twelfth-century woman who complained to the head of the Jewish community about her husband: "he hit me with something that cannot be mentioned." At the same time he notes that among the well-to-do Jews of the Geniza there was "a real cult of footwear," namely an indulgence in high-end shoes that were ordered and imported from overseas.

Although footwear figured prominently in the Muslim division between consecrated and defiled spaces, the actual switch between wearing shoes and barefootedness was swift, dictated by the custom of shedding shoes before entering a house or mosque, and facilitated by a relatively conducive climate in many Muslim lands. This resulted in the practice of wearing shoes pressed down at the heel, which was common to all classes. The *babouche*

Figure 1.3   Photograph of an Indian-Jewish family. Courtesy of the Library of the Jewish Theological Seminary, New York.

slipper, worn by Muslims and Jews, serves an excellent example for this liminality (see Figures 1.4 and 1.5).

The nexus of sacredness, divine revelation, and shoelessness is paradigmatic to Jewish culture and has been evoked directly or subversively by Jewish poets of different ages and sensibilities. The American Emma Lazarus (1849–1887), most famous for "The New Colossus," concluded her poem "In the Jewish Synagogue at Newport," written in July

Figure 1.4   Pair of woman's shoes, Marrakesh (Morocco), late nineteenth century. Silk embroidered with silk and gold threads; leather soles; 24.9 × 9.8 cm. Courtesy of the Jewish Museum, New York.

Figure 1.5   Print of a North African Beit Midrash [study hall]. Courtesy of the Library of the Jewish Theological Seminary, New York.

1867, with "Take off your shoes as by the burning bush / Before the mystery of death and God" (Lazarus 2005, 9). A century later, Yehuda Amichai writes in his poem "And That Is Your Glory":

> Underneath the world, God lies stretched on his back
> Always repairing, always things get out of whack.
> I wanted to see him all, but I see no more
> than the soles of his shoes and I'm sadder than I was before.
> And that is his glory. (Amichai 1986, 11–12)

The removal of shoes has also been associated since biblical times with bereavement and mourning (Ezek. 24:17, Isa. 20:2–4, Jer. 2:25). Jews are buried barefoot, covered by a simple white shroud. Yet the Jews of Tripoli in the nineteenth century were the exception to this rule, burying their dead with all the shoes they possessed (Nacht 1915, 14). This may be regarded as the remnant of an ancient custom, exemplified in the Talmudic story about the prophet Jeremiah, who was said to have left instructions that he be buried in his clothes, with his shoes on and his staff in his hands so he would be completely ready for the day of resurrection (Kolatch 1985, 181). At times, barefootedness was also required of the living, as if by this act of self-affliction mourners paid special respect to the dead. In the first century, it was customary for coffin bearers to walk barefoot as a sign of mourning (Safrai 1976, 778). Funerary barefootedness was still practiced occasionally in the mid-nineteenth century by London's Indian Jews. Rabbi Yitzhak ben Yehuda, head of the yeshiva in Mainz, Germany, during the second half of the eleventh century, urged his son to show particular deference to his deceased mother by walking barefoot to the cemetery where she was to be buried, even though the obligation to walk barefoot applied only to the return home after the burial. To this day, during *shiva,* a seven-day period of intense mourning after the death of a close relative, when mourners are confined to the house and prohibited from engaging in business or labor, sexual relations, or such physical comforts as bathing and cutting their hair, they are not allowed to wear shoes or sandals. This, writes Maurice Lamm, in his manual *The Jewish Way in Death and Dying,* is "symbolic of personal mortification and a disregard of vanity and comfort, in order better to concentrate on the deeper meaning of life" (Lamm 2000, 121). When exceptions must be made, and the mourner must leave the house, he or she is allowed to wear shoes but must place in a bit of earth the leather shoe "to keep the bereaved ever mindful that he is in mourning" (Lamm 2000, 122).

Barefootedness typified communal mourning over the destruction of Zion, notably on Tisha b'Av (the ninth day of the Hebrew month of Av, which occurs in July or August), a fast day that commemorates the destructions of the First and Second Temples. In the fourth and fifth centuries Jerusalem's Jews would pay an excessively heavy fee for the annual Tisha b'Av privilege of walking barefoot on the Temple Mount dressed in mourners' garments and rolling themselves in the dust (Kraus 1894, 227). Centuries later the great Spanish philosopher and Hebrew poet Judah Halevi (c. 1075–1141), yearning to visit the Holy Land, wrote in a similar vein: "It would delight my heart to walk naked and barefoot

Figure 1.6 A worshipper reading Lamentations on Tisha b'Av. Illumination from The Rothschild Machzor (Florence, 1490). Courtesy of the Library of the Jewish Theological Seminary, New York.

among the desolate ruins where your shrines once stood" (Halevi 2006, 349). To this date it is customary in some synagogues for worshippers to remove their shoes on Tisha b'Av and sit on low benches while the book of Lamentations is read (see Figure 1.6). The Jews of Kurdistan, reports Eric Brauer, "go to the synagogue barefoot, or else they wear only black stockings or (most frequently of all) the Kurdish cloth shoes" (Brauer 1993, 301). Likewise the Indian Jews of Cochin do not wear shoes on that day (Daniel 2001, 163). Liya Mikdash-Shamailov described the customs of the mountain Jews of the Caucasus, still practiced during the second half on the nineteenth century: "Men gathered in the synagogue, which remained in darkness. Worshippers sat on the floor; the community rabbi recited the book of Jeremiah and the Scroll of Lamentations in a tearful voice. Congregants repeated the verses, beating their breasts, and many rubbed ashes on their forehead and went barefoot" (Mikdash-Shamailov 2003, 91).

It seems that Jews originally went barefoot or semi-barefoot on Yom Kippur, the solemnest day of the year (Ben Ezra 2003, 275). A French church document dated 1733 refers to the custom of going to the synagogue wearing untied slippers (Schechter 2003, 30). A similar description comes from Constantinople during the mid-nineteenth century (Ben

Oliel 1852, 211). Some rabbis explained this custom by comparing the intensely spiritual Jews on Yom Kippur to angels, who have no need for shoes (Henkin 2003, 82). Following Kabbalistic strands, some equated the shoe with the human body: just as the shoe protects the body, so the body protects the soul. Hence, on a day of all-consuming spirituality there is no need for the materiality of shoes. Others explained barefootedness as dissociation from Joseph's brothers' criminal shoe transaction and the havoc it caused. However, normative custom eschewed barefootedness, settling on the avoidance of leather shoes in favor of canvas footwear, symbolizing the removal of the animalistic from people, of intentionally creating vulnerability and discomfort on a day that is full of denial of the physical self.

Female footwear has long been associated with sexual allure. William A. Rossi in his book *The Sex Life of the Foot and Shoe* cites an orthopedic surgeon as follows:

> Human gait is much more than locomotion. Since perhaps the earliest days of mankind women have used it as an erotic instrument, with great success, in the same way as some forms of dancing have always been used to arouse male sexual response. The eroticism of the gait is most influenced by the way the feet are used, often with the aid of a certain kind of footwear. The foot and the shoe—those are the real roots of erotic gait. (Rossi 1976, 139–40)

Rossi emphasizes repeatedly the sexual kinship of foot and shoe and rhapsodizes over the "erotic magic of high heels" (Rossi 1876, 121). He dwells on the sexual attractiveness of a leggier look, a smaller-looking foot, and enhanced height, and explains that "It causes postural changes that accentuate voluptuousness in the shape and movement of the lower limbs, the pelvis and the buttocks, the abdomen and bosom, the curve of the back, the carriage" (Rossi 1976, 121). Long before him, the ancients were fully aware of the titillating effect of a well-placed shoe and its impact on the sexually charged female gait. We are told in the apocryphal book of Judith that Holofernes, the enemy general she would seduce and behead, was greatly impressed by Judith's attire and that "her sandals ravished his eye" (Jdt. 16:9) (Goodspeed 1962, 163). The bride in the *Song of Songs* is met with exclamation: "How beautiful are thy steps in shoes, O prince's daughter! The roundings of thy thighs are like the links of a chain, the work of the hands of a skilled workman" (Song 7:1). Moralists took a dimmer view of this metonym of female sexuality. The prophet Isaiah put much of the blame for the chaos and ultimate destruction of Zion on the erotic strutting of its daughters:

> Moreover the Lord said: because the daughters of Zion are haughty, and walk with stretched-forth necks and wanton eyes, walking and mincing as they go, and making a tinkling with their feet; Therefore the Lord will smite with a scab the crown of the head of the daughters of Zion, and the Lord will lay bare their secret parts. In that day the Lord will take away the bravery of their anklets, and the fillets, and the crescents; the pendants, and the bracelets, and the veils; the headties, and the armlets, and the sashes, and the corselets, and the amulets; the rings, and the nose-jewels; the aprons, and the

mantelets, and the cloaks, and the girdles; and the gauze robes, and the fine linen, and the turbans, and the mantles. And it shall come to pass, that instead of sweet spices there shall be rottenness; and instead of a girdle rags; and instead of curled hair baldness; and instead of a stomacher a girding of sackcloth; branding instead of beauty. Thy men shall fall by the sword, and thy mighty in the war. And her gates shall lament and mourn; and utterly bereft she shall sit upon the ground. (Isa. 3:16–26)

The rabbis who expounded on this text conjured even more fantastically damning details. "Tinkling with their feet," one rabbi explained, meant that the woman "used to have a picture of a serpent on her shoe" (Midrash Eichah Rabbah IV: 18); at the time the depiction of serpents was associated in rabbinic culture with idol-worship, and Jews were commanded to destroy vessels bearing this shape by either grinding them to dust or throwing them into the Dead Sea (Mishnah Avodah Zarah 3:3). Out-fantasizing him, his colleagues suggested steamier details: "She took a hen's gullet, filled it with balsam and placed it between her heel and her shoe; and when she saw a band of young men, she pressed upon it so that the perfume went through them like the poison of a snake" (Midrash Eicha Rabbah IV:18).

While Rossi and the rabbis regard the female as seducer, author Susan Brownmiller applies a feminist gaze to the sexually charged high-heel shoe. To her "the overall hobbling effect with its sadomasochistic tinge" suggests "the restraining leg irons and ankle chains endured by captive animals, prisoners and slaves who were also festooned with decorative symbols of their bondage" (Brownmiller 1984, 184). In his Freudian analysis of shoes as sexual fetish, Berkeley Kaite discusses the combination of fragility and strength of the high-heel female shoe, which, he says, suggests sexual ambivalence, explaining "in the pornographic instance, what makes it signify is its masculine heel, but a heel within a feminine frame of reference" (Kaite 1995, 96). This ambisexuality, he notes, is conspicuous in women's high-heel sandals, whose design mixes the hardness of the leather and heel, the shaky footing resulting from the high heel, and the lack of support offered by the straps of leather that extend over the instep, with the toe protruding phallically from the front.

These qualities as well as the fetishized aspect of the single shoe need to be kept in mind when approaching artist Nechama Golan's provocative sandal, which tackles issues of religion, male authority, and feminism (see Figure 1.7). Golan's journey from secular Israeli to Orthodox feminist Jew and cutting-edge artist is fascinating, and her work, grounded in her religious commitment while challenging rabbinic tenets especially as they relate to women, is unsettling. Her sandal, made of paper, ink, and glue, uses for its insole and heel a well-known sacred rabbinic text from late antiquity, now often criticized as sexist and emblematic of religious male authority. It begins with "A woman is acquired in three ways and she acquires herself in two ways. She is acquired through money, document, or sexual intercourse" (Mishnah 1:1). The voice of woman, explains the artist, is silenced between the male rabbinic authority represented by the text and the sandal, shaped by the secular Western male whose aim is to endow woman with the seductive appearance of a sexual object. The will of woman, be she religious or secular, is absent here. The construction of the

גניזה

Figure 1.7   Nechama Golan, *Untitled*. 2002. Paper, ink, glue. Courtesy of the artist.

sandal from the perspective of the male concept of woman, says Golan, makes it a critical work that questions the position of woman. In the original work the sandal is of the same size as the artist's foot. Golan notes that by basing her works on the actual dimensions of her own body she makes it the point of departure for her artistic and critical statement as her (unseen) foot imprints itself on the shoe's insole while metaphorically erasing the rabbinic text (Golan 2007). At the same time, Golan stamped the provocative image with the designation *geniza* (storage), referring to the prohibition against discarding documents that include the name of God in Hebrew letters. Before receiving a cemetery burial such papers are kept in a synagogue depository, called the *geniza*. Golan says this is the price she is willing to pay for using "holy texts." With this she confirms her respect for and acceptance of the religious worldview she had adopted.

From Freud to Derrida shoes have been equated with the vagina, with the penis located in either the heel or the foot. It is thus interesting that a baby shoe is often employed as a decorative prop in the "Brita" celebration in which the baby girl is welcomed into the world and into Judaism. Because the concept is not grounded in Jewish law and does not inherently suggest a specific date or a dictated procedure, it gained popularity among secular Israelis and was inspired by an egalitarian desire to create a parallel to the baby boy circumcision celebration. The *Brita* and various feminist religious celebrations of baby girls, are invented traditions that leave the door open for new liturgy and a choice of ceremonial symbolism. Of the latter the most striking are the frequency of the shoe image on invitation and decorations, and the immersion of the feet of the infant girl in water, alluding, according to one Web site, to "Miriam's song at the Red Sea, or Rebecca at the well," noting that the covenant with Noah after the flood is the second covenant involving all humanity" (http://www.traditionsrenewed.com/lifecycle/trlifecycle.html).

Shoes function as metonyms for personhood and as markers of identity both by choice and coercion. They are a rich source of information for a person's age and gender, occupation, economic and social status, and religious and ideological position, as well as a host of personal characteristics. Shoes, as the only article of clothing that retain their shape and position even when not worn, are never truly empty. They are always in waiting for their actual or imagined owner, serving as biographical documents of their wearer. In his terse "The Man Who Stepped Out of His Shoes" (1953), Uri Zvi Greenberg (1896–1987), a towering figure in modern Hebrew poetry, wrote of a man who on a golden morning goes out to the electric pole, steps out of his shoes, and begins to walk barefoot into the distance, "without the memory of his shoes, / which wait for him here" (U. Greenberg 2006, 532). Shoes as metonym for the full human being appear in "The Blind Woman," a brilliant short story by Jacob Steinberg (1887–1947) that tells the tragic story of Hannah, a young blind woman who is tricked into marrying a man she is told is a young well-to-do widower engaged in the tobacco business but who turns out at the end to be an elderly grave-digger (Steinberg 1966, 70–88). Suspecting her husband's identity, Hannah waits for him to fall asleep, crawls off her bed, and feels his boots with her hands. Wrinkled and made of rough leather, they lead her to imagine the totality of the man's appearance, age, and economic circumstances: tall, thin, and bent, wearing worn and patched-up traditional Jewish clothes. In light of the near symbiotic relation between shoe, foot, and the physical and spiritual totality of one's being, it is not surprising that people are greatly disturbed by the idea of wearing the shoes of the dead, more so than any other garment.

This is reflected in the custom, still in practice in some religious circles, of destroying the shoes of the deceased to ensure that no other person would wear them. The shoes are either thrown into separate cans of garbage, cut up into pieces, or even set on fire. An Israeli Web site recounts the following story: subsequent to a discussion on what to do with the personal effects of Hassidic yeshiva student who had been killed in a 2006 road accident, the latter appeared to a fellow student in a dream and clarified that it was appropriate to use all his belongings with the exception of his slippers. When the dream was related to the head of the yeshiva, he instructed that the slippers be burned ("The Dream That Rouses the Yeshiva"). A radically different opinion appears in a responsum written in 1992 by David Golinkin, an Israeli Conservative rabbi. After surveying various rabbinic explanations, Golinkin rules that the custom contradicts the dictum against wanton destruction (*Lo Tashkhit*) and recommends that the shoes of the dead be donated to the needy (Golinkin 1992, 73–77).

Jews generally wore the same style of shoe as the general population, albeit with some minor modifications such as the avoidance of shoes with laces on the Sabbath so as to not be involved in knotting, or a preference for black laces as a sign of mourning (Bava Kama

59b). In one Talmudic exchange between a rabbi and a fellow Jew (Ta'anit 22a), the latter is asked why he is wearing black shoes although he is not in mourning. The response is that he does so in order to mask his identity when he travels among the Gentiles so he can find out in advance of any harsh measures that are planned against Jews.

In Muslim lands footwear and barefootedness were at times imposed on Jews as part of a dress code system intended to mark the differentiation and humiliation of *dhimmi* (non-Muslim protégés of the Domain of Islam). Some decrees required the use of visibly coarse and unpleasant materials, others specified color, and the most outlandish one, enacted in 1121 by the Seljuk Sultan of Baghdad, required women to wear mismatched-colored shoes, one red, the other black, and a small brass bell on either neck or shoes (Baron 1980, 259; Stillman 2000, 108; Ye'or 1972, 66, 191, 203). Some of the clothing restrictions were either short-lived or not enforced, fluctuating according to regional policies and individual rulers, with Muslim Spain the most liberal in this respect. Yet in Morocco's imperial cities—Fez, Marrakesh, and later Menkes—Jews were not allowed to wear shoes when walking in Muslim streets, a practice strongly objected to by Sir Moses Montefiore in 1864 (Stillman 2000, 114, 119). In 1820 the *Boston Recorder,* in an account of the discriminatory treatment of the Jews in Tangier, explained,

> In some towns they must walk barefoot, and everywhere they take off their shoes when passing before a mosque, or the house of any Mussulman of distinction. When they meet a Moor of high rank, they must hastily turn away to a certain distance on the left of the road, leave their sandals on the ground, several paces off, bend the body forward, and in that humiliating posture remain till he passes forward. ("Condition of the Jews at Tangier" 1820, 5, 17)

Some seventy years later J. E. Budgett Meakin reported that, except in coastal towns where there was a strong Western influence, most Moroccan Jews walked barefoot outside their quarter and needed to remove their shoes before certain mosques. He notes that this used to be required of women as well, but they were exempted as the sight of their calves was deemed indecent and devotionally disturbing (Budgett Meakin 1892, 381).

A Sephardic folk story highlights the shoe as emblem for the relation between Jews and Muslims. Its main character is Don Isaac Abravanel (1437–1509)—scholar, statesman, and close advisor to the king and the person in charge of the royal wardrobe. Abravanel's Muslim rival tries to cause his downfall by tricking the shoemaker to put a piece of paper with the Prophet's name into a royal shoe, so that the king will unknowingly step on it. The act of sacrilege would be blamed on Abravanel, resulting in his elimination. Things turn out differently as the true culprit is exposed and executed in the fire he had prepared for Abravanel (Sadeh 1983, 223–24).

While most of the vestimentary discriminatory practices were terminated by the early twentieth century due to pressure exerted by the West, barefootedness did not cease in parts of Yemen. Max Lapides, instrumental in the organization of the immigration of Yemenite Jews to Israel in the aftermath of independence in 1948, noted that "shoes always present a special ticklish problem since our guests never wore any before" (Ahroni 2001, 75). Images of Yemenite Jews walking barefoot toward the Holy Land became staples of modern Zionism's visual canon (see Figure 1.8). Yemenite barefootedness was seen through the double and ambivalent lens of Zionist romanticism and European elitism. On the one hand Yemenites were recognized as descendants of the oldest Jewish diaspora and indeed, dressed in long tunics and wearing long curly side-locks, they looked like embodiments of biblical characters, picturesque figures who provided geographic and historical authenticity to the Zionist enterprise. On the other, these "exotic" Jews were dark-skinned and not versed in modern Western culture, and thus regarded as "primitive" by the secular, mostly European *yishuv* (Jewish community in pre-state Israel).

At the same time, pioneering Zionism, with its rejection of bourgeois European values, its yearning for biblical roots, dreams of pre-exilic sovereignty and mythical devotion to the reclamation of the land through intense and painful physical labor, was not inimical to barefootedness. British writer Anita Engle, in an enthusiastic essay titled "Halutziuth" (pioneering) written in the 1940s, recalled she was told, "Take off your shoes....One should walk barefoot on the land" (Engle 1943, 210). It is perhaps that in its quest to interface with the physical land while still protecting the foot that the sandal, a quasi-shoe, became the definitive footwear of the first native-born generation of young Israelis. In a sentimental essay titled "Summer, Sandals, and the Zionist Dream," written in 1996, novelist Ehud Ben-Ezer (born in 1936 in Petach Tikva, the first Zionist colony) eulogized the disappearance of sandals from the Israeli shoescape (Ben-Ezer 1996, 20). "During my youth," he wrote, it was adults who wore shoes while the young generation was in sandals, which became one of the symbols of the *sabra* (native born). The adults of the present, he mourned, "are us," and, clinging to a style that is mostly outdated, he insisted, "we refuse

Figure 1.8   The Zabeb family arrives at camp Hashed near Aden, Yemen. Run by the Joint Distribution Committee, the camp served as a transit center for emigrants. The photograph was taken in November 1949. Courtesy of the Central Zionist Archives, Jerusalem.

to give up the pleasure of the naked foot in summertime and with it the sense of annually revived youth." As for today's youth, those boys in "huge sneakers" without socks or even laces, and the girls in platform shoes or army-like boots, he suggests, are cretins who imitate foreign fashions that do not fit the weather and "the wonderful native Israeli sense of barefootedness" (Ben-Ezer 1996, 20).

The rich metaphoricity of shoes attracted the imagination of artists and storytellers. Hasidism, with its populist approach and emphasis on spirituality, attached great importance to storytelling, particularly of the wonders of Hasidic saints and the noble deeds of common people. The Ba'al Shem Tov (Master of the Good Name, also known acronymically as the Besht, 1698–1760), the founder of the movement, himself a gifted storyteller, was the subject of many such tales. One entails a shoe that flew off the foot of Dov-Baer of Mezeritch, the Besht's student and successor. Dov-Baer danced enthusiastically during *Simchat Torah* (Joy with/of the Torah), a day of rejoicing that follows the eighth day of Sukkot, on which the annual cycle of public Torah readings is completed and begun again. The Besht, however, did not participate in the dance. He later explained to his followers

Figure 1.9   Yosl Bergner, from the *Lost Shoe* series, 2005. Oil on canvas, 50 × 40 cm. Courtesy of the artist.

that while the Hasidim were dancing he had entered the Garden of Eden. There he saw an assemblage of scattered fringes of prayer shawls, worn *tefillin,* heels of shoes, shoelaces, and even whole shoes, all glowing with a special light. While surveying the scene, Dov-Baer's shoe suddenly flew into the Garden, joining the holy litter. When two angels came to sweep and collect the strewn objects, the Besht asked what they were going to do with them. An angel responded, "These shoes have flown here from the feet of Jews dancing with the Torah. They are very precious to God, and soon the angel Gabriel will make a crown out of them for God to wear on His Throne of Glory" (Schwartz 1993, 194–95).

Yosl Bergner (1920–), one of Israel's most celebrated artists, recently produced a series of eighteen paintings titled "A Lost Shoe." Bergner, whose work has remained figurative throughout his career, settled in Israel in 1950 and features significantly in the mainstream of Israeli artistic discourse. Yet he has retained his identity as a non-native, a Diaspora Jew grounded in the vanished Yiddish world of Eastern Europe. His shoe series was inspired by a lonely black shoe he found on a Tel Aviv street, which in his drawings became saturated with the images that constitute what he calls in Yiddish *"mayn medine"* (my country): gray walls, mysterious windows, a crucifixion poll, birds, and blurred graffiti (see Figures 1.9 and 1.10). Danny Kerman, an artist friend who wrote the introduction

Figure 1.10 Yosl Bergner, from the Lost Shoe series, 2005. Oil on canvas, 50 × 35 cm. Courtesy of the artist.

for the shoe exhibition catalogue, noted that Bergner, in typical fashion, treats his objects with kindness (Kerman 2005, 2–3). In some of the paintings, he writes, Bergner rescues the shoe from its loneliness and provides companion shoes; in others the shoe dialogues with birds or gives life to a plant. Kerman notes that, although Bergner's still life is never still, but full of dynamism, his lost shoe does not walk. Perhaps, he ruminates, "the birds took it with them to the horizon, which Yosl likes so much, and perhaps an invisible hand crucified it on some piece of wood" (Kerman 2005, 2–3).

* * *

The story of Jewish shoemakers is part and parcel of the history of Jewish artisans, a vast topic that stretches over two millennia and spans diverse geographical terrains. Moreover, shoemaking encompasses a wide range of specialization and working conditions. Although generalizations are clearly problematic, it is helpful to situate them within the distinct patterns that present themselves in the practice of Jewish crafts prior to the modern era. In the areas of the Jewish "first settlement" outside Palestine—namely Mesopotamia, Egypt, the Byzantine lands, Italy, Provence, Spain and North Africa—Jews were considered part of the indigenous population and constituted a natural segment of the artisan class, and, despite their outsider status, Jewish craftsmen in Muslim lands were not seriously hampered by guild restrictions as in Christian Europe (Baron 1980, 202). This was not so in the "second settlement" in Northern and Western Europe, where Jews, from the Middle Ages until the Emancipation, were shunned and assailed by Christian guilds and relegated to the role of petty traders and moneylenders and artisans of a ritual nature that served a predominantly Jewish clientele. The most numerically significant Jewish artisan class was created during the "third settlement" in Eastern Europe, where a large Jewish population provided it with an economic base.

The scant statistics we have demonstrate that shoemakers occupied a significant place among Jewish artisans in both the Christian and Muslim worlds, outnumbered only by tailors, the paradigmatic Jewish craftsmen.[5] Indeed, in an attempt to reduce the overabundance of Jewish tailors, modern-day Jewish benevolent associations promoted shoemaking along with other crafts.[6] In the interwar period ORT, a Jewish society devoted to training and education, promoted the professionalization of shoemaking, as seen from the poster designed by artist Issachar Ryback (1897–1935) (see Figure 1.11).

In some places, notably the Iberian Peninsula, local conditions enabled Jews to establish their own craft associations. The shoemakers guild in Saragossa, with a constitution confirmed in 1336 by Pedro IV, king of Aragon, was a benevolent association, whose bylaws focused on social and religious welfare. Perhaps the guild also had un undeclared professional agenda not unlike the Saragossa Jewish tanners guild that, among other things, protected its members from the hostile policies of the Christian guilds (Assis 1996, 116).[7] Additional shoemakers guilds existed at the end of the fourteenth century in Perpignan, and the *confraria de los judios çapateros* (guild of the Jewish shoemakers) of Huesca owned shops into the fifteenth century (Assis 1996, 116).

Figure 1.11 Propaganda poster for ORT (the Society for Trades and Agricultural Labor) training program, 1920s. Artist: Issachar-Ber Rybak. Courtesy of YIVO Institute of Jewish Research, New York.

It was suggested that following the exile from Spain, the paradigm of guild as a fraternal association traveled with the Spanish exiles to Italy and other countries in the Mediterranean basin and was eventually transmitted to the rest of Central and Eastern Europe (Ruderman 1976, 223–24). Prague, where ten or eleven Jewish craft guilds operated during the seventeenth and eighteenth centuries, is a good case in point. The city's Jewish shoemakers guild was formed in 1730. According to its statutes it included master shoemakers, cobblers, and heel makers. Applicants had to prove that they were natives of Prague, a reflection of the desire of the local authorities to reduce the city's Jewish population, and, as was a general rule in all guilds, they had to be married, so that bachelors with smaller financial needs would not compete with heads of families. Some exceptions regarding the latter were made for journeymen who were sons of a deceased master, and similarly, for widows of a master, who were allowed to carry on his work with the help of a journeyman as long as they did not remarry. The census of the Prague ghetto taken in 1729 confirms these arrangements: it lists 105 shoemakers, 5 of them women, and 11 heel makers (Wischnitzer 1965, 174).

The guild's statutes also spelled out the three-tier organization of the profession, at the top of which stood the master. At the bottom was the apprentice, a boy whose family paid the master a fee in exchange for two or three years of training, including board and lodgings, and, in between, the journeyman, who usually hired himself out to a master for a specified period (see Figure 1.12). Jewish journeymen and apprentices worked from early in the morning until eight at night, except on Jewish holidays. They were required

Figure 1.12   Shoemaker's workshop. Postcard with photograph
that shows the master, the woman of the house (presumably
his wife or daughter), journeymen, and apprentices. Prague,
ca. 1900. Courtesy of the Visual Documentation Center, Beth
Hatefutsoth, the Nahum Goldmann Museum of the Jewish
Diaspora, Tel Aviv.

to attend daily morning services, as well as lectures on religious law given by a rabbinic
scholar. All guilds maintained a mutual aid system and a strong sense of group identity,
symbolized by flags and emblems that they proudly displayed on festive occasions and
pageants. The emblem of the Prague Jewish shoemakers guild was a goblet in the shape of
a large boot, made of pewter, about 70 centimeters tall (see Figure 1.13).

The Jewish guild system was also prevalent in Poland and Lithuania, although with a
difference. Unlike the autonomy enjoyed by guilds in Spain, in Poland they were greatly
dependent on the *Kahal,* the community council whose sanction they needed before being
approved by the ruling authorities. This led at times to intra-Jewish conflicts, as the councils
were controlled by an elite that had little respect for the artisans' low socioeconomic status.
Consequently, artisans often established their own craft-based synagogues (see Figure 1.14).
There are little data on Jewish shoemakers in eighteenth-century Poland, one explanation

Figure 1.13   Sketch of the guild cup emblem of the Jewish Shoemakers of
Prague, eighteenth century (1920). Reconstructed drawing by
Adolf Kaspar (1877–1934).

Figure 1.14   Shoemakers' synagogue, Birze (Birzai), Lithuania,
ca. 1930. Courtesy of Basil Baruch Sandler.

being that due to the discriminatory policies of the Polish shoemakers guilds, they were careful not to disclose their trade to the authorities (Wischnitzer 1965, 226).

By the late nineteenth century, the largest segment of world Jewry lived within the czarist empire. In 1880, Russia included four million Jews, 95 percent of them confined to a
government-designated area known as the Pale of Settlement, where they constituted only
12 percent of the entire population but 38 percent of urban residents. It was estimated
that by the turn of the century there were 500,000 Jewish artisans in the Pale, representing 44 percent of the Jewish labor force. Of those, 25 percent were tailors and 14 percent
shoemakers (Liebman 1979, 82). The latter were often also petty traders who hawked
their products in the local marketplace or peddled from house to house (see Figure 1.15).
From the 1880s onward the wages and standard of living of Jewish artisans rapidly de-
clined due to a confluence of economic developments, governmental anti-Jewish measures,
and an increase in the birthrate that raised the number of Jews from 1,600,000 in 1820
to 4,000,000 in 1880. Jewish artisans were exposed to competition from both peasant

Figure 1.15   Customer looking over shoes in outdoor marketplace. Kazimierz, Poland, 1925. Courtesy of YIVO Institute of Jewish Research, New York.

workers who came from the ranks of the serfs (liberated in 1861), and the rise of capitalism in Russia, which led to the establishment of large industrialized factories reluctant to employ Jews. Though some 20 percent of the Jewish workforce was employed in factories, these tended to be small-scale operations with relatively primitive machinery. All this led to widespread poverty, an unemployment rate of 40 percent or more, and the pauperization of a large part of the artisan class (Marks 2003, 143).

The conditions of Jewish artisans worsened during the interwar period. The newly independent states of Lithuania and Poland wished to advance the economic interests of their own (non-Jewish) nationals, often at the expense of Jewish artisans. Economic crises during the 1920s reduced Jewish artisans, including the high numbers of shoemakers, to abject poverty. In 1929, in the city of Brest, only 50 of the 300 local Jewish shoemakers earned a reasonably sufficient income. Many worked in their cramped homes, with lasts more conspicuous than food in their meager kitchens (see Figure 1.16).

There is little wonder that shoemakers emigrated en masse and featured prominently in the immigrant neighborhoods of England, Western Europe, and America. Jacob Riis's 1889 photo of a poor Jewish cobbler (see Figure 1.17) and the 1907 Broadway play *The Shoemaker* by James Halleck Reid, the story of a Jewish shoemaker that extends from the Bowery to a Rocky Mountain mining town, confirm the Jewish shoemaker's visibility to

Figure 1.16 Young boy in shoemaker's apartment. Lithuania, ca. 1935. Courtesy of YIVO Institute of Jewish Research, New York.

Figure 1.17 Itinerant cobbler living in a coal cellar, Ludlow Street, New York City. From Jacob Riis, *How the Other Half Lives: Studies Among the Tenements of New York* (1890).

the general population (Bordman 1994, 607). Some plied their craft in New York, Philadelphia, and other major northern and midwestern urban centers. Others, like journalist Paul Greenberg's father, a shoe repairman, established themselves in remote towns, often augmenting their income by becoming part-time itinerant artisans. Greenberg reminisces fondly about his father, who during the war years, when new shoes were rationed, used to get into his old Chevy on Sundays and drive to little towns in Arkansas, Louisiana, and East Texas where he sold the used shoes he had mended, for which no ration points were required (P. Greenberg 2006, 2).

Many flocked to the "shoe cities" in Massachusetts, of which the most prominent was Lynn, which in 1910 produced some 40 percent of the nation's shoes.[8] Gradually they made the shift from workers to management and owners: in 1910 there were approximately 400 Jewish shoe workers in Lynn; in 1918 their number had swelled to 800, representing more than a third of Lynn's employed Jews; by the 1930s the local shoe and leather trade were regarded as Jewish industries, with nearly half of the city's shoes produced under Jewish ownership and management. This began to change in the postwar era, as cheap imports and the introduction of nonleather materials reduced demand for American-made shoes. In 1968 there were 146 plants manufacturing nonrubber footwear in Massachusetts; by 1981 only 38 remained. Globalism had its final victory in 2000, when the last shoe plant to survive, Barry Manufacturing Company, established in 1946 by Samuel Rothbard, shut down. The owners, Samuel's grandchildren, could no longer keep the plant going. They likened the closing of the factory and the loss of 150 jobs to a death in the family.

The centuries-long journey of the Jewish shoemaker was depicted in a deceptively naïve story, "The Little Shoemakers" (Singer 1982, 39–56), by Isaac Bashevis Singer (1902–1991). It is a simple tale that begins in Frampol, a small village, after the 1648–1649 Khmelnytsky massacres that decimated about half of the Ukraine's Jews, and ends in the immediate aftermath of the Holocaust in a manicured New Jersey suburb. Abba, the central character, is a pious old-world Jew, the descendant of a long line of righteous shoemakers. He sees all his children break the ancestral chain and emigrate to America, his wife dies, his community is destroyed, and finally, a broken survivor, he arrives at his Americanized son's home. A lost soul, he stumbles into his old shoemaking equipment—last, hammer and nails, knife and pliers, file and awl—which become the tools of his salvation. The story ends on an idyllic Sunday morning, when his seven successful sons join him in his work for a session of traditional shoemaking and singing, as was their practice in the old country. Though Singer's story is a paean to old-time shoemakers, he was not unaware of the low regard in which they were held, often mentioned in contrast to the learned and wealthy. When interviewed about his Yiddish readers he said, "I feel that my readers are not simple people. They may not have doctor titles but I understand that they are Jewish people. The father may be a shoemaker, but his son is already a professor. Potentially, the shoemaker could also be a professor if he would have studied" (Singer 1974, 30).

The shoemaker's low social status in Jewish society engendered many folktales—in both Eastern and Western communities—where he is compensated either in this world or the next for his generosity, courage, and wisdom. His meek position also invited interpretations of hidden saintliness and invisible mystical powers, his stitching of the upper and lower parts of the shoe carrying metaphysical significance. The prime example for the metaphysical cobbler is Enoch, originally a bland biblical figure who in Kabbalistic literature attains the highest juncture where human and divine wisdom unite.[9] Enoch was glorified in Hasidism, representing the simple, pure of heart, barely noticeable man, the very antithesis of the rich and mighty of the community. Abraham Joshua Heschel, one of modern Judaism foremost theologians, began his book *Man's Quest for God* with a story told by the Hasidic rabbi of Ger about a shoemaker who used to work all night so that his poor customers, who owned only one pair of shoes, would have them in the morning when they needed to go to work. The shoemaker skipped his morning prayer, although every so often, when he raised his hammer from the shoes, he uttered a sigh: "Woe unto me, I haven't prayed yet!" The rabbi commented, "Perhaps that sigh is worth more than prayer itself" (Heschel 1954, 3–4). A recent embodiment of the otherworldly shoemaker appears in Erri de Luca's fantastic novel *God's Mountain*. Situated in a poverty-stricken Naples neighborhood, it features Don Rafaniello, a hunchbacked Holocaust survivor whose hump, he says, conceals angel wings that would one day fly him to Jerusalem. Rafaniello, it is said, is "master of all masters and even makes the lame walk" (de Luca 2002, 54). By repairing the shoes of the poor, he fixes and transforms their lives.

Jewish shoemakers have their own hall of fame. It includes Luis Diaz, the "Messiah of Sentubal," Portugal, who proclaimed himself heir to King David's throne and was burned at the stake in 1542; David Levi (1742–1801) of London, an important theologian who authored the immensely influential three-volume *Dissertation of the Prophecies of the Old Testament;* Samuel Gompers (1850–1924), first president of the American Federation of Labor; Lazar Kaganovich (1893–1991), Bolshevik leader, secretary-general of the Moscow party and member of the Politburo.

Shoemakers had a certain reputation as folksy intellectuals with an affinity for the printed word (Hobsbawm and Scott 1980, 90–93). The great Yiddish poet Mani Leyb (1883–1953) was a poor lad who rose from the shoemakers' ranks. Sick and nearing his fiftieth birthday, he wrote of his two conflicting craft identities in the poem "I Am...,"

> I am Mani Leyb, whose name is sung—
> In Brownsville, Yehupets, and farther, they know it:
> Among cobblers, a splendid cobbler; among
> Poetical circles, splendid poet.

The poem concludes:

> In Brownsville, Yehupets, beyond them, even,
> My name shall always be known, O Muse.
> And I am not a cobbler who writes, thank heaven,
> But a poet who makes shoes. (Leyb 2001, 219–20)

Nineteenth-century shoemakers had a reputation for radicalism and were a significant presence within the German revolution of 1848, the Swing Riots in England, and the Paris Commune. In their analysis of this phenomenon, Hobsbawm and Scott explain that the village shoemaker was self-employed, and his clientele consisted of humble people, frequently poor (Hobsbawm and Scott 1980, 89). This gave him license and enabled him to express his opinion with little fear that it would cost him his job or his clientele, and his shop often functioned as a local meeting place. The growth of industrialism, which undermined the position of independent artisans, heightened their political radicalism. Rising industrialism was particularly injurious to the Jewish artisan, and it was only natural for Jewish shoemakers to become active participants in revolutionary circles, and in the Bund, the Jewish socialist party formed in Vilna, Lithuania, in 1897. From this cradle of workers' radicalism came an icon of Jewish working-class martyrdom: Hirsh Lekert (1879–1902) (see Figure 1.18), a poor 22-year-old shoemaker's apprentice, who in May 1902 shot Victor von Wahl, the ruthlessly anti-labor governor of Vilna, in retaliation for his brutal flogging of anti-government protestors.

Lekert's was a public act of defiance, carried out in the theater. Von Wahl was slightly wounded. Lekert was arrested, court-martialed, and sentenced to death. The execution was cunningly postponed to allow Lekert's pregnant wife and the local rabbi to pressure the defiant convict into sending a petition to the czar, which the authorities assured them would spare his life. Lekert finally yielded to the pressure. As soon as his petition was submitted, the Vilna authorities broke their word and carried out the execution. Lekert was secretly buried in an unmarked grave. Although the Bund was strongly opposed to acts of terror, popular sentiment was with the poor shoemaker who had stood up to oppression. Lekert became a mythologized figure of the left. Two Yiddish plays, one by Aron Kushnirov, and

הירש לעקערט
22 יאהר אלט.
האט געשאסען דעם 5־טען מאי 1902 יאהר אין
דעם ווילנער גובערנאטאר 6 אום 11 אוהל.
אויפגעהאנגען געווארען דעם 28־טען מאי 1902 יאהר, אין ווילנא.

Figure 1.18   Portrait of Hirsh Lekert. Courtesy of YIVO Institute of Jewish Research, New York.

the other by H. Leivick, were written about him in conjunction with the twentieth anniversary of his execution. A shoemaking workshop was named after him, (see Figure 1.19) and a commemorative monument was erected in Minsk. In 1928 Lekert's story was the subject of a soviet film, *His Excellency,* also known as *Hirsh Lekert.*

On May 10, 1943, in the darkest days of the Vilna ghetto, Yiddish poet Avraham Sutzkever (1913–) wrote of a heroic teacher, Mira, who amidst the doom and devastation tries to keep the spark of life in her young charges. She tells them a local story of defiance: "She bites her lip of courage she will tell: / About Hirsh Lekert, how he fought and fell" (Sutzkever 1991, 161).

* * *

It is impossible to conclude an essay on Jews and shoes without referring to the Holocaust. Heaps of empty shoes have become its visual icon, an assemblage of death that represents lives barbarously brought to their final destination, each shoe a story into itself. In his chilling poem "A Load of Shoes," written January 1, 1943, Avraham Sutzkever writes about the disembodied footwear transported from Vilna to Berlin. A witness, his tongue "like meat," he cannot help asking the question for which he knows the answer: "but the

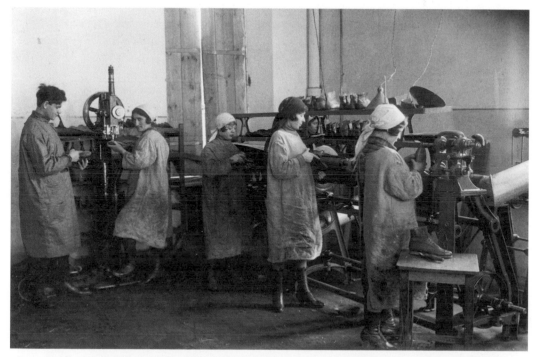

Figure 1.19 At the job in a shoemaking workshop named after Hirsh Lekert. Kiev, 1920s. Photograph by M. Z. Pashker. Courtesy of YIVO Institute of Jewish Research, New York.

truth, shoes, / where are your feet?" As he begins to catalogue the shoes' missing owners, he recognizes:

> Slippers and pumps,
> Look, there are my mother's:
> her Sabbath pair,
> in with the others. (Sutzkever 2001, 1162–63)

The recently created memorial to the Jews of Budapest who were killed by the Hungarian fascists highlights the iconicity of the shoe as Holocaust metonym (see Figure 1.20). Randolph H. Braham, in his magisterial recording of the Holocaust in Hungary, meticulously records the minutest details, including names and addresses, of the events that took place near the end of the war, when most Hungarian Jews had already been deported to death camps and the Russians were practically at the city gates:

> In the last few weeks before the liberation *Nyilas* [Arrow Cross] gangs invaded a large number of Jewish-inhabited buildings.... Usually, the Jews were first robbed of their last remaining valuables. Many were shot on the spot; others were taken to the banks of the Danube and shot into the river. The method of execution was to tie three people together, place them at the edge of the Danube, and shoot the middle one in the back of

Figure 1.20   "Shoes on the Danube Bank," Budapest. Gyula Pauer and Can Togay. Courtesy of the artists.

his head at close range so that the weight of his body would pull the other living victims into the river. (Braham 1994, 998)

Artists Gyula Pauer and Can Togay explained that the impetus for their "Shoes at the Danube Bank" memorial was the public debate generated by the inauguration of the House of Terror in 2002.[10] The museum contains exhibits related to the fascist and communist regimes of twentieth-century Hungary. Some critics argued the museum was politically slanted in its overemphasis on Hungary's victimhood and minimization of the role played by Hungarians. When Can Togay, film director, actor, and poet, was asked for his opinion he responded, "first there should be a statue depicting the shoes at the Danube bank, and then everything would fall automatically to its right place." The visual image was inspired by the 1955 Félix Máriássy film *Budapesti tavasz* (Springtime in Budapest), based on a novel by Ferenc Karinthy (1921–1992). The film tells the story of the last two months of the war in Budapest through the love affair between a Jewish girl and a runaway soldier, and it includes a scene that shows a long line of abandoned shoes that the Jews had been forced to remove before being shot and dumped into the river. Togay approached conceptual artist and set designer Gyula Pauer, with whom he had worked on several films. Their collaboration on the shoe project began with a search for a suitable location. The initial intention to build it near Margaret Bridge, where most of the killings took place, was soon abandoned, and they chose a part of the Pest quay, which offered visual clarity and was still paved with stones that were historically correct. The proximity of the location to the Hungarian Parliament highlighted the importance of the monument. The aim of the artists was "to create an object that would raise questions *in* and present questions *to* the observer," be that a native or tourist who strolls down the popular Danube bank. They decided on the use of iron, its material simplicity and roughness deemed most appropriate to portray these historical events.

Financial backing was not easy to come by. Seed money came from art collector Peter Kornai and the Ministry of Culture's Sixtieth Anniversary Holocaust Fund. Small amounts were sent in by many elderly people. Yet private businesses known for their contributions to cultural enterprises failed to respond. It was finally Hungary's Prime Minster Ferenc Gyurcsány who secured most of the funding, to which was added support from the city of Budapest.

During the planning stage the artists foresaw the possibility of politically motivated vandalism. Thinking of graffiti or paint spray, they were not quite prepared for the physical extraction of four of the shoes—probably requiring a metal chain tied to a motorized vehicle—that occurred shortly after the memorial's inauguration on April 16, 2005, as part of the official commemoration of the sixtieth anniversary of the Holocaust. The shoes were later found in the river.

NOTES

1. All biblical quotes in this essay are taken from the 1917 Jewish Publication Society (JPS) translation of *The Holy Scriptures,* chosen for its close literal adherence to the original Hebrew text.

2. Stillman notes that in Muhammad's time *na'l* was a sandal made of palm fiber, smooth leather, or leather with animal hair, and was considered by the Prophet as the norm in male footwear, unlike the more luxuriant *khuff,* a shoe or boot made of leather.

3. Turim cites Cawthorne and Pattison 1997.

4. It makes the exception by allowing one who has nothing to eat to sell his shoes in order to provide for a meal.

5. In 1724, of the 586 Jewish artisans in provincial Bohemia, 62 were shoemakers, saddlers, and belt makers (Wischnitzer 1965, 177); and Prague in 1729 had 100 male and 5 female shoemakers, compared with 158 male and 17 female tailors and 36 seamstresses (Wischnitzer 1965, 174). In 1777 Mikulov (Moravia) there were 13 shoemakers compared with 20 tailors (Wischnitzer 1965, 179). In 1870 Pest had 316 shoemakers compared with 1,688 tailors, and a year earlier Vienna listed 119 shoemakers and 505 tailors (1891, 26). The British Board of Guardians' register of Jewish occupations in London (1879–1882) lists 98 boot finishers and 44 boot and shoe makers, compared with 384 tailors. The city of Brest (in Belarus) had 300 Jewish shoemakers, though only 50 had a reasonably sufficient income (Bauer 2001, 152), and in 1939, on the brink of World War II, Soviet Jewry included 536,845 furriers and shoemakers (Altshuler 1998, 179). Shoemaking was equally popular among Jews in the Orient: in 1899 Algiers supported 45 Jewish tanners and 730 Jewish shoemakers (Laskier and Simon, 2003, 30); of the 416 Jews living in Jerusalem in the 1880s, 60 were shoemakers as compared to 87 tailors (Jacobs 1891, 26).

6. In 1879 Vienna the 422 apprentices of the *Handwerkeverein* included 58 shoemakers, second only to 84 locksmiths; in 1882 the *Alliance Israelite,* active in North Africa and Asia Minor, reported 67 bootmakers apprentices compared with 49 tailors. See Jacobs 1891, 27.

7. For the text of the Saragossa charter see Wischnitzer 1965, 278–79.

8. Most of the information on Lynn, Massachusetts is based on Keva 2000.

9. For a detailed discussion see Idel 1996, 265–86.

10. Most of the information on the monument is based on the 2007 essay by Gyula Pauer and Can Togay.

BIBLIOGRAPHY

Ahroni, Reuben. 2001. *Jewish emigration from the Yemen 1951–98.* Richmond, Surrey: Curzon.

Altshuler, Mordechai. 1998. *Soviet Jewry on the eve of the Holocaust.* Jerusalem: The Centre for Research of East European Jewry and Yad Vashem.

Amichai, Yehuda. 1986. *The Selected Poetry of Yehuda Amichai.* Eds. and trans. Chana Bloch and Stephen Mitchell. New York: Harper and Row.

The Apocrypha. 1962. Trans. Edgar J. Goodspeed. New York: Vintage Books.

Assis, Yom Tov. 1996. *Jewish economy in the medieval crown of Aragon, 1213–1327: Money and power.* New York: E. J. Brill.

Baron, Salo Wittmayer. 1980. *A social and religious history of the Jews.* New York: Columbia University Press.

Bat Ye'or. 1972. *The Dhimmi: Jews and Christians under Islam.* Rutherford, NJ: Farleigh Dickinson University Press.

Bauer, Yehuda. 2001. *Rethinking the Holocaust,* New Haven, CT: Yale University Press.

Bellow, Saul. 1976. *To Jerusalem and back.* London: Penguin Classics.

Ben-Ezer, Ehud. 1996. "Summer, sandals and the Zionist dream" [in Hebrew]. *Hed HaKhinukh* (July/August): 20–21.

Ben Ezra, Daniel Stökl. 2003. *The impact of Yom Kippur on early Christianity.* Tübingen: Mohr Siebeck.

Ben Oliel, Abraham. 1852. "Journal of Mr. Abraham Ben Oliel." *The Christian miscellany and family visiter.* Vol. 7, 120–22, 157–60, 180–83, 218–21. London: John Mason.

Bordman, Gerald. 1994. *American theatre: A chronicle of comedy and drama, 1869–1914.* New York: Oxford University Press.

Braham, Randolph L. 1994. *The politics of genocide: The Holocaust in Hungary.* Vol. 2. New York: Columbia University Press.

Brauer, Eric. 1993. *The Jews of Kurdistan,* completed and ed. Raphael Patai. Detroit, MI: Wayne State University Press.

Brownmiller, Susan. 1984. *Femininity.* New York: Simon & Schuster.

Budgett Meakin, J. E. 1892. "The Jews of Morocco." *Jewish Quarterly Review,* 4 (3): 369–96.

Budilovsky, Joan, and Eve Adamson. 2003. *The complete idiot's guide to meditation.* Harmondsworth: Alpha Books.

Carmichael, Calum M. 1977. "A ceremonial crux: Removing a man's sandal as a female gesture of contempt." *Journal of Biblical Literature* 96 (3): 321–36.

Cawthorne, Nigel, and Pattison, Angela. 1997. *A century of shoes: Icons of style in the twentieth century.* Edison, NJ: Charwell Books.

Chinitz, Jacob. 2007. "The role of the shoe in the Bible." *Jewish Bible Quarterly* 35 (1): 41–46.

"Condition of the Jews at Tangier." 1820. *Boston Recorder* (Apr 22): 5, 17.

Crombie, James E. 1895. "Shoe-throwing at weddings." *Folklore* 6 (3): 258–81.

Daniel, Ruby. 2001. *An Indian Jewish woman remembers.* Skokie, IL: Varda Books.

de Luca, Erri. 2002. *God's mountain.* New York: Riverhead.

"The dream that rouses the yeshiva." [in Hebrew] Chabad On-Line. Available at http://www.col.org.il/show_news.rtx?artID=26420. Accessed March 2, 2008.

Engle, Anita. 1943. "Halutziuth." In *The Jewish National Home,* ed. Paul Goodman, 187–215. London: J. M. Dent & Sons.

Epstein, Louis M. 1923. "Legal conception of marriage in ancient Israel." *Jewish Quarterly Review* 14 (2): 269–74.

Ginzburg, Louis. 1956. *Legends of the Jews.* Vol. 2. New York: Simon and Schuster.

Goitein, Shelomo Dov. 1983. *A Mediterranean society.* Vol. 4. Berkeley: University of California Press.

Goitein, Shelomo Dov. 1997. "Three trousseaux of Jewish brides from the Fatimid period." *Association for Jewish Studies Review* 2: 77–110.

Golan, Nechama. 2007. Private correspondence. Sept 27, 2007.

Golinkin, David. 1992. "A responsum concerning disposing of shoes in the garbage." In *Responsa of the Law Committee of the Rabbinical Assembly in Israel.* Vol. 4, 1990–1992 [in Hebrew], 73–77, Jerusalem: The Rabbinical Assembly in Israel and the Masorti Movement.

Gordis, Robert. 1979–80. "Studies in the book of Amos." *Proceedings of the American Academy for Jewish Research* 40: 201–64.

Greenberg, Paul. 2006. "Shoes and me." *Jewish World Review* (November 29): 1–3. Also available at http://www.jewishworldreview.com/cols/greenberg1.asp. Accessed February 27, 2008.

Greenberg, Uri Zvi. 2006. "The man who stepped out of his shoes." In *The Penguin Book of Hebrew Verse,* ed. and trans. T. Carmi, 532. London: Penguin Classics.

Halevi, Judah. 2006. "Ode to Zion." In *The Penguin book of Hebrew verse,* ed. and trans. T. Carmi, 347–49. London: Penguin Classics.

Hebrew/English Babylonian Talmud, ed. Isidore Epstein. 30 vols. London: Soncino Press, 1935–1948.

Henkin, J. H. 2003. *Responsa on contemporary Jewish women' issues.* Jersey City, NJ: Ktav.

Heschel, Abraham Joshua. 1954. *Man's quest for God.* New York: Charles Scribner and Sons.

Hobsbawm, E. J., and Joan Wallach Scott. 1980. "Political shoemakers." *Past and Present* 89: 86–114.

Holy Scripture, The. 1917. Philadelphia: Jewish Publication Society.

Hundert, Gershon David. 2004. *Jews in Poland-Lithuania in the eighteenth century: A genealogy of modernity.* Berkeley: University of California Press.

Idel, Moshe. 1996. "Enoch was a stitcher of shoes" [in Hebrew]. *Kabbala* 5: 265–86.

Jacobs, Joseph. 1891. *Studies in Jewish statistics.* London: D. Nutt.

Kaite, Berkeley. 1995. *Pornography and difference.* Bloomington: Indiana University Press.

Katz, Nathan. 2000. *Who are the Jews of India?* Berkeley: University of California Press.

Kerman, Danny. 2005. "Introduction." In *Yosl Bergner, lost shoe.* Exhibition Catalogue, Tel Aviv: Dan Gallery, 2005.

Keva, Bette Wineblatt. 2000. "Shoe City's last holdout, Barry Manufacturing, to close in June." *Jewish Journal Archives* (March 31–April). Available at http://www.jewishjournal. org. Accessed February 26, 2008.

Kister, M. J. 1989. "Do not assimilate yourselves…" *Jerusalem Studies in Arabic and Islam* 12: 321–71.

Kolatch, Alfred J. 1985. *The second Jewish book of why.* Middle Valley, NY: Jonathan David Company.

Kraus, S. 1894. "The Jews in the works of the Church Fathers." *Jewish Quarterly Review* 5: 122–57.

Lamm, Maurice. 2000. *The Jewish way in death and mourning.* New York: Jonathan David.

Laskier, Michael Menachem, and Reeva Spector Simon. 2003. "Economic life." In *The Jews of the Middle East and North Africa in modern times,* ed. Reeva Spector Simon, Michael Menachem Laskier, and Sara Reguer, 29–48. New York: Columbia University Press.

Lazarus, Emma. 2005. "In the Jewish synagogue at Newport." In *Emma Lazarus: Selected poems,* ed. John Hollander, 9–10. New York: Library of America.

Levi, Primo. 1979. *The truce,* trans. Stuart Wolf. London: Abacus.

Levine, Lee. 2003. "Contextualizing Jewish art." In *Jewish culture and society under the Christian Roman Empire,* eds. Richard Kalmin and Seth Schwartz, 91–131. Leuven: Peeters.

Leyb, Mani. 2001. "I Am…," trans. John Hollander. In *Jewish American literature: A Norton anthology,* ed. Jules Chametzky, 219–20. New York: W. W. Norton & Company.

Liebman, Arthur. 1979. *Jews and the Left,* New York: John Wiley.

Marks, Steven G. 2003. *How Russia shaped the modern world: From art to anti-Semitism, ballet to Bolshevism.* Princeton, NJ: Princeton University Press.

Mikdash-Shamailov, Liya. 2003. *Mountain Jews: Customs and daily life in the Caucasus.* Hanover, NH: University Press of New England.

Midrash Rabbah. 1939. Vol. 7, trans. J. Rabinowitz. London: Soncino.

Nacht, Jacob. 1915. "The symbolism of the shoe with special reference to Jewish sources." *Jewish Quarterly Review* 6 (1): 1–22.

Patrick-Hughes, Thomas. 1995. "Shoes." In *A Dictionary of Islam,* 580–811. New Delhi: Asian Educational Services.

Pauer, Gyula, and Can Togay. 2007. "Shoes at the Danube bank." Private correspondence, Jan 30.

Perris, George Herbert. 2001. *Russia in revolution.* Boston: Elibron Classics. Facsimile reprint of 1905 edition, London: Chapman and Hall.

Pritchard, James B. 1969. *The Ancient Near East in pictures.* Princeton, NJ: Princeton University Press.

Ringgren, Helmer. 1977. *"na'al."* In *Theological dictionary of the Old Testament.* Vol. 9, ed. G. Johannes Botterweck, Helmer Ringgren, and Heinz-Joseph Fabry, trans. David E. Green, 465–67. Grand Rapids, MI: William B. Eerdmans.

Rosner, Fred. 1995. *Medicine in the Bible and the Talmud: Selections from classical Jewish sources.* Jersey City, NJ: Ktav.

Rossi, William A. 1976. *The sex life of the foot and shoe.* New York: Saturday Review Press, E. P. Dutton & Co.

Rubenstein, Jeffrey. 1992. "Purim, liminality and communitas." *Association for Jewish Studies Review* 17 (2): 247–77.

Ruderman, David B. 1976. "The founding of a Gemilut Hasadim Society in Ferrara in 1515." *Association for Jewish Studies Review* 1: 233–67.

Sadeh, Pinhas. 1983. "Rabbi Isaac Abravanel and the King's shoe" [in Hebrew]. In *The book of Jewish imaginations,* ed. Pinhas Sadeh, 223–24. Tel Aviv: Schocken.

Safrai, Shemuel. 1976. "Home and family." In *The Jewish people in the first century,* ed. Shemuel Safrai and M. Stern. Vol. 2, 728–92. Assen, The Netherlands: Van Gorcum.

Schechter, Ronald. 2003. *Obstinate Hebrews: Representations of Jews in France, 1715–1815.* Berkeley: University of California Press.

Schwartz, Howard. 1993. "A crown of shoes." In *Gabriel's palace, Jewish mystical tales,* ed. Howard Schwartz, 194–95. New York: Oxford University Press.

Singer, Isaac Bashevis. 1974. Interviewed by Sander L. Gilman. *Diacritics* 4 (1): 30–33.

Singer, Isaac Bashevis. 1981. "The little shoemakers." In *The Collected Stories of Isaac Bashevis Singer* trans. Saul Bellow, 38–56. New York: Farrar, Strauss, Giroux.

Steele, Valerie. 1985. *Fashion and eroticism: Ideals of feminine beauty from the Victorian era through the Jazz Age.* New York: Oxford University Press.

Steinberg, Jacob. 1966. "The blind woman." [in Hebrew.] In *A collection of stories by Jacob Steinberg,* ed. with an introduction by Gershon Shaked, 76–88. Tel Aviv: Yakhdav.

Stern, David, and Mark Jay Mirsky, eds. 1990. *Rabbinic fantasies, imaginative narratives from classical Hebrew literature.* Philadelphia: Jewish Publication Society.

Stillman, Yedidda Kalfon. 2000. *Arab dress: A short history from the dawn of Islam to modern times.* Leiden: Brill.

Sutzkever, Abraham. 1991. "Teacher Mira." In *A. Sutzkever: Selected poetry and prose,* 160–611 trans. Barbara Harshav and Benjamin Harshav. Berkeley: University of California Press.

Sutzkever, Abraham. 2001. "A load of shoes," trans. C. K. Williams. In *Jewish American literature: A Norton anthology,* ed. Jules Chametzky, 1162–63. New York: W. W. Norton & Company.

Traditions Renewed "Birth/Bris/Birth of a Daughter/Naming." Available at http://www.traditions renewed.com/lifecycle/trlifecycle.html. Accessed Feb 26, 2008.

Turim, Maureen. 2001. "High angels on shoes." In *Footnotes: On shoes,* ed. Shari Benstock and Suzanne Ferriss, 58–90. New Brunswick, NJ: Rutgers University Press.

Turkle, Sherry, ed. 2007. *Evocative objects.* Cambridge, MA: MIT Press.

Wexler, Paul. 1996. *The non-Jewish origins of the Sephardic Jews.* Albany: State University of New York Press.

Wischnitzer, Mark. 1965. *A history of Jewish crafts and guilds.* New York: Jonathan David.

Wright, Thomas. 1927. *The romance of the shoe: Being the history of shoemaking in all ages, and especially in England and Scotland.* London: C. J. Francombe and Sons.

Zeitlin, Solomon. 1948. "The Halaka, introduction to Tannaitic jurisprudence." *Jewish Quarterly Review* 39 (1): 1–40.

PART I: RELIGION AND THE BIBLE

2 THE BIBLICAL SHOE

ESCHEWING FOOTWEAR: THE CALL OF MOSES AS BIBLICAL ARCHETYPE

ORA HORN PROUSER

When Moses met God for the first time, in what is commonly referred to as the scene of the burning bush, he was immediately directed to remove his shoes because of the holiness of the ground on which he was to walk: "Remove your sandals from upon your feet, for the place upon which you stand is holy ground" (Ex. 3:5).[1] This is one of the most famous phrases and scenes in the Bible, referred to and repeated within the biblical text itself, emphasized in later Jewish literature, and even a phrase that has made its way into modern Hebrew. (See Figure 2.1.)

Moses, who had fled Egypt, was living a pastoral life with his Midianite family. While working as a shepherd, he was called by God to return to Egypt to lead the Israelites to freedom. This was quite a momentous meeting. It was Moses's first introduction to God. It was the first step of what would become one of the most significant stories in the Bible, as well as in Jewish thought and theology—the Exodus from Egypt. And it was God's opportunity to consecrate and direct one of the most important prophets and leaders in the Bible. Given all that God needed to ask of Moses and to explain to him at that most significant meeting, it is remarkable that the initial directive involves so seemingly mundane a matter as the removal of an article of clothing. Due to the import and placement of this statement, it becomes eminently clear that God's command involved significantly more than the simple physical removal of footwear, and even more than establishing the holiness of a moment or piece of land.

Introductions between God and an individual human being are highly instructive in regard to the future relationship that person will have with the Deity. God's first directive to Abraham is to travel and move to a new location: "Go forth from your native land, and from your father's house to the land that I will show you" (Gen. 12:1ff). This order is immediately obeyed. Subsequently, throughout their relationship God made demands on Abraham that were almost consistently obeyed without question.[2] God's first introduction to Ezekiel is an awesome vision that overwhelms him physically and emotionally (Ezek. 1–3). It is thus no accident that throughout Ezekiel's career he performed symbolic acts that engulfed his entire physical being.[3] Similarly Jeremiah's introduction to God consists of intense dialogue (Jer. 1), and Jeremiah's relationship with God throughout his career was one of conversation and passionate discourse.[4] Thus, while God's directive to Moses may simply appear to be about holiness, as specifically stated in the verse, upon closer

Figure 2.1   Title Page of Passover *Haggadah* with detail (right). (Amsterdam, 1712). Courtesy of the Library of the Jewish Theological Seminary, New York.

analysis it becomes evident that this removal of the shoes holds clues to the very nature of the relationship God is establishing with Moses and the Israelites.

Although Moses had been raised as royalty, he was living the life of an exile, not imagining his destiny as anything beyond a pastoral existence. The reader's knowledge of Moses until that point includes a few brief scenarios in which Moses showed an interesting combination of impulsive behavior and passivity. Both in Egypt and in Midian he was shown to be someone who defended the underdog through physical prowess and bravery (Ex. 2:11–17). When his actions in Egypt were discovered, however, he fled in fear (Ex. 2:14–15). In Midian there was no need to flee, but it is interesting that he did not try to build upon his heroism at the well by becoming part of Jethro's family until, after some time, he was specifically invited (Ex. 2:18–21). These contradictions make it difficult to know what to expect from Moses as we approach the burning bush episode.[5]

It is similarly difficult to know what to expect from God at this critical juncture. God hears the cries of the Israelites and decides to take action because of fidelity to the patriarchal covenant (Ex. 2:24–25). Given the history of God's relationship with humankind, it is logical that God will redeem the Israelites and save them from slavery; at the same time it cannot be ignored that God has allowed this situation to carry on for some time without intervening. Given this knowledge of God and Moses, this introduction lays the groundwork for the future relationship between God and Moses, which will have tremendous impact on the relationship between God and Israel as well.

God called to Moses, repeating his name, while Moses responded, *hineni* (Here I am) (Ex. 3:4). This models Moses squarely after the paradigm of Abraham, who was called by God with similar repetition and responded using the same word (Gen. 12:1, 22:1).[6] The very next directive to Moses demanded that he remove his shoes and not come any closer (Ex. 3:5). God immediately articulated a covenantal bond with Israel rooted in relationships with the patriarchs. Only after these introductions did God explain the divine plan to deliver the Israelites from Egypt. The removal of shoes, therefore, is bracketed by two elements connecting God to the patriarchs. Its significance, therefore, cannot be overestimated, and its meaning must be understood in order to make sense of the divine encounter with Moses.[7]

The removal of shoes evokes several meanings throughout the Bible.[8] The most famous removal of shoes—except for the call of Moses—occurs in the ceremony that formalizes a man's refusal to engage in a levirate union with his deceased brother's childless widow (Deut. 25:5; Ruth 4:7). We will not expand on this topic, as it is discussed elsewhere in this book. For our purposes, though, it is sufficient to note that there are legal implications in the removal of a shoe.[9]

Barefootedness also occurs in the context of the humiliation of captives.[10] When the release of prisoners is described, the conditions include clothing the naked among them and providing them with shoes (2 Chr. 28:14ff). It was customary for captives to be kept barefoot. This served multiple purposes, providing booty for the winners and making escape difficult (Ryken, Wilhoit, and Longman 1998, 74). Similarly, there are examples of prophetic figures performing symbolic acts, including walking naked and barefoot, to express the shame inherent in their situation of captivity and subjugation (Isa. 20:2–6).

Walking barefoot can suggest lack of readiness. David fled barefoot from his son Absalom (2 Sam. 15:30). This could be seen as a sign of mourning, as in the same verse David is described as weeping and covering his head, familiar indicators of bereavement. Given the emphasis on the haste involved in the flight (2 Sam. 15:14), however, David's shoelessness can also be seen as signifying a lack of preparation. Conversely, the wearing of shoes can be understood as a symbol of preparation. In describing the readiness of an army to destroy Israel, Isaiah emphasized that their "belts on their waists do not come loose, nor do the thongs of their sandals break" (Isa. 5:27). Similarly, Israelites were to eat the Paschal sacrifice wearing sandals and holding their staffs, to symbolize their readiness for the journey ahead of them (Ex. 12:11).

All of these meanings of being barefoot resonate in God's introduction to Moses. By asking Moses to remove his shoes as the first act in their relationship, God was setting the tone for their future interaction. God was establishing a relationship with legal significance. The patriarchal references allude to the covenant, but the removal of the shoe magnifies the legal force of this interaction. God was placing Moses on the level of a lowly captive. Moses was being humbled before God; he was being shown that his future was no longer in his own control. He was the equivalent of a prisoner, subjugated to God's will, and needed to act accordingly. Finally, Moses was being told that he was not prepared for this job. He was being asked to act "with his shoes off." There was no way he could possibly be fully prepared for this task. It is not that he was unwilling or inadequate to the task. Rather, no human being could be prepared for the enormity of this prophetic mission. It is thus in no way surprising that Moses's response to this initial contact was to hide his face in fear (Ex. 3:6) and then continue to argue his unworthiness to God (Ex. 3:11–4:17). This scene then repeats itself with Joshua soon after the Israelites entered Israel. Joshua was confronted by an angel who also told him to remove his shoes from his feet (Joshua 5:13–15).[11] The repetition of this scene serves to legitimize Joshua's status as successor to Moses and therefore to the patriarchs, and to emphasize the Israelites' new and intimate connection to the land.[12]

All of this applies not only to Moses but to the Israelites as a whole. They were all being told that this was the relationship they could have with the Divine: a covenantal legal relationship, humility, lack of choice, and lack of readiness all play themselves out further when the Israelites received their own revelation from God at Sinai (Ex. 19). The entire Sinai experience was the establishment of a legal relationship that included covenantal responsibilities and the delivery of the Decalogue, along with other laws. The Israelites experienced God's intense power, and thus they felt humbled in the Divine Presence. Finally, despite the fact that they were given elaborate preparation instructions (Ex. 19:10ff.), they were in fact totally unprepared for their experience of God. They, as Moses had, stood back in fear (Ex. 20:15).

In addition to these symbolic meanings, there is a physical role to the shoe. A major purpose of shoes is to provide protection for the feet. It is highly unusual that God should ask Moses to remove his shoes in a command to lead people on a long journey through the desert. Shoes would be most necessary for such a journey. Yet God began this call by telling Moses to remove his shoes, the very shoes he would need in order to be successful in his prophetic mission. This contradiction makes sense, however, when put in the context of Moses's call as a whole. Moses was being asked to be God's spokesman to the Israelites and to Pharaoh, and yet Moses had a severe speech defect. God often chose leaders who possessed deficits of some sort, or caused Israel to fight against great odds in unusual ways, to make clear that the victory was due to God's power and will and not to human activity.[13] Moses's success would not be due to his eloquence, his physical prowess, or his material equipment. He would succeed because of God's help and sustenance. This can be further supported in that at the end of Deuteronomy, the miraculous nature of the Israelites' journey through the desert is characterized by the state of their shoes despite the arduous nature and length of the trip: "I led you through the wilderness forty years; the clothes on your back did not wear out, nor did the sandals on your feet" (Deut. 29:4). Thus God's command to Moses to remove his shoes is also a statement that he would be protected by God throughout his journey and that he need not fear the dangers and hazards of the voyage.

The focus on shoes and feet is also especially noteworthy at this most critical juncture in the establishment of God's relationship with Israel. When looking at the role of shoes in the Bible it becomes clear that there are references to shoes in several decisive moments in the development of God's connection with Israel. Shoes are mentioned in conjunction with Abraham, Moses, Aaron, and Joshua. Shoes are also present in prophetic and poetic texts in the Prophets and Writings. The role of shoes at these critical moments could point to a larger theme of mobility and wandering, which are so much a part of biblical thought. Abraham, Moses, Aaron, and Joshua all spend significant amounts of time traveling, moving themselves, and, often, others with them, at God's direction. Shoes can symbolize this wandering, and the protection and support necessary, provided by God, during these times of travel.

This idea is further emphasized when Ezekiel tells the story of God and Israel as that of God's noticing and caring for an abandoned child (Israel) who grows into womanhood. In the description of divine choosing and support, God provided the young woman, that is, Israel, with clothing and shoes (Ezek. 16:10). As this text is meant to tell the "history" of Israel, the providing of shoes once again calls attention to the role of mobility in the story of Israel. It is equally significant, however, that in this allegory God eventually rejected the woman, Israel, because of her infidelity, and this rejection involved the removal of that same clothing (Ezek. 16:35ff.).[14]

This perspective indicates the establishment of a somewhat distant and difficult relationship between God and Moses and the Israelites. Within the text itself, however, the stated reason for Moses's removal of his shoes was that the land upon which he was standing was holy. So too, when the priests entered the Tent of Meeting, did they do so after their bare feet had been ceremonially washed (Ex. 30). They were the only ones who were allowed to enter, and they needed to be barefoot, as would later be required of the high priest upon his entry into the Holy of Holies in the Temple. There was not to be anything separating the person from the holy ground. Dealing with holiness usually involved respecting separation and distinctions, but in this case the holiness demanded a lack of separation from the land—an intimate connection between human skin and holy ground.

The removal of clothing in times of contact with the Divine resonates in several ways. The removal of clothing may be accompanied by increased intimacy. Requesting or demanding the removal of shoes indicates that God is seeking further intimacy with humans when they meet in places of holiness.[15] This theme can also be traced back to the very beginning of God's relationship with humankind. In the Garden of Eden the humans were notably naked and comfortable (Gen. 2:25). They were also in a very intimate relationship with God at that point, feeling the Divine Presence throughout the garden. Yet when they were banished from the garden, God provided them with clothing (Gen. 3:21). This is generally understood as a loving, protective act that God performed to prepare the humans for their new lives in a less protected environment. It is also possible, however, to see the clothing as a lowering of the intimacy between God and humans, and their separation into a place that is less holy. God's desire was for the humans to live in Eden, on a higher level of holiness, and a greater level of intimacy with the Divine. Once that was not to be the case, this impaired status was expressed by the humans' wearing of clothing, and the providing of that clothing by God.[16]

While nakedness is often used to express intimacy, it also places people in a more vulnerable state, leaving them open to dangers from the physical elements, and humiliation from other human beings. Indeed, full intimacy is only possible by willingly entering such a vulnerable state, trusting that, although exposed, one need fear no harm.[17]

When God commanded Moses to remove his shoes, God was inviting him to enter into a more intimate mutual relationship. God was expressing that the increased closeness carried with it the possibility, and the hope, of a very special bond—but also of specific responsibilities and clear physical and emotional dangers. God was revealing the nature of their relationship to Moses and the Israelite nation, a liaison marked by intimacy and distance, privileges and responsibilities. The study of shoes and barefootedness in the biblical text becomes a window onto an understanding of the divine connection with Israel.

NOTES

1. All biblical quotations are taken from *Tanakh—The Holy Scriptures*.
2. See, for example, Gen. 21:9ff; 22:1ff.
3. See, for example, Ezek. 4:1ff, 11:1ff, 12:17ff.
4. See, for example, Jer. 15:1ff, 20.
5. For interesting analyses of Moses as he first met God, see, for example, Fox 1995, 269–72; and Kirsch 199, 93f.
6. For more on the comparison between Moses and Abraham, see Fishbane 1974, 66f.
7. The significance of the donning and removal of shoes can be compared to the significance of wearing and removing clothing in biblical narrative texts. See Prouser 1996, 27–37. See also the importance of a spiritual, metaphorical understanding of shoes in Roth 1992, 170–82.
8. Several of these meanings are mentioned in Jacob Nacht's early article about the symbolism of shoes in many Jewish texts (Nacht 1915, 1–22). See also Ryken, Wilhoit, and Longman 1998, 74.
9. For more on this topic, see, for example, Chinitz 2007, 43ff, and Roth 1992, 174.
10. For further discussion about this topic, see, for example, Lemos 2006, 225–41.
11. Several commentators assume that Joshua was only asked to remove one shoe because of the singular form of the word *naʿalka* (your shoe) (Roth 1992, 178). Note, however, the plural form of the word *ragleka* (your feet), supporting that here too Joshua is asked to remove both shoes.
12. Martin Buber suggests further that Moses is being asked to separate himself from material goods (Buber 1988, 42). This is echoed by Jacob Chinitz (2007, 44–45) and Ariel Roth, who supports this contention through rabbinic material (Roth 1992, 177ff).
13. This thrust permeates the book of Judges, for example, in which Ehud is left-handed, Jephthah is illegitimate, and Deborah is a woman.
14. This chapter of Ezekiel, together with small sections of Hosea and Jeremiah, have been described as "pornoprophetics" by many feminist critics, as the chapters use sexual and violent metaphors in their descriptions of Israel as a woman. This discussion is beyond the scope of the present paper, but for more discussion see the many articles in Brenner 1995.

15. The relationship of nakedness and connection with the Divine finds further expression in 1 Sam. 19:24, in which Saul encounters the Divine Spirit and prophesies in naked ecstasy as a result. Saul's two cases of going into ecstasy with a group of prophets highlights his intense desire for, and love of intimacy with, the Divine (Hertzberg 1964, 167–68).

16. Mary Douglas makes the case that atonement in Leviticus is characterized by covering, as seen in priestly garments, coverings on the Tabernacle, and the like. This idea enhances the significance of those holy moments of nakedness and bare feet (Douglas 1999, 244–47).

17. Nakedness used as a method of humiliating people in the Bible can be seen in 2 Sam. 10:4, and Hos. 2:11–12.

BIBLIOGRAPHY

Brenner, Athalya, ed. 1995. *A feminist companion to the Latter Prophets,* Sheffield, UK: Academic Press.

Buber, Martin. 1988. *Moses.* New York: Prometheus Books.

Chinitz, Jacob. 2007. "The role of the shoe in the Bible." *Jewish Bible Quarterly* 35: 41–46.

Douglas, Mary. 1999. *Leviticus as literature.* New York: Oxford University Press.

Fishbane, Michael. 1974. *Text and texture.* New York: Shocken Books.

Fox, Everett. 1995. *The Shocken Bible: The five books of Moses.* New York: Shocken Books.

Hertzberg, Hans William. 1964. *I and II Samuel.* Philadelphia: Westminster John Knox Press.

Kirsch, Jonathan. 1998. *Moses: A life.* New York: Ballantine Books.

Lemos, T. M. 2006. "Shame and mutilation of enemies in the Hebrew Bible." *Journal of Biblical Literature* 125: 225–41.

Nacht, Jacob. 1915. "The symbolism of the shoe with special reference to Jewish sources." *Jewish Quarterly Review* 6: 1–22.

Prouser, O. H. 1996. "Suited to the throne: The symbolic use of clothing in the David and Saul narratives." *Journal for the Study of the Old Testament* 71: 27–37.

Roth, Ariel. 1992. "The definition and meaning of the term 'shoe' in Judaism" [in Hebrew]. *Nizanei Aretz* 8: 170–82.

Ryken, Leland, James C. Wilhoit, and Tremper Longman III, eds. 1998. *Dictionary of biblical imagery.* Westmont, IL: Intervarsity Press.

Tanakh—The Holy Scriptures. 1985. Philadelphia: Jewish Publication Society.

3 THE *HALITZAH* SHOE
BETWEEN FEMALE SUBJUGATION AND SYMBOLIC EMASCULATION

CATHERINE HEZSER

The biblical book of Deuteronomy requires a man who is unwilling to enter levirate marriage, that is, to take his deceased childless brother's widow as his wife, to create offspring for him and to perpetuate his name, to undergo the so-called *halitzah* ceremony (Deut. 25:5–10). The "unshoeing"—the widow's removal of her brother-in-law's shoe—plays a prominent role in this ritual, which was originally meant to punish and humiliate the *levir* (brother-in-law). From biblical to rabbinic, medieval, and modern times many changes in the practice, interpretation, and valuation of this ritual occurred that reflect developments in the structure of the Jewish family and the role of women in Judaism. In Roman-Byzantine and medieval times the biblical propagation of levirate marriage eventually gave way to rabbis' preference for *halitzah*, and *halitzah* rather than levirate marriage became the common practice in the state of Israel from 1950 onwards. American progressive congregations went even one step further and abolished (Reform) or avoided (Conservative) *halitzah* altogether, viewing it as part of a patriarchal social system incongruous with the status and role of women in modern society.

In the following we shall trace the development and interpretation of the *halitzah* ritual, paying particular attention to its reflection of the role of women in the respective societies. A ritual that once served to express female anger at being refused by the most natural suitor, indicating her liberation from male domination, may over time have become a meaningless formality, a means of coercion, and an affront to the sensibilities of both parties involved.

One may speculate why a shoe is used as the central ritual object in the *halitzah* ritual. Explanations range from associating the shoe with ancient forms of property transaction to seeing it as a symbol of the female sexual organ. It will be necessary to analyze the *halitzah* texts within the context of other literary references to shoes to arrive at conclusions in this regard.

THE *HALITZAH* SHOE IN THE HEBREW BIBLE

Only one biblical text deals with the *halitzah* ritual explicitly, namely the already mentioned Deuteronomy 25:5–10:

> (5) If brothers dwell together, and one of them dies, and he does not have a child [or: son, *ben*], the wife of the deceased shall not be married outside [the family] to a stranger [*le'ish sar*]. Her brother-in-law shall come upon her and take her as his wife and perform

the duty of the brother-in-law. (6) And the first-born that she gives birth to shall be installed in the name of his dead brother, and his name shall not be erased from Israel. (7) And if the man should not desire to take his sister-in-law, his sister-in-law shall go to the gate to the elders and say: My brother-in-law refuses to set up for his brother a name in Israel. He will not perform the duty of a brother-in-law unto me. (8) And the elders of the city call him and talk to him. And [if] he stands [firm] and says: I do not desire to take her—(9) his sister-in-law shall approach him under the eyes of the elders and tear [*ve'haltzah*] his shoe from his foot and spit in his face [or: in front of him, *be'fanav*]. And she shall answer and say: Thus shall be done to a man who does not build the house of his brother. (10) And his name shall be called in Israel "House of the Unshoed [*bet halutz ha-na'al*]." (Author's translation)

This text was formulated in the context of a patriarchal and patrilineal society in which a married woman would automatically become a member of her husband's family and remain within this family even after his death. In a patriarchal society the family name and the family property could be transmitted from one generation to the next through male heirs only (Epstein 1942, 98). Therefore it is most likely that the childlessness of the deceased in the text above refers to his lack of sons in particular. Susan Niditch has pointed to the anomalous situation of the childless widow in a society where women's identity "depends upon their bearing their husband's children" (Niditch 1979, 144). A childless widow could neither be a virgin in her father's house nor a mother in her husband's family, the two roles available to women in patrilocal societies. The levirate marriage and the *halitzah* rite were two possibilities to rectify her situation and to enable her to assume a legitimate place within the social structure of the time (Niditch 1979, 145–46). In a society that allowed polygamy and put a lot of emphasis on bonds among members of the extended family, the brother-in-law would be the most suitable partner to replace the deceased. As wife of her husband's brother, the widow would be able to fulfill her duty of procreation and in turn be maintained by her husband's family.

The Deuteronomistic account, as well as the stories about Judah and Tamar in Genesis 38 and Ruth and Boaz in the book of Ruth, indicate that men were not very keen on entering levirate marriages in biblical times (see also Weisberg 2004, 405). Tamar and Ruth had to disguise themselves to entice their kinsmen (however, men other than their brothers-in-law) in order to make them enter into unions with them. The Deuteronomistic enactment of the *halitzah* rite is meant to punish and humiliate men who refuse to enter levirate marriages. In the Hebrew Bible the levirate is presented as positive for women but disadvantageous for men: it would ensure widows' maintenance and proper status within society but constitute a financial burden and disadvantage for the male. Unless the widow is beautiful and the *levir* desires her, he has nothing to win. He can only lose: the son he procreates and raises would bear the name of his deceased brother and this son would inherit his deceased brother's part of the family property, which would otherwise be distributed among the brothers immediately. We do not know whether, and to what extent, the shameful aspects of the *halitzah* rite were effective in increasing instances of levirate marriage in biblical times. It is probably indicative that aside from the three mentioned texts no traditions about levirate marriage are transmitted in any of the biblical writings.

According to Deuteronomy 25:7 the *levir* is free to refuse levirate marriage without having to convince the elders of his reasons.[1] If he refuses to marry his brother's widow, the *halitzah* ceremony is supposed to take place. Only Deuteronomy 25:9 presents the ceremony of unshoeing, which seems to be a specifically Deuteronomistic innovation missing in Genesis 38 and Ruth. In Ruth 4:4–7 a custom "of former times" is mentioned: "to confirm all matter [of transaction] a man would pull off his shoe and give it to his [business] partner, and this was the confirmation [of a transaction] in Israel." Since the near kinsman is unwilling to perform the rite, Boaz is asked to do it for himself (v. 8): by taking off his shoe (and presumably taking it back himself) in the presence of elders Boaz is said to have acquired Elimelech's property, including Ruth his widow. This ritual does not contain any of the humiliating aspects of the unshoeing described in Deuteronomy 25:9.[2] It is also not the woman but the man himself who loosens his shoe. The fact that the Deuteronomist ascribes the action of the unshoeing to the woman—and it should be noted that the woman is the main actor in the entire ceremony—must make it especially humiliating for the *levir*.

SHOE SYMBOLISM AND *HALITZAH*

If we take into consideration that shoes were valuable objects, symbols of prestige, and means of exerting power in biblical antiquity,[3] taking off the *levir*'s shoe and revealing his naked foot would have constituted a serious offense to his manhood. Not everyone will have been able to afford shoes, and those who did would probably wear them for many years until they fell apart (Deut. 29:4: wearing the same shoes for forty years in the wilderness).[4] Slaves and members of the poorer strata of society went barefoot (Baker 1996–1997, 197). Shoes served as means to transfer property (Ruth 4:7–8) and to claim territory (Ps. 60:10: "over Edom I will cast my shoe"), that is, they were associated with property ownership. Therefore we have to assume that becoming barefoot did not merely mean "being deprived of normal dress" (Chinitz 2007, 41), but being deprived of an emblem that signified dignity, honor, and power within the ancient social unit.

That the unshoeing is ascribed to a woman could, on the one hand, be understood in a Freudian sense as permission to divest him of the means of exerting male power, a female revenge against his unwillingness to share his semen with her and allow her to bear children. The unshoeing could then be considered a symbolic emasculation, and the "House of the Unshoed" a disparaging name for the household whose patriarch's manly pride and dignity was lost. On the other hand, one also has to be aware of the fact that the unshoeing itself was a slavish gesture in antiquity. Slaves would take off their master's shoes: "To loosen a person's shoe-strings . . . is equivalent to subjugation. The master gains authority over his servant as soon as the latter loosens his shoestring" (Nacht 1915–1916: 4–5).[5] Could this association also have played a role in the *halitzah* rite? Would the woman's loosening of the levir's shoe (also) be an expression of her subjugation under him, of a normal female duty turned upside down?

Based on an earlier article by Ludwig Levy, Calum Carmichael has suggested that the foot may be understood as a symbol of the male sexual organ, while the shoe symbolizes the vagina (Carmichael 1977, 323).[6] In the *halitzah* ritual the woman would then be seen to "withdraw symbolically from him by removing his shoe [i.e., herself]. She thereby breaks off the potential marital relationship" (Carmichael 1977, 323). There are no biblical texts that would support this equation, so that Carmichael has to base his argument on "almost universal folk usage" and an Arab (Bedouin) form of divorce (Carmichael 1977, 323). But the later rabbis were well aware of the sexual symbolism of the foot and shoe. For example, in Midrash Genesis Rabbah, Pharaoh's being afflicted with lupus is explained as follows on the basis of his relations with Abraham's wife (cf. Gen. 12:15–17): "R. Berekiah said: Because he dared to approach the shoe of that lady" (Gen. R. 41:2), the shoe obviously denoting her vagina, that is, the text suggests that they had sexual intercourse.[7] A similar imagery appears in the Zohar, where a divine messenger's command to Joshua, "Take your shoe from off your foot" (Josh. 5:15), is explained: "for the reason that he separated himself from his wife only at certain times" (Zohar, Soncino ed., vol. 3, p. 148a).

The symbolism can also be used in a reversed direction, however. According to a passage in the Babylonian Talmud, a woman might reject suitors from a superior family background by saying: "I do not want a shoe too large for my foot": if the bridegroom pretends to be of a higher status than he actually is, the betrothal is invalid (b. Qid. 49a). Here the man is compared with the shoe and the woman with the foot. This would also fit the general symbolism of the shoe, mentioned earlier, as an instrument of power and conquest. Based on this imagery, the shoe would symbolize male power over his wife and the unshoeing the undoing of it.

Paul A. Kruger has criticized Calum Carmichael's interpretation by questioning the original audience's proper understanding of the sexual symbolism (Kruger 1996, 536). He suggests understanding the biblical *halitzah* rite as a rite of passage instead: through the unshoeing, the widow liberates herself from the *levir*'s authority and becomes free to begin a new life based on her own choice (Kruger 1996, 536). Viewing the *halitzah* as a rite of passage does not necessarily contradict our understanding of it as an emasculation, explained earlier. Rather, these two ways of understanding complement each other and provide a more comprehensive interpretation: the ritual emasculation of the *levir* is necessary as a rite of passage for the woman to regain her own identity from the time before she was married. Such a ritual is both humiliating (for a final time it puts her into the position of the wife/slave) and liberating (it divests her of her husband's/*levir*'s authority over herself); it marks the boundary between her status as married woman and independent widow, between being maintained within and by her (deceased) husband's family and having to find her own means of support. One should refrain from viewing the biblical institutions of levirate and *halitzah* from a modern perspective, though: for biblical women the levirate may well have been preferable to an independent and unsupported status.[8] This situation would have given the *halitzah* ritual its violent character as a genuine expression of anger, the shoe being torn off the *levir*'s foot rather than merely being unloosened, an action supported by spitting into the *levir*'s face.[9]

RABBINIC VIEWS ON *HALITZAH*

Not much is known about levirate marriage and *halitzah* in Second Temple times. Because levirate marriage is mentioned or implied a few times in Josephus, the New Testament, and tannaitic sources referring to Temple times, Tal Ilan assumes that "levirate marriage was more frequently practiced than *halitzah*" at that time (Ilan 1995, 155).[10] The sparse references do not allow us to determine, however, whether levirate marriage was the general practice; it may well have been limited to the propertied strata of society, to men who could support more than one woman. If the biblical form of levirate was maintained, there would be little incentive for men to enter such unions, besides piety and concern for the widow's subsistence.

What is striking is that the rabbis of the first four and a half centuries C.E. reinterpreted and changed the biblical rules to adapt them to their own circumstances. Although the three biblical texts discussed previously indicate that levirate marriage was not particularly favored by men, rabbis tried to make the levirate attractive to their contemporaries. At the same time rabbis acknowledged the equal validity of *halitzah* and removed all of the negative connotations of humiliation and denunciation that were an essential part of the biblical rite. Their transformation of the character of levirate marriage almost renders it meaningless, hardly distinguishable from any other marriage. The original intention, to raise an heir to the deceased man's name and property, would be lost in the process.

Deuteronomy 25:2 explicitly states that the first-born son of the widow and the *levir* "shall be installed in the name of his dead brother, and his name shall not be erased from Israel," that is, he will bear the name of his deceased uncle and inherit his portion of the family property when he is sufficiently mature. As Samuel Belkin has pointed out, "the desire to ensure the continuity of the family name and to preserve within its midst ancestral property is a common phenomenon among all people" (Belkin 1970, 275). All the more surprising are the Mishnah's rulings, which suggest that the newborn son would be the proper child of the *levir* and that the *levir* and not the son would become owner of the deceased brother's property (M. Yeb. 4:7). The rabbis thereby provide the *levir* with a "financial incentive for levirate marriage" and render levirate marriage almost indistinguishable from other marriages in which the husband has full authority over his minor children and over his wife's earnings (Weisberg 1998, 47, 50).[11] They normalize levirate marriage, but this normalization leads to the loss of its original purpose, namely the maintenance and continuation of the deceased brother's name and property (see also Weisberg 1998, 50–51).

Despite the changes to make levirate marriage more attractive to men, rabbis do not seem to put any pressure on men to enter it. Rather, they limited its applicability and considered *halitzah* similarly appropriate, albeit with a financial disadvantage: if he refused to marry his deceased brother's widow the brother-in-law would not receive his deceased brother's entire property; the property would go to the father of the deceased or be distributed among all surviving brothers (M. Yeb. 4:7).[12] *Halitzah* itself seems to have become a mere formality, "a useful, and sometimes necessary procedure" (Weisberg 1998, 53).[13] In M. Yebamot 12:3, where the ritual is discussed in more detail, the spitting is not even required by all rabbis to render the ritual valid.[14] But the unshoeing is; it remains the one essential part of the process acknowledged as necessary by all rabbis.

Would *halitzah* have maintained its original meaning at a time when the refusal to enter levirate marriage was no longer seen as objectionable by the religious authorities, at a time when rabbis might even argue against levirate marriage on the basis of its possible violation of the Levitical incest laws? An argument that comes up frequently in later discussions may be posed here as well: "if levirate is not a viable option for him, . . . why should he suffer humiliation during the *halitzah* ceremony?" (Weisberg 1998: 59). If the humiliating aspects are removed from the ritual, if the ritual has become a mere formality rather than a violent expression of anger against the brother-in-law's refusal to fulfill his obligations toward the deceased, one may well argue that the ritual has lost its proper purpose, together with the levirate union itself.[15] The scholarly discussion about whether rabbis preferred *halitzah* over levirate marriage becomes obsolete then.

Why would rabbis have introduced such radical changes to the institution of levirate marriage? According to Dvora Weisberg, rabbis cared more for the living than for the dead: they allowed the levirate widow to achieve a socially legitimate status but were no longer concerned about memorializing the dead through children (Weisberg 1998, 67).[16] Belkin points to the "natural aspect" of fatherhood: "the deceased male was not the natural father of the new born child," and adoption did not exist as a legal option in ancient Jewish society (Belkin 1970, 290). He also suggests that a "moral sentiment" may have been the primary motivation for maintaining levirate marriage (Belkin 1970, 320). We would argue that socioeconomic reasons may have been relevant as well. The fact that the brother-in-law may take possession of the deceased brother's wife and property suggests that rabbis were mostly concerned about keeping his property intact within the family. Is the wife merely seen as part of the family property then, as Judith Romney Wegner has suggested (Wegner 1988, 97)? Until the brother-in-law submits to the *halitzah* ceremony she is legally bound to him, and her body can be used to increase the number of children within the family. Yet tannaitic rabbis' attempts to render the *halitzah* ceremony a mere formality might also have increased potential *levirs'* willingness to set the widow free.

THE *HALITZAH* SHOE AND THE ROMAN SANDAL

Deuteronomy 25:9 merely says that the widow shall "tear his shoe from his foot" but does not specify what kind of shoe could be used. According to the plain wording of the text one would assume that any shoe belonging to the *levir* could be employed in the ritual.

The rabbis of the Mishnah already considered it necessary to specify the nature of the shoe. M. Yeb. 12:1 rules that

> [If] halitzah [was performed] with a shoe [*man'ol*], her *halitzah* is valid; with felt shoes [*anfilin*, from Greek *empilion*, Lat. *impilia*], her *halitzah* is invalid. With a sandal [*sandal*] which has a heel, it is valid; and [if] it does not have a heel, it is invalid. From the knee and below, her *halitzah* is valid; from the knee and above, her *halitzah* is invalid.

On the one hand, the biblical reference to a shoe is expanded to include sandals. On the other hand, certain types of shoes are considered inappropriate for the rite, namely those made of felt cloth (i.e., socks) and sandals without heels. That the shoe or sandal as well as the straps should be made of leather is not specified here. The Talmud Yerushalmi (y. Yeb. 12:1, 12c) even transmits a story according to which "the brother of the mother of R. Kahana performed *halitzah* by night, with a single judge, on the Sabbath, with a sandal made of cork, standing up" and without spitting. Obviously, everything was wrong about this procedure and some rabbis did not like it, but there is no reference to anyone declaring it invalid. It seems that these matters were not strictly regulated in late Roman Palestine, that rabbis were not unanimous about them, and that they had little authority in enforcing their teachings anyway.

The next Mishnah (12:2) provides a rather broad understanding of the biblical reference to "his shoe":

> [If] she performed *halitzah* with a sandal that did not belong to him, or with a sandal [made] of wood, or with [a shoe] for the left foot on the right foot, her *halitzah* is valid. [If] she performed *halitzah* with a [too] large [shoe] in which he can walk, or with a [too] small one which covers the larger part of his foot, her *halitzah* is valid.

According to this text, the brother-in-law does not need to own the sandal himself but can use someone else's as well. The shoe or sandal does not even need to fit him properly, the only requirements being that it cover his foot and that he can walk a few steps in it. Even a wooden shoe can be used. In the Yerushalmi a statement transmitted by R. Hela in the name of R. Yochanan declares that "even if the whole of it is made out of wood, it is valid" (y. Yeb. 12:2, 12d). Rabbis allegedly disagreed concerning straw sandals: R. Aqiba considered them valid for *halitzah*, whereas sages considered them invalid (see the *baraita*, the tannaitic tradition, quoted previously from the Talmud Yerushalmi).

This general expansion of the variety of shoes that can be used in the *halitzah* ceremony and the broad understanding of "his shoe," that he can walk in it but does not need to own it, is probably related to the actual use of shoes in ancient Jewish society. As already pointed out, shoes were quite valuable, and not everyone would have owned a proper pair of leather shoes. The cheaper and less elaborate sandals would have been much more prevalent and were worn by many more people (Baker 1996–1997, 199; Krauss 1910, 177–78). The Babylonian Talmud even says explicitly that sandals were customarily used for *halitzah*

(b. Yeb. 102a: "for the people have long ago adopted the practice [of *halitzah*] with a sandal"). It seems that rabbis did not want to make the validity of the ritual dependent on the *levir*'s ownership of expensive leather shoes. Therefore they allowed shoes of different forms and materials to be used, even if they were merely borrowed for the occasion.[17] Only certain types that might not be considered shoes at all (felt socks) or that might fall apart during the tearing (straw sandals) were excluded, but even in some of these cases rabbis disagreed among themselves about what was permissible and what should be prohibited. Again, the Babylonian Talmud spells out the motives behind rabbis' specifications: they want to prevent the use of faulty or damaged shoes (b. Yeb. 102a) and footwear that may not be regarded as proper shoes at all (b. Yeb. 102b).[18]

Whereas rabbinic sources distinguish between shoes and sandals only, Roman sources know of a great variety of shoes. By Hellenistic times, shoemaking had become a highly specialized profession, and shoes of different forms, materials, and qualities for different genders, occupations, and purposes were made. Shoes would also serve as status symbols; on the basis of their shape, material, color, and craftsmanship one's association with the lower or higher strata of society could be discerned (Baker 1996–1997, 198). Among the various types of Roman shoes were the *calceus,* a heeled shoe that covered the whole foot and would normally reach to the calf, fastened with laces or straps in the center. Different forms of *calcei* for women, senators, patricians, and so on existed. The term *carbatina* seems to have been used for shoes cut from one piece of leather, fastened by a lace. Distinguished from these proper shoes were the various types of sandals: the simple leather-soled sandals with a thong between the toes called *soleae* and the more elaborate *crepidae* and *caligae.* The latter two seem to have covered more of the foot than the *soleae;* they would enclose the heel and have leather uppers and/or straps fastened around the sides of the foot, but they were nevertheless partly open.[19] At Masada, women's and children's shoes as well as Roman soldiers' sandals, which usually had nails fastened to them, were found.[20]

Baker points out that the *calcei,* ankle-high boots laced in the front, "were the forerunners of most of the shoes worn in Europe during the Middle Ages" (Baker 1996–1997, 198). Through Roman conquests, Roman-style shoes would be brought into and copied throughout the provinces. They would have been the common type of footwear in Roman Palestine as well.[21] Baker even suggests that "much of the world's footwear in succeeding periods derived from Roman shoes. The concept of closed footwear, especially military boots modeled after the *caliga,* was carried by the Roman legions to distant lands" (Baker 1996–1997, 199). Some of the illustrations of *halitzah* shoes in early modern books resemble Roman shoes (see Figure 3.3). Whether this is due to a certain conservativism in the manufacture of ritual artifacts or illustrations or whether such traditional-style shoes were still worn in the respective time periods can be determined only once all existing *halitzah* shoes have been dated, catalogued, and compared with the shoe fashions of the times in which they were used.

Figure 3.1 Halitzah Ceremony, Germany, eighteenth century. Source: Kirchner (1734). Courtesy of the Library of the Jewish Theological Seminary, New York.

Figure 3.2 Halitzah ceremony, Germany, eighteenth century. Source: Adler (1773). Courtesy of the Library of the Jewish Theological Seminary, New York.

Figure 3.3   Halitzah shoe. Source: Calmet (1732). Courtesy of the Library of the Jewish Theological Seminary, New York.

HALITZAH IN THE MIDDLE AGES

In the past scholars have argued for significant differences between Ashkenazic and Sephardic communities with regard to levirate marriage and *halitzah*. In particular, it was suggested that levirate marriage would have been more frequently practiced by Sephardic Jews, who lived in an environment in which polygamy was common (Epstein 1942, 123–24). The ban against polygamy is usually associated with Rabbenu Gershom (c. 960–1028) in sources from the twelfth century C.E. (Falk 1966, 16–17). Occasionally, levirate marriages seem to have been conducted in German communities even after that time, on the basis of the assumption that the biblical commandment of levirate marriage was more authoritative than the ban.[22] But in general Ashkenazic rabbis tended to prefer *halitzah* to levirate marriage: "The ban was accepted by the French/German communities, who all considered themselves to be Gershom's disciples" (Falk 1966, 33). Accordingly, in Ashkenazic communities *halitzah* became the customary ritual if a levirate situation arose.

With reference to the situation in Italy from the late fifteenth century onwards, Howard Adelman has pointed out that "it is necessary to read rabbinic literature as responses to a much more variegated reality than the rabbis wanted" (Adelman 1994, 117). There seem to have been disagreements among rabbis and variant local customs, which led him to the conclusion that "neat categorizations of Ashkenazim and Sephardim do not hold up in light of findings about *yibbum* and polygyny in Italy" (Adelman 1994, 117). Even in areas where Jews lived under Islamic rule, such as Egypt and Palestine, it seems to have become customary in the twelfth century not to take a second wife during the first wife's lifetime (Falk 1966, 10).

In Italy and elsewhere financial aspects were very important, and if no compromise could be achieved rabbis had to use bribes or threats of excommunication to persuade brothers-in-law to perform *halitzah*.[23] Interestingly, *ketubbah* clauses in which the brother-in-law agreed to release the widow willingly after her husband's death, and others granting divorce under certain circumstances such as serious illness or long journeys, were already introduced in Italy at that time (Adelman 1994, 110).[24] They would prevent the occurrence of the problem of the *agunah,* the widow unable to remarry, which prevails in orthodox communities today.

In classical rabbinic literature the choice between levirate marriage and *halitzah* was the *levir*'s only (Weisberg 2000, 59). In his *Mishneh Torah,* Maimonides (1135/38–1204) maintains that view (2:16) but also states that a woman had to agree to levirate marriage; otherwise *halitzah* should be performed (1:2).[25] He nevertheless insists on the precedence of the "*mitzvah*" of levirate marriage over *halitzah* (1:2), and this view is quoted in the *Shulchan Aruch* (Even HaEzer 165:1). Maimonides limits the applicability of levirate marriage by a broad understanding of "child" in Deuteronomy 25:5: if there is any child of a Jewish wife, even a daughter or illegitimate progeny, neither levirate marriage nor *halitzah* is necessary (1:3).

Maimonides also specifies the procedure of *halitzah:* a ninety-day interval between the death of the husband and levirate marriage or *halitzah* should be maintained (1:19). After the widow has approached the judges at the *levir*'s place of residence, the judges determine the place where the ceremony should take place (4:1–2). The *levir* and the widow are instructed in their respective declarations beforehand, and three more individuals who can read must be present (4:5). Concerning the shoe Maimonides states that

> a leather shoe with a heel, that is not sewn with linen threads, is brought to [the *yavam,* her brother-in-law, the brother of the deceased husband]. He places it on his right foot and ties its straps around his foot.... He then presses his foot to the ground. She sits [on the ground], extends her hand before the court, loosens the straps of his shoe, removes it, and throws it to the ground. At the moment she removes the majority of the heel..., she becomes free to marry another man. (4:6)

Maimonides thereby establishes the proper protocol and procedure for the *halitzah* ritual. He also removes the ancient rabbinic permission to use a variety of shoes and sandals by specifying that a heeled leather shoe with leather straps should be used.[26] Shoes made of cloth, without a heel, sewn with linen threads, made from goat's hair, the inner balk of a palm tree, cork, or wood are unacceptable (4:18). The form of the shoe is not further determined, and we have to assume that it could vary from one locality to the next. The shoe should be "brought to" the brother-in-law; it does not have to be his own shoe, as stated explicitly later on (cf. 4:19), but it should "belong" to him at the outset of the ceremony. Today rabbinic courts own *halitzah* shoes, but "it is customary to give it to the *yavam* as a present before the ceremony."[27] Since the *yavam* must be able to make a few steps in it only, one may assume that a standard size shoe would be suitable in most cases.

HALITZAH IN MODERN TIMES

Levirate marriage was practiced in Sephardic and Mizrachi communities until 1950, when the Israeli Chief Rabbi Herzog, supported by the Sephardi Chief Rabbi Uziel, prohibited its practice in Israel (Katz 1994, 28). This prohibition was criticized by Mizrachi Jews, who saw it as an expression of Ashkenazic Jews' dominance in the newly founded state (West-reich 2003–2004, 426). The main reason for the abolishment of the biblical regulation was that two different family law traditions could hardly coexist in harmony in a modern state, and that levirate marriage conflicted with the position of women in modern society (Westreich 2003–2004, 426). From that time onward *halitzah* became customary in cases in which the husband died childless, a circumstance more prevalent in Israel than in the Diaspora because of the military situation.[28]

The German Reform movement had already abolished both levirate marriage and *halitzah* in the nineteenth century. As a rabbi Abraham Geiger would conduct the *halitzah* ritual, if a community member wished to perform it, but "he was persuaded that its social function had long ceased to exist" (Meyer 1988, 113). Michael A. Meyer points to an 1837 article in which Geiger suggested the abolition of both the *halitzah* ritual and the status of the *agunah*, "which imposed indignity or cruelty on Jewish women" (Meyer 1988, 140). In 1839, M. Gutmann, district rabbi of Redniz, published a detailed article on levirate marriage and *halitzah*, in which he argued for the abolition of these institutions, because they had lost their meaning in modern times (Gutmann 1839, 61–87). Since medieval times polygamy has been prohibited, and even in cases where it did not apply, Ashkenazic rabbis argued against levirate marriage. If the brother-in-law is not able to enter levirate marriage, he cannot reject it; if he does not reject it, one cannot legitimately require him to undergo the *halitzah* ritual (Gutmann 1839, 64, 77–78). At a time when levirate marriage has practically been abolished for a long time already, *halitzah*, meant as a punishment for the *levir's* rejection of the levirate, is pointless. To continue performing it under entirely changed circumstances is to disregard the Torah's plain meaning (Gutmann 1839, 65–66). At the Leipzig synod's second meeting in 1871, there was "near unanimous consent" that the traditional halakhic necessity of the *halitzah* ritual (as it was upheld by the orthodox) should not prevent a widow's remarriage, now that *halitzah* was rarely practiced by Jews anymore (Meyer 1988, 190).

The American Conservative Movement has not abolished *halitzah* as has the Reform movement, but tries to avoid it nevertheless. The Committee on Jewish Law and Standards has discussed the issue time and again since the 1930s. In 1934 it was already suggested to introduce "a premarital agreement between husband and wife to obviate the Halitzah ceremony" (Golinkin 1997, vol. 1, 77). In an article on the "Adjustment of the Jewish Marriage Laws to Present-Day Conditions" (1935), Louis Epstein emphasizes that "the Committee is unanimous in wishing to make an end to *Halitzah*, if it can be done within the limits and through the instrumentality of the Law itself" (Epstein 1997, vol. 2, 664). Nevertheless, he argues against the committee's suggestion that all marriages should be conditional—with a clause inserted into the *ketubbah* (marriage contract) stating that if the husband dies childless, the marriage has no effect—by declaring conditional marriages unethical (Epstein 1997, vol. 2, 666–67).[29] Epstein proposes a different formula, in which the husband declares that, if he is still childless after ten years of marriage, "I shall cause a divorce to be written for my wife…to be effective one hour before my death" (Epstein 1997, vol. 2, 666).

In a 1951 statement by Rabbi Isaac Klein on "The problem of chalitzah today," the issue was brought up again (Klein 1997, vol. 2, 757–61). Klein stresses the "indignities and injustices" the childless widow often has to deal with: "extortion and blackmail" may be used against her by her brother-in-law, while rabbis are unable to force him to agree to *halitzah* (Klein 1997, vol. 2, 757). In addition, "more and more women are unwilling to submit to the obligation. The ceremony has become repugnant and meaningless to the modern mind" (Klein 1997, vol. 2, 757). He rejects Rabbi Henry Fisher's suggestion to abolish *halitzah* because levirate marriage has been abolished (see also the Reform argument presented earlier), however, by saying that it "has been discontinued only *de facto* but not *de jure*" (Klein 1997, vol. 2, 757–58). Halakhically one can only argue for certain preventive measures to avoid *halitzah,* by inserting a respective clause into the *ketubbah,* as already suggested before.

Conservative rabbis would agree with Reform rabbis that *halitzah* originated and was practiced in social conditions that were entirely different from ours today: at a time when polygamy was common, when women could not inherit and make a living themselves, when people believed in immortality through children (Golinkin 1997, vol. 1, 434: Report of the CJLS, 1958). Yet only individual Conservative rabbis were willing to abolish this ritual altogether, whereas the CJLS (Committee on Jewish Law and Standards) preferred to evade it in a halakhically justifiable way.[30]

Since the nineteenth century, progressive Jews have seen the *halitzah* ritual as a symbol of women's subjugation within ancient patriarchal society rather than as a ritual of liberation from marital restrictions. As we have seen, *halitzah* had lost its original radical meaning in rabbinic times already, when it became a mere formality. In the Middle Ages, when polygamy was outlawed and levirate marriage not practiced anymore, *halitzah* had entirely lost its original meaning. Within the modern context, at a time when women refuse to identify themselves on the basis of their ability to bear children and when they are financially independent, the meaning of *halitzah* is overturned: it has become a reminiscence of patriarchal oppression and female dependence on men.[31]

NOTES

1. Yoffie 2000, 22 stresses that the "Torah allows the man to refuse this marriage though the process of *halitzah* but provides no such avenue for the woman."
2. Differences between the ceremonies described in Ruth and Deuteronomy have already been noticed by several scholars; see, for example, Carmichael 1977, 324; Kruger 1996, 535; Chinitz 2007, 44.
3. Nacht 1915–1916, 2: "The shoe denotes supreme power and possession."
4. Nacht 1915–1916, 10 points to rabbinic sources that suggest that the same shoes would be worn on weekdays and Sabbath, by father and child. A tradition in b. Git. (Babylonian Talmud tractate Gitin) 68b suggests that a pair be worn for seven years. According to b. Shab. (Babylonian Talmud tractate Shabbat) 112a, "Rab Judah…had a pair of sandals, at times he went out in them, at others

his child." According to a story tradition in Lam. R. (Midrash Lamentations Rabbah) 1:13, sandals might be sold for seven to ten dinars, that is seven to ten daily wages of a day laborer.

5. See, for example, b. B.B. (Babylonian Talmud tractate Bava Batra) 53b: "If the slave fastens or undoes his master's shoe." See also Mark 1:7, parallel to Luke 3:16 and John 1:27: John the Baptist is not even worthy enough to loosen the laces of Jesus' shoes. This is meant as an expression of self-humiliation, because loosening other people's shoestrings was one of the most lowly tasks. Krauss 1910, 180 points out that this task could be quite arduous and time-consuming due to the complicated network of laces typical of Roman shoes and sandals.

6. See also Levy 1918, 182–83. Nacht 1915–1916, 15 also refers to the foot as a "symbolic designation for the man."

7. The text has a parallel in Gen. R. 52:13.

8. Roth 1988, 61–73 shows that various forms of levirate marriage were and are still practiced in many societies.

9. Hasan-Rokem 2003, 68–69 sees a connection between spitting in the *halitzah* rite and spitting in a story transmitted in Lev. R. (Midrash Leviticus Rabbah) 9:9. When a woman goes to listen to R. Meir's teachings against her husband's wishes, he locks her out of her home until she has spit into the rabbi's face to humiliate him. He seems to have seen the Torah scholar as a competition to his power as a husband. In the story the meaning of the spitting is reversed by the rabbi: it serves healing purposes, that is, the association of spitting and humiliation is subverted here.

10. See Josephus, Ant. 4.8.23 (254), where *halitzah* is also mentioned; also Mark 12:19–25, where levirate marriage seems to be implied.

11. Interestingly, "the responsibility for the marriage contract falls on the estate of the deceased" (M. Yeb. 4:4), thereby increasing the financial advantages of levirate marriage.

12. See Weisberg 1998, 46, 52–57 for a discussion of the restrictions on levirate marriage introduced by rabbis. While this article focuses on the Mishnah, the rabbis of the Babylonian Talmud similarly considered levirate marriage and *halitzah* equally valid; see Weisberg 2000, 60.

13. See also Ilan 1995, 153.

14. See also Sifre Deut. 291, where the spitting is reinterpreted: it has to be before the elders, but not necessarily into the brother-in-law's face.

15. It should be noted that, in contrast to rabbis, Josephus has maintained and even intensified the aspect of humiliation when writing: "The wife of his brother shall loosen his sandals (note that the plural is used here!) and spit in his face and declare that he merits this treatment from her for having outraged the memory of the departed. Then let him quit the council of elders and carry this reproach throughout his life" (Ant. 4.8.23, 254).

16. See also Weisberg 2000, 65, where she suggests that "rabbinic Judaism, with its de-emphasis on material goods, its focus on Torah study, ... may regard childlessness as a personal tragedy rather than a kind of death or uprooting." Therefore "reproduction was seen as a less than certain way of transmitting one's values; if so, reproducing for the deceased might seem less urgent."

17. Cf. b. Yeb. 103b: "His shoe implies one which he can wear." See also b. Qid. 14a.

18. In b. Yeb. 102b even sandals of cork or bast and felt socks with foot support are declared valid.

19. On the various types of shoes see Baker 1996–1997, 198–99. There are a number of Web sites with images of Greek and Roman shoes.

20. See Baker 1996–1997, 200–201 for images of the excavated shoes.

21. Unfortunately, no detailed study of footwear in Hellenistic and Roman Palestine exists to date.

22. See Falk 1966, 17, on the judgment of the council of Speyer, Worms, and Mainz in 1160; Falk 1966, 31, on Eliezer of Metz at the end of the twelfth century; Falk 1966, 32, on Jacob Segal Moeln at the beginning of the fifteenth century.

23. See the cases described by Adelman 1994, 107–10, 114–15.

24. Similarly, a letter of *halitzah* dated Breslau 1765, commissioned by the husband's brothers and signed by the scribe and beadle of the community, confirms that *halitzah* will be given to the wife if the husband should die childless; see Duschinsky 1920, 448.

25. The references refer to Maimonides 1995.

26. See also the Shulchan Aruch, Even HaEzer 169:15.

27. R. Eliyahu Touger's comment on Maimonides's text in Maimonides 1995, 67, n. 59.

28. The Israeli film *I Love You Rosa* (1972), directed by Moshe Mizrahi and set in Jerusalem at the end of the nineteenth century, thematizes the problematics of the levirate institution, when the brother-in-law is still a child and the widow has to wait for him to become an adult. Interestingly, the widow makes the real decisions on entering and breaking up levirate marriage here, while the *levir* merely follows her wishes. She is very concerned about remaining within the parameters of Jewish law and asks for *halitzah* when realizing that her relationship to the *levir* is based on mutual love and attraction rather than on duty to the deceased. Nevertheless, the *halitzah* ceremony remains incomplete (she is unable to take off his shoe) and they become a couple at the happy end.

29. For the wording of the formula see Epstein 1997, 664–65.

30. In his response to Rabbi Klein's statement (1951), Rabbi Henry Fisher reemphasized his earlier view that *halitzah* "no longer has any validity in our own day" (cited in Golinkin 1997, vol. 2, 763); in a "Responsum on the Status of Women" (1984) Rabbi Phillip Sigal suggested declaring *halitzah* "inoperative," but the suggestion was not accepted by the majority (Rabbinical Assembly 1988, 288).

31. I would like to thank Sharon Mintz of the Rare Book Room at the Jewish Theological Seminary, Gabriel Goldstein of the Yeshiva University Museum, Melissa Crespy of the Rabbinical Assembly, and especially Edna Nahshon for their suggestions and support.

BIBLIOGRAPHY

Adelman, Howard. 1994. "Custom, law and gender: Levirate union among Ashkenazim and Sephardim in Italy after the expulsion from Spain." In *The Expulsion of the Jews: 1492 and after,* ed. Raymond B. Waddington and Arthur H. Williamson. New York and London: Garland 107–25.

Adler, Jacob Georg Christian. 1773. *Sammlung von gerichtlichen jüdischen Contracten.* Hamburg: Buchenröder and Ritter.

Baker, Shane A. 1996–1997. "Loosing a shoe latchet: Sandals and footwear in the first century." *Brigham Young University Studies* 36: 196–206.

Belkin, Samuel. 1970. "Levirate and agnate marriage in rabbinic and cognate literature." *Jewish Quarterly Review.* New Series 60: 275–329.

Calmet, Augustin. 1732. *A historical, critical, geographical, chronological, and etymological dictionary of the Holy Bible.* London: J.J. and P. Knapton.

Carmichael, Calum M. 1977. "A ceremonial crux: Removing a man's sandal as a female gesture of contempt." *Journal of Biblical Literature* 96: 321–36.

Chinitz, Jacob. 2007. "The role of the shoe in the Bible." *Jewish Bible Quarterly* 35: 41–46.

Duschinsky, C. 1920. "The rabbinate of the Great Synagogue, London, from 1756–1842." *Jewish Quarterly Review.* New Series 10: 445–527.

Epstein, Louis M. 1942. *Marriage laws in the Bible and the Talmud.* Cambridge, MA: Harvard University Press.

Epstein, Louis. 1997. "Adjustment of the Jewish marriage laws to present-day conditions." In *Proceedings of the Committee on Jewish Law and Standards of the Conservative Movement, 1927–70,* ed. David Golinkin, vol. 2. Jerusalem: The Rabbinical Assembly 664–672.

Falk, Ze'ev W. 1966. *Jewish matrimonial law in the Middle Ages.* Oxford: Oxford University Press.

Golinkin, David, ed. 1997. *Proceedings of the Committee on Jewish Law and Standards of the Conservative Movement, 1927–70.* 3 vols. Jerusalem: The Rabbinical Assembly.

Gutmann, M. 1839. "Über die Leviratsehe und die Ceremonie des Schuhausziehens." *Wissenschaftliche Zeitschrift für Jüdische Theologie* 1: 61–87.

Hasan-Rokem, Galit. 2003. *Tales of the neighborhood: Jewish narrative dialogues in late antiquity.* Berkeley: University of California Press.

Ilan, Tal. 1995. *Jewish women in Greco-Roman Palestine: An inquiry into image and status.* Tübingen: Mohr-Siebeck.

Katz, David S. 1994. *The Jews in the history of England, 1485–1850.* Oxford: Clarendon.

Kirchner, Paul Christian, 1739, *Jüdisches Ceremoniel.* Nürnberg: P.C. Monath.

Klein, Isaac. 1997. "The problem of chalitzah today." In *Proceedings of the Committee on Jewish Law and Standards of the Conservative Movement, 1927–70,* ed. David Golinkin. vol. 2. Jerusalem: The Rabbinical Assembly 757–61.

Krauss, Samuel. 1910. *Talmudische Archäologie.* Vol. 1. Leipzig: Gustav Fock.

Kruger, Paul A. 1996. "The removal of the sandal in Deuteronomy XXV 9: 'A rite of passage?'" *Vetus Testamentum* 46: 534–39.

Levy, Ludwig. 1918. "Die Schuhsymbolik im jüdischen Ritual." *Monatsschrift für die Geschichte und Wissenschaft des Judentums* 3: 178–85.

Maimonides. 1995. *Mishneh Torah: Hilchot yibbum va'chalitzah. The laws of Yibbum and Chalitzah.* A new translation with commentaries and notes by R. Eliyahu Touger. New York and Jerusalem: Ktav.

Meyer, Michael A. 1988. *Response to modernity: A history of the Reform movement in Judaism.* New York and Oxford: Oxford University Press.

Nacht, Jacob. 1915–1916. "The symbolism of the shoe with special reference to Jewish sources." *Jewish Quarterly Review* 6: 1–22.

Niditch, Susan. 1979. "The wronged woman righted: An analysis of Genesis 38." *Harvard Theological Review* 72: 143–49.

Rabbinical Assembly, ed. 1988. *Proceedings of the Committee on Jewish Law and Standards of the Conservative Movement, 1980–1985.* Jerusalem: Rabbinical Assembly.

Roth, Ernst. 1988. "Die Geschichte der Leviratsehe." *Udim* 13: 59–97.

Wegner, Judith Romney. 1988. *Chattel or person? The status of women in the Mishnah.* Oxford and New York: Oxford University Press.

Weisberg, Dvora E. 1998. "Levirate marriage and *halitzah* in the Mishnah." In *The Annual of Rabbinic Judaism. Ancient, medieval and modern,* ed. Alan J. Avery-Peck, William Scott Green, and Jacob Neusner. Vol. 1, 37–69. Leiden: Brill.

Weisberg, Dvora E. 2000. "The Babylonian Talmud's treatment of levirate marriage." In *The Annual of Rabbinic Judaism. Ancient, medieval and modern,* ed. Alan J. Avery-Peck, William Scott Green, and Jacob Neusner. Vol. 3, 35–66. Leiden: Brill.

Weisberg, Dvora E. 2004. "The widow of our discontent: Levirate marriage in the Bible and ancient Israel." *Journal for the Study of the Old Testament* 28: 403–30.

Westreich, Elimelech. 2003–2004. "Levirate marriage in the state of Israel: Ethnic encounter and the challenge of a Jewish state." *Israel Law Review* 37: 426–99.

Yoffie, Adina M. 2000. "Refusal of the levirate marriage: A woman's rights." *Conservative Judaism* 52: 22–29.

Zohar, The. 1931–1934. 5 vols. Trans. Harry Sperling and Maurice Simon. London: The Jewish Publication Society.

4   THE TOMBSTONE SHOE

SHOE-SHAPED TOMBSTONES IN JEWISH CEMETERIES IN THE UKRAINE

RIVKA PARCIACK

Visitors to the numerous Jewish cemeteries in Western Ukraine, Kiev, and the regions of Volhyn and Podolia are struck by the unique sight of tombstones in the shape of a boot or shoe. Made of cement, dark granite, or a soft white local stone, they stand on the graves of women, men, and children without distinction of gender or age (see Figure 4.1). Despite their visual conspicuousness these tombstones have not been written about, with the exception of a brief mention by Boris Chaimovitsh and Valeri Dimshits, members of recent ethnographic expeditions (1988–1993) to the Ukraine (Chaimovitsh and Dimshits 1994, 130). Unfortunately they offer no explanation for the extraordinary shape of the stones. These stones are referred to by local Ukrainians as *bashmak,* a word of Turkish origin, which means "workshoes," or *valonki,* meaning "high felt shoes" in Russian, Ukrainian, and Polish.[1]

The typical shoe tombstone looks as though it was placed on the grave lying on its back so that its sole is positioned at the front of the grave, facing the observer, serving as a vertical tablet. Engraved on it are basic information about the deceased and the date of burial in the familiar customary format. The horizontal section of the tombstone is shaped like a cylinder, about 160 centimeters long, and widens gradually toward the end as it approaches what may be described as the shoe's vamp. The base of the upright section adds a further 20 centimeters to the length. The upright section's height is about 85 centimeters, while its width normally ranges from 40 to 50 centimeters. More often than not the exact measurements of the original size and width of the tombstone cannot be determined due to damage caused by such natural forces as erosion, breakage, and subsidence, and by humans, notably the wartime German occupiers and local authorities who transported tombstones from one location to another in order to clear space for road construction. Stonecutters may also have used some of the markers for their material and farmers used them to sharpen tools.

Most of the shoe-like tombstones discussed in this essay are simple constructions, almost entirely devoid of ornament.[2] They are located in the same communal cemeteries as conventional tombstones built along standard lines, and are decorated with traditional symbols.[3] Epitaphs on shoe-shaped markers are usually brief. They begin with the traditional Hebrew letters *Peh Nun* (equivalent to RIP), then continue with the details of the dead person's identity (his or her name, that of the father, dates of birth and death) and end with the customary Hebrew letters *Taf, Nun, Tsadi, Bet* and *Heh,* which stand for "May his (or her) soul be

Figure 4.1   Shoe-shaped tombstones in Berdichev. Photographed by the author.

bound up in the bond of everlasting life." Only a few honorary words—such as "important man" or "important woman"—are engraved, and there is a total absence of the acrostics that often appear on conventional East European Jewish tombstones (Figure 4.2).

Unfortunately, most of the letters in the epitaphs are nearly indecipherable due to deterioration: the upright section of many tombstones is often detached and either missing or left lying around near the grave, with details relating to the deceased frequently worn away or missing altogether.

Shoe-shaped tombstones are found throughout cemeteries in Balin, Bar, Berdichev, Deraznia, Felsztajn (now known as Kosgirka), Kaminits-Podolsk, Kiev, Mechanovka (now known as Komsomolsk), Medzyboz, Mezeritsh, Mohylov Podolski, Ostrog, Polonne, Satanov, Skvyra, Sudilkov, Spetivka, Ternopol, and Zhitomir, as well as in other small towns and villages in the various districts of Volhyn and Podolia (see Figure 4.3). In some of these cemeteries there are only a small number of shoe-shaped tombstones among a large number of conventional ones. Other cemeteries contain a somewhat larger although still proportionately small number of them. However, in Berdichev and Medzyboz there are hundreds of shoe-like tombstones that constitute an overwhelming majority. They are also in the majority in some places like Mechanovka, but, as only a fraction of the cemetery has survived, we have no way of knowing the shape of the cemetery's missing markers. In some instances such an assemblage is located mainly along the cemetery's perimeter, as in the Satanov cemetery, or adjacent to the access paths heading toward the heart of the cemetery and close to the fence, as in the cemetery in Bar. Such distinctions are difficult to make, because it is no longer possible to clearly delineate the original borders of the cemetery at the time of the burials.

Shoe-shaped tombstones are generally grouped together, but they are found on isolated graves located amidst conventional stones, even when the same cemetery has an assemblage

Figure 4.2   Shoe-shaped tombstones in Berdichev. Photographed by the author.

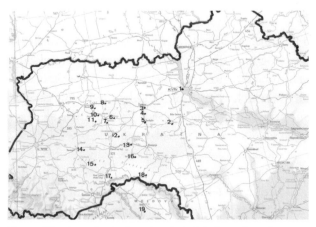

Figure 4.3   Locations of cemeteries with shoe-shaped tombstones. 1 = Kiev, 2 = Skvyra, 3 = Zytomir, 4 = Michalovka (now Komsomolsk), 5 = Berdichev, 6 = Polonne, 7 = Spetivka, 8 = Medzybozhe, 9 = Mezeritsh, 10 = Ostrog, 11 = Sudilkov, 12 = Balin, 13 = Deraznia, 14 = Ternopol, 15 = Satanov, 16 = Bar, 17 = Kamenets Podolski, 18 = Mohylov Podolski, 19 = Felsztain.

of shoe-shaped markers in another location. This is the case in Kaminits-Podolsk, where four are found at the far edge of the cemetery, with a similar stone located centrally. Overall, shoe-shaped markers throughout Volhyn and Podolia number in the thousands. However, they are not found in northern and eastern Ukraine.

It is difficult to establish the precise date when many of the tombstones were crafted. Although tombstone texts often give the date of death at the bottom of the epitaph, this particular part has often sunk deep into the ground and become inaccessible. The stones themselves, which have suffered from the effects of acid rain, leaves, and soil, are often eroded, with inscriptions now obscure and indecipherable. Additionally, the top of the upright section of many tombstones, upon which information about the dead person was inscribed, is often lopped off. Given that, the oldest tombstone I located was in Balin cemetery and was dated 1848–1849. Various sources suggest that shoe-shaped tombstones first appeared in the Ukraine in 1840.[4] All tombstones where it was possible to ascertain specific dates were erected in the twentieth century. Shoe-shaped stones in Spetivka, Medziboz, and other towns were erected as late as the 1980s.

HOW CAN ONE EXPLAIN THE PECULIAR SHAPE OF TOMBSTONES?

Attempts to locate relevant written documents, certificates, or testimonies that might shed light on these unique structures proved fruitless. The records of many communities in the Ukraine were lost in a fire that broke out in the central archives in Lvov after World War II. No references were found of the Jewish burial societies in the Ukraine, in *pinkasim* (memorial volumes of the communities) nor in *Yizkor* (Remembrance) books, personal memoirs, literary works, or other kinds of documentation. This made the study of these tombstones a challenging enterprise, although the fact that it has not even been undertaken heretofore is surprising.

I propose that a possible explanation for the distinct form of shoe-shaped tombstones can be found in a yearning for and anticipation of approaching redemption, and this view is supported by the historical context. As mentioned, shoe-shaped markers first appeared in the Ukraine in 1840, which is the year 5600 by the Jewish calendar.[5] In a period suffused with messianic expectations among both Jews and Christians, it was considered a momentous year, regarded by Jews as the advent of the new century of the sixth millennium. The shift from one era to another, and especially the beginning of a new epoch, often gives rise to mystical and Messianic ferment. This was particularly the case in 1840, because during the preceding two hundred years Jewish communities of Eastern Europe had experienced the impact of messianic movements and seen the rise of widely accepted theories about arcane matters and numerology. Great mystic significance was assigned to 5600.[6] Indeed, according to the Talmud, the *Zohar*, the most important work of Kabbalah, and various numerological calculations, 5600 was the year when the Messiah would arrive.[7]

During this period many Jews believed in numerological calculations of the End of Days and in the imminent arrival of the Messiah. Because they believed this would occur in 5600 (1840), they became known as *Tarniks,* a term derived from the Hebrew letters denoting the number 5600.[8] Two missionaries of the Scottish Church traveling in the region during 1839 confirmed in their writings that even Jews in geographical areas outside the Ukraine (Galicia, Prussia, Rumania, Moldavia, and Turkey) were totally convinced of the imminent appearance of the Messiah. Some stated that should this not occur they would abandon their faith and convert to Christianity. We know of Jews who sold their houses to be ready to move at a moment's notice, and commercial agreements between Jews were signed with a provisionary rider holding that their validity would expire should the Messiah arrive (Morgenstern 1985, 58). This conviction was so widespread that those who did not adhere to it were vilified and their religious faith disparaged. The passionate feuds between Tarniks and their opponents point to the centrality of the subject of approaching redemption both within Jewish religious thought and everyday life.

In trying to understand the origin of shoe-shaped tombstones, we must look at some crucial biblical verses that deal with the subject of redemption. The book of Isaiah addresses the similarity between revelation and redemption during the Exodus from Egypt and the redemption that would occur at the End of Days (11:16); the same parallelism is also evoked in Jeremiah (16:14–16):

> Assuredly, a time is coming—declares the Lord—when it shall no more be said, "As the Lord lives who brought the Israelites out of the Land of Egypt" but rather "As the Lord lives who brought the Israelites out of the northland, and out of all the lands to which He had banished them." For I will bring them back to their land, which I gave to their fathers.[9]

Rabbi Schneur Zalman of Liadi (1745–1813), the founder of the Hassidim *Chabad* movement,[10] addressed this in his discussion of ultimate redemption, a parallelism enhanced by Isaiah 11:11–12:

> In that day, my Lord will apply His Hand again to redeeming the other part of His people from Assyria—as also from Egypt, Pathros, Nubia, Elam, Shinar, Hamath, and the coastlands. He will hold up a signal to the nations and assemble the banished of Judah from the four corners of the earth.

The prophet Micah suggested that not only would the Israelites be redeemed, but there would be a vast migration of multitudes of pilgrims marching toward Zion:

> And many nations shall come, and say, Come, and let us go up to the mountain of the Lord, and to the house of the God of Jacob. (Mic. 4:2)

They who march to Jerusalem would include, according to the prophet Ezekiel, those redeemed from their graves:

> Thus said the Lord God: "I am going to open your graves and lift you out of the graves, O, My people, and bring you to the land of Israel." (Ezek. 37:12)

The analogy between the Exodus and a vast migration at the End of Days is extended to footwear. Just as the ancient Hebrews were commanded to have their shoes on in readiness for their journey as explained in Exodus 12:11—"Your loins girded, your sandals on your feet and your staff in your hand"—so will the redeemed make their way and cross rivers with shoes on, encasing their feet, as written in Isaiah 11:16:

> The Lord will dry up the tongue of the Egyptian sea.—He will raise His hand over the Euphrates with the might of His wind and break it into seven wadis, so that it can be trodden dry-shod. Thus there shall be a highway for the other part of His people out of Assyria, such as there was for Israel when it left the land of Egypt.

The parallelism between the original Exodus and future redemption was expounded by Rebbe Menachem Mendel Schneersohn (1902–1994), the last spiritual leader of Chabad Lubavitch. In 1959, when his Hassidim convened for a meeting on the final day of the Passover holiday, he spoke of the Exodus and the parting of the Red Sea, interpreting them as a paradigm for the redemption to come. He based his explication on the exegesis of the biblical portion *Bo* (Hebrew for "Come unto"), recited on the final day of the Passover holiday, which outlines the instructions given to the Israelites on the eve of the departure from Egypt (Ex. 12:11): "Your loins girded [i.e., prepared to travel], your sandals [or shoes] on your feet, and your staff in your hand."[11] Like Rabbi Schneur Zalman of Liadi before him, he linked it to Isaiah's prophecy of the End of Days.

Jews were not the only ones intently focused on redemption. Following the defeat of Napoleon and the failure of the Polish revolution in 1831, a stream of exiles departed Poland headed mainly for France.[12] There, a mystically inclined group of exiles emerged who sought to identify Poland as the crucified Jesus of nations, whose return would herald national liberation. This messianic movement was fostered by the religious, national, and social ideas of Giuseppe Mazzini and the utopian Saint-Simon and was led by Andrzej Tomasz Towiański (Aeskoly 1933, 26–29). As the notion of forthcoming redemption was also current among the Gentiles among whom the Jews lived, it may be assumed that mutual influences permeated both cultures and strengthened their respective beliefs. Still, one must keep in mind that they occurred against different backgrounds and carried different meanings and implications.

We find then during the second half of the nineteenth century, an interesting connection between the Tarniks' intense messianism, the Polish school of Towiański and his followers, the outlook of the Hassidim, and Isaiah's influential prophecy of the End of the Days. All these elements combine to suggest an explanation for the construction of shoe-like tombstones whose shape may reflect the belief in the coming of the Messiah and the resurrection of the dead, when God will guide the resurrected with shoes or sandals on their feet on their journey to Zion. Interestingly, this interpretation was confirmed by both Jews and non-Jews who live in the Ukraine in immediate proximity to the shoe-shaped stones. They responded unequivocally to queries regarding the meaning of the tombstones by explaining that they were built when the arrival of the Messiah was believed to be imminent.

There are other hints at a possible solution to the riddle of the enigmatic origins of shoe-shaped markers. Shoes are an important symbol in Kabbalah. The explanation goes as follows: the upper part of the shoe is made of coarse leather that enwraps and protects the concealed foot, but it is the foot's sole enclosed within the shoe that leads and determines the way one walks. The Chabad Rabbi Menachem Mendel (1789–1866), known as the Zemach Zedek (plant of righteousness), explained: "Indeed it guides the footwear to the same side that directs the foot according to the will of the divine existence that lies within the foot...it [the shoe] is utterly subject to the foot and to whatever it [the foot] wishes, it will tend to go" (Zemach Zedek 1991, 186). In Kabbalah, the angels Sandal (Sandalfon) and Mattat (Matatron) are described as God's footwear, for they function as separators and filters that mediate between God and the material world. It is through these "shoes" that the overwhelming intensity of divine power is reduced, preventing it from reaching revelation (Zemach Zedek 1991, 14).

The foot/shoe metaphor compares the foot to the divine presence, which the shoe conceals within it. The Zemach Zedek, who studied the symbolism of the shoe, explained that unlike garments, which conceal the body partially, the shoe conceals the foot completely. It thus serves as a metaphor for the limitedness of the Divine Presence (Shekhinah), which is concealed and reveals itself only indirectly and to a limited degree, and evokes Psalms 13: "How long, O Lord, will you forever hide Your face." The Zemach Zedek explained that, just as the leather of footwear conceals the foot completely, "so the divine light is well hidden and may only be seen partially in the way that nature behaves" (Zemach Zedek 1991, 186).

In this vein, the leaders of Chabad interpreted the biblical verse "How lovely are your feet in sandals, O daughter of nobles" (Song 7:2) as referring to the time of redemption, namely "How lovely are feet of Israel when climbing the Mount of Zion."[13]

The Zemach Zedek wrote, "Now...the question of the shoes that cover the feet of the *Shechinah*...has become clear...and they are dressed for the souls in the sense of the signs of the Messiah...the meaning of all this refers to the footwear that the *Shechinah*...wears, as a metaphor for the feet, is none other than what is lowered down in the CFD" (Zemach Zedek 1991, 186).[14] CFD is an acronym for Creation, Formation and Doing (in Hebrew, *Bet-yod-Ayin = briah-yetzirah-asiya*). According to Kabbalah these are the lowest and meanest three parts in the Chain of Sacredness in the world to which our evil generation belongs, and they are therefore full of *klipot* ("peels," namely evil demons). The Zemach Zedek went on to say that was the case "in order to revive a spirit of degradation in the sense of exile, because then the *Shekhinah* must wear the attire of footwear" (Zemech Zedak 1991, 186). Thus the Divine Presence itself, upon descending, wants additional protection so that the *khitzonim* (lit: deamons) should not exploit the feet of the Shekhinah, when they descend into death, a place filled with the evil of the *khitzonim*.[15]

The fear of the harmful actions of the *khitzonim* was well known and had already been mentioned in the introduction to the book *Ma'avar Yabbok* (1626) by Aharon Berachiah, who explained that the *khitzonim* may appear in a cemetery together with the angel of death and try to grab and take possession of the body of the deceased.[16]

The Zemach Zedek regards the metaphoric shoe as attire for the soul, the cover for the divine presence when it descends into a contaminated area, such as a cemetery. Although he certainly did not intend for this metaphor to be understood on a concrete level, it well may be that some of his followers translated his metaphysical imagery into realia, erecting shoe-shaped tombstones so as to protect their dearly departed. Hiding them in the protective encasement of a shoe would guard them from falling prey to the evil demons thought to exist within cemetery soil. For if the Divine Presence needed such protection, all the more so dead humans. In this sort of reasoning, death and life are not truly separated, the dead, just like the living, face dangers, and the heavenly world is not cut off completely from the material world—both being controlled by the same system.

* * *

Shoe-shaped tombstones present many questions. What distinguished the communities that contained them from neighboring ones that did not? What distinguished the deceased buried under a shoe-like marker from others buried nearby who were apparently members of the same community and were buried in conventional graves under traditional markers? The previously mentioned concentration of shoe-shaped tombstones along the edges of the old Jewish cemetery in the city of Bar in Podolia could possibly provide some answers. The individuals buried there had not been banished from the community, as proven by the fact that they were buried within the boundaries of the cemetery, albeit in separate, distant locations. It seems almost certain that, owing to some degree of hesitation, the graves with shoe-shaped tombstones were not mixed with those of other deceased individuals.

In other cemeteries too, some separation is evident between traditional graves and the ones with shoe-shaped stones, although this could not be determined with certainty, as noted previously. Did some individuals seek to use their tombstones to dissociate themselves, perhaps only to a limited extent, from the rest of the community? Have we come across evidence indicating an unresolved argument, a hint at the fact that perhaps the community did not take a firm stand with respect to this style of burial and to what it symbolizes, and therefore the community allocated a separate place for those individuals but did not prevent their burial at the same location? The allocation of separate burial plots for people whose beliefs were rejected by the community was not a widespread phenomenon. This can be exemplified by the register of the deceased among the families of Shklov dated 5590 (1829/30), where it was noted, "The conflict between the Hassidim and Mitnagdim [their opponents] in Shklov [Belarus] still rages fiercely, so much so that a special section has been allocated in the cemetery solely for Hassidim, so that they should not be mixed together with the Mitnagdim." (Halpern 1969).

CONCLUSIONS

Many issues are raised by the phenomenon of shoe-shaped tombstones, yet there are no conclusive and definitive answers. I suggest two explanations. The first looks at the shoe-shaped markers in the context of the emergence of the messianic Tarnik movement. Based on texts from the Talmud, the Zohar, and numerological accounts, this Jewish movement expected the redemption of the Jews to occur in 1840, the same year in which the first shoe-shaped tombstones appear. A central text in this redemptive scheme was the prophecy of Isaiah (11:12–16) about the end-time apocalypse. In it God is guiding the redeemed—whose feet are shod—on their return to Zion.

The second explanation is suggested by the teachings of the leaders of the Chabad Hassidim movement. Building upon Cabbalistic metaphors, Chabad ascribed to shoes a protective power against demons who live in the cursed, contaminated soil of the earth and who try to harm both the living and the buried dead. Chabad suggested that metaphorically even God would need the protection of shoes in contaminated areas. The reasoning went as follows: if God needs footwear protection, this holds all the more so for the buried dead. This protection was to be found in shoe-shaped stones.

These two explanations for the construction of shoe-shaped markers in Jewish graveyards in the Ukraine point to an intimate link between the worlds of the living and the dead and a great yearning for redemption. While shoes often serve as a means to separate the profane and the sacred, in this case they transcend these counterposed categories in anticipation of the final redemption in Zion.

ACKNOWLEDGMENTS

My research was made possible by a grant from the Memorial Foundation for Jewish Culture. I wish to express my gratitude to Professor Olga Goldberg for her important comments. I am indebted to Professors David Asaf and Marcin Wodziński, Prof. Hania Zaremska, who traveled with me all over Ukraine, and Mr. Binyamin Lukin of the Central Archives for the History of the Jewish people, for sharing their invaluable knowledge.

NOTES

1. *Bashmak* = boots, according to Podverko and Balla (1974). The term *Valonki* (compacted felt boots) is widely used in the local Russian, Ukrainian, and Polish vernacular but does not appear in the dictionary.
2. Only a minuscule number of the more than a thousand tombstones I examined in the Ukraine bore decorations. They included the following images: a human face (at Berdichev), priestly hands (at Balin and Berdichev), a candlestick (*menorah*) and candles, a dove (on women's graves), a bird and a deer on men's (at Satanov), lions and a crown (at Ostrog), curtains, and nonspecific decorations on women's tombstones (at Medzyboz).
3. For images of decorated "conventional" tombstones in cemeteries in the Ukraine and Moldova see Goberman (1993).
4. This information derives from Binyamin Lukin of the Central Archives for the History of the Jewish People, who, together with Boris Chimovitsh, surveyed a hundred Jewish small towns in the Ukraine (Lukin and Khaimovitsh 1997).

5. For conversion of the Gregorian to the Hebrew calendar and vice versa see http://www.hebcal.com/converter.

6. Every letter of the alphabet in Hebrew has a numerical value. In the Hebrew calendar years are usually given in letters, not numbers; thus the year He (5 × 1000) + Tav (400) + Resh (200) equals 5600.

7. Duker (1953) describes the highly charged messianic atmosphere among Jews and Gentiles.

8. The depth of this conviction is reflected in the tale about the *tzaddik* (holy man) Rabbi Abraham of Buczacz, who kept a set of white clothes and a *shofar* (ram's horn) ready at his bedside, with the synagogue beadle (*shamash*) seated and up all night in order to wake the rabbi when the Messiah came.

9. All biblical quotations are from *The Holy Bible,* King James Version.

10. *Chabad* is a Hebrew acronym, its initials taken from the first three kabbalistic schemes of the world: *Chochmah, Binah* and *Da'at,* that is, Wisdom, Understanding, and Knowledge.

11. See Schneersohn 2003: Book 9, part 2, p. 235. The book includes sermons of Rabbi Menachem Mendel Schneersohn, translated into Hebrew from the original Yiddish.

12. Poles regarded Napoleon as a savior and had high hopes that he would bring them political redemption. In Adam Mickiewicz's *Pan Tadeusz* (1834), Poland's national epic, Yankel the Jew has a role to play in confirming this conception.

13. The need to protect the feet in shoes, in order to keep them from dirt or thorns at the symbolic level is found in Cordovero 1999, 154. Moshe Cordovero (1522–1570) was a major Kabbalist in Spain and later in Safed, Palestine.

14. The explanation is given by Menachem Mendel (Zemach Zedek) in *Derech Mitsvotekha* (1991, 350), by Shemuel Schneersohn in 1945, *Torat Shmuel* [the *Torah* of Samuel], and later by Menachem Mendel Schneersohn in *Torat Menachem, Hitva'adut.*

15. In his introduction (1996, 12–72) Aharon Berachiah of Modena describes the danger of the *chizonim*, the demons that accompany the Angel of Death and wish to grasp the deceased body. Many of the customs around the Jewish cemetery are connected with this belief.

16. The *klipot* demons are found in the cemetery. For a recounting of their deeds see Nigal (1995).

BIBLIOGRAPHY

Aeskoly, Aharon Zeev. 1933. *Towiański movement among the Jews—A messianic episode* [in Hebrew]. Jerusalem: Benny Bezalel.

Berachiah, Aharon (of Modena). 1996. *Ma'avar Yabbok* [*The passage of Yabbok*] [in Hebrew]. Jerusalem: Ahvat Shalom.

Chaimovitsh, Boris, and Boris Dimshits. 1994. "In the footsteps of An-Sky" [in Hebrew], trans. Yossi Rusink. In *Back to the shtetl: An-Sky and the Jewish ethnographic expedition 1912–14* [in Hebrew with English synopses], ed. Rivka Gonen, 121–32, Jerusalem: Israel Museum.

Duker, Abraham G. 1953. "The Tarniks: Believers in the coming of the Messiah in 1840." In *Conference of Jewish Relations: The Joshua Starr Memorial Volume,* 191–201. Studies in History and Philology. New York: Conference on Jewish Relations.

Goberman, David. 1993. *Jewish tombstones in Ukraine and Moldava.* Moscow: Imidzh. Translated into English in 2000 under the title *Carved memories: Heritage in stone from the Russian Jewish Pale,* trans. Lina Lezhneva. New York: Rizzoli.

Gonen, Rivka, ed. 1994. *Back to the shtetl, An-Sky and the Jewish ethnographic expedition, 1912–1914, from the collection of the Russian Museum of Ethnography in St Petersburg.* Jerusalem: The Israel Museum.

Halpern, Israel. 1969. *Jews and Judaism in Eastern Europe* [in Hebrew]. Jerusalem: Magnes Press.

Lukin, Binyamin, and Boris Chaimovitsh. 1997. *100 Evreiskikh mestechek Ukrainy: Istoricheskii Putevoditel.* Jerusalem: Ezro.

Morgenstern, Abraham. 1985. *Messianism and the settlement of the land of Israel.* Jerusalem: Yad Ben-Zvi.

Nigal, Gedaliah. 1995. *Magic, mysticism and Hasidism: The supernatural in Jewish thought,* trans. E. Levin. Northvale, NJ: Jason Aronson.

Podverko, L., and M. I. Balla. 1974. *English–Ukranian Dictionary.* Lvov, Ukraine: Radyanska Shkola Publishing House.

Schneersohn, Menachem Mendel. 2003. *Torat Menachem* [in Hebrew]. Brooklyn, NY: Sifriyat Otsar ha-Hasidim.

Schneersohn, Shemuel. 1945. *Likutey Torat Shmuel* [*Selection of Shmuel's teachings*] [in Hebrew]. Brooklyn, NY: Sifriyat Otsar ha-Hasidim.

Zemach Zedek (Menachem Mendel). 1991. *Derekh Mitsvotecha* [*The way of your commandments*] [in Hebrew]. Brooklyn, NY: Sifriyat Otsar ha-Hasidim.

5 THE ISRAELI SHOE
BIBLICAL SANDALS AND NATIVE ISRAELI IDENTITY

ORNA BEN-MEIR

PROLOGUE

In a nation involved in a constant struggle for its very existence, the topic of sandals recently stirred up quite a public debate. The ethics committee of the Israeli parliament, the Knesset, submitted a draft for a dress code, with special emphasis on footwear. A ban on wearing sandals in the Knesset chamber became an explosive issue. It was especially irritating for two members, who both wear sandals year-round for personal reasons, and as a recognizable sign of their ideological and political identities. Chaim Oron, a left-wing kibbutz member, and Uri Ariel, a rightist settler, were both representatives of the Israeli pioneering ethos, but from opposite sides of the political fence (Meranda 2007).

The notion of impropriety that this sandals debate engendered is related to the much wider concept of "undressing the foot." Sandals are an item of clothing that stresses the fluidity of the body. Cavallaro and Warwick argue that "[dress] *frames* the body and insulates private fantasies from the Other, yet it simultaneously connects the individual self to the collective Other and fashions those fantasies on the model of a public spectacle" (Cavallaro and Warwick 1998, xvi). The complex meaning that has been imbued in footwear within Jewish tradition (Roth 1992, 170–82) was here transformed in the secular Israeli culture. Labor Knesset member Shelly Yechimovitz summarized the issue thus: "the so-called 'biblical sandals' are more representative of Israeli culture and are therefore more acceptable than 'luxury brand shoes manufactured by children in a sweatshop in China'" (Shakhar 2007, 4). This debate expresses only a few of the myriad meanings that have been encapsulated in the footwear commonly called "Biblical Sandals." This will be discussed here in the context of a sartorial declaration of the 'New Hebrew' identity that has evolved in Israel: renouncing the shoes of a wandering Jew without a land, in favor of the sign of a native Israeli, whose feet are planted upon his ancestors' land.

WHAT IS BIBLICAL ABOUT THE SANDALS?

Biblical Sandals are not merely footwear but have evolved into a cultural symbol. This term actually encompasses several types of sandals, which all share three common features: thin leather soles, horizontal straps made of coarse-cut brown leather, sometimes buckled, and much exposure of the foot (Figure 5.1). This kind of footwear made its debut in

Figure 5.1   Handmade Israeli sandals worn by their original owner. Sandals were made at Kibbutz Yakum, 2007. Courtesy of Dr. Shlomo Lee Abrahmov.

Israel during the second decade of the twentieth century. In the late 1920s they were called Khugistic Sandals.[1] As a result of their institutionalized popularity, they were renamed Biblical Sandals around the time of World War II. Renaming was part and parcel of an appropriation strategy of the 'New Hebrew' entity, which had crystallized in the first half of the twentieth century in the land of Israel, not yet a nation. The secular entity sought to separate itself from its Jewish shadow. Biblical Sandals were thus an inevitable counterpart to the *blorit,* the locks of curly hair that symbolized the *sabra,*[2] the native Israeli, in the sartorial dichotomy "from the sole of thy foot unto the crown of thy head" (Deut. 28:35). Schroer and Staubli, who discuss body symbolism in the Bible, argue that the foot, the lowest part of the body and a symbol of oppression, is in direct contrast to the head, the highest part, and is by itself a symbol for the entire human (Schroer and Staubli 2001, 184–91). In native Israeli iconography, baring the head—renouncing the Jewish religious skullcap (*kippah*)—was conceptually parallel to the idea of undressing the foot, that is, wearing sandals.

One may ask why the footwear that symbolizes Israeli secular identity should be given a name that connotes Judaism's most sacred book. Moreover, in the Bible there is no mention of sandals, yet its frequent use of the Hebrew word *na'al,* which refers to both sandal and shoe, points to the symbolic significance that had been attached to the foot and the practices of dressing the feet. Schroer and Staubli say that no other part of the human body is thought of in so close connection with its clothing.[3] The wealth of footwear practices illuminates the importance attached to this article of clothing in the Bible. Rabbi Ariel Roth compares the many biblical shoe references to those in later scriptures and argues that all indicate a higher "spiritual meaning of wearing shoes" (Roth 1992, 175). Schroer and Staubli find common meaning in all the references to shoes in the Bible: that of power (Schroer and Staubli 2001, 181–93). Possession, domination, subjugation, and seizure of all things that had been created are thus described by their creator: "the heaven is My throne, and the earth is My footstool" (Isa. 66:1–2). In this biblical manner of thought, becoming a nation for the Israelites meant adherence to this foot symbolism:

> if thou wilt not hearken unto the voice of the Lord thy God, to observe to do all his commandments...The Lord will smite thee in the knees, and in the legs...whereof thou canst not be healed. (Deut. 28:15, 35)

In this context renaming Khugistic Sandals as Biblical Sandals invested them with symbolic imagery. Moreover, it simultaneously established a firm link to the sandals of the ancestors, not that such an artifact has been actually found at biblical archaeological sites. However, excavations in Syria between 1928 and 1937 in a third-century synagogue in Dura Europos uncovered murals that depicted biblical Israelites wearing sandals. This example of ancient Jewish art showed thong-type sandals, with a vertical strap passing between the first two toes. This leads to the conclusion that the term "biblical" attached to horizontally strapped sandals is not related to a time period but represents a more abstract concept.

The addition of the term "biblical" is significant within the context of the genesis of Israeli culture. It was meant as a revolution in the definition of Jewish identity, declared by the new Jewish culture that had been crystallizing in Palestine from 1882 through to the foundation of the Israeli state in 1948. The goal of this distinct and self-aware culture was the replacement of the then-current identifications of "Jew" and "Jewish" with "Hebrew" (Even-Zohar 1990, 175–76). The 'New Hebrew' culture sought to free Jewish life of the restrictions of religion, that is, observance of the Torah and the commandments. For those Jews who did not accept the authority of the Talmud, the Oral Law, the Bible offered a new genealogy, says historian Anita Shapira. It served as a mythological-historical foundation for the new national entity—"a primordial moment that lends the people the legitimacy to demand from the family of nations its own place in the sun" (Shapira 2004, 13). Footwear, as an intimate body covering and an article of locomotion, was thus a highly appropriate material symbol of nationality. It linked three components of national identity: the man, his ancestral land, and the Bible, wherein the promise to the patriarch Abraham served as proof-text to possession of the land for his offspring: "Rise up, walk through the length and the breadth of the land, for I will give it to you" (Gen. 13:17).[4]

THE ZIONIST ETHOS

Taking possession by walking "the length and breadth of the land" has become a central concept of the Zionist ethos, in which the Biblical Sandals play a dramatic role. The Zionist movement had evolved from a growing interest in nationalism in late nineteenth-century Europe. From its onset the Bible acted as a motor of cultural evolution. It supplied the national language, Hebrew, and provided the Zionist founding narrative, in which the Jewish people had a glorious past on their own land. Zionism aimed at reconstructing that narrative by moving the Jews from the Diaspora to Palestine. Two prerequisites were needed for the ambitious Zionist project: evolution of a "New Man"[5] who would take on the revolution, and an appropriation process. As the biblical landscape was no longer merely a literary fantasy, the land should be possessed physically, on foot and with hands, by walking and working.

The initiation rite for members of the Second Aliyah[6] was walking through the land to discover the biblical scenery of their ancestors. And "walking by foot" was taken literally, that is, going barefoot or with minimal foot covering so as to be connected more intimately to the land (Ben-Zvi 1959). Around this time, some improvised sandals had begun to appear on the feet of the people of the Second Aliyah.

This footwear matched the proletarian spirit of the nationalistic and socialist youths who came from Eastern Europe to Palestine to build a new life. They heard the call of Martin Buber: "Just as the Jewish people need the land to live a full life, so the land needs the Jewish people to be complete" (Buber 1948, 12). Their ascetic spirit, the tough physical conditions in Palestine, and the shortage of resources all led to adoption of a frugal lifestyle. These conditions helped make these sandals the ultimate footwear for the land of Israel. On one hand walking in sandals was almost like going barefoot, traditionally a low-status vestimentary sign. In addition, undressing the feet alluded to the then-admired model of the native Bedouin (Shavit 1997, 483–93). On the other hand, sandals symbolized rejection of shoes that, especially for women, had signified the modern conspicuous consumption of the bourgeoisie, from which they had escaped (Perrot 1994, 104–6).

The sandals were also linked to another foundation of the Zionist movement: working the land—"only labor could embroider for us the threads that will connect us to the land internally."[7] This ideal was adhered to literally, as the working shoes that the pioneers brought with them began tearing apart:

> From the train came down a nice looking man, whose shoes were broken with his toes open. . . . Is there a more supreme thing than these broken shoes on the feet of a leader? It is the symbol of symbols of pioneering. (Rand 1981, 198)

Open-toed shoes were a step toward the creation of sandals, thus exemplifying the two-sided motto of "conquering the land"—an allusion to the biblical commandment to Adam after the creation: "have dominion . . . over every living thing . . . upon the earth" (Gen. 1:28). During the 1920s sandals became a status symbol of the proletarian elite, although this category included several versions of strapped shoes. At work sandals were worn over socks, after work without;[8] both options went with European clothes. Later in the decade, credit for the "invention" of straight horizontally strapped sandals was taken by a commune called the Khugim, so they were called Khugistic Sandals (Franco 1981, 308). At the same time this type of sandal with a buckle had been brought to Palestine from Germany, probably by members of Zionist youth movements (e.g., Ha'shomer Ha'tzair).[9] Indeed, in the 1920s German schoolchildren wore *Jesuslatchen* [sandals worn by Jesus] (Rosenthal, 2007).[10]

NONGENDERED LOOK

In discussing sandals one may refer to their symbolic contribution in creating the visual stereotype of the *chalutz* (pioneer). The Zionist self-transformation demanded disposal of former identities. Clothing was the first social rule reinforced by this new society. Elizabeth Wilson emphasizes the important place that nineteenth-century socialists gave to dress in their condemnation of capitalism and their vision of possible alternatives (Wilson 1985, 208). A famous ceremonial act in pioneer circles was the "Execution" (Pinski 1981, 208)— relegating personal clothes to the collective public wardrobe, while bourgeois wardrobes were set on fire (Kibbutz Beit Alpha 1981, 206–7). However, renouncing a private wardrobe in favor of sharing clothes with collective members gave rise to problems when it came to footwear. Shoes tend to adapt to the shape of the wearer's foot, and different wearers never could get the used shoes to fit snugly. Obviously, sandals were a less painful alternative.

A distinct style of pioneering dress evolved by the 1930s. Its institutionalized uniformity was influenced by the strict dress code of the Zionist youth movements. The most important of these was Ha'shomer Ha'tzair, whose first members settled in Palestine in 1917. They believed that the liberation of Jewish youth could be accomplished by moving to Palestine and living in an agricultural collective, or kibbutz. In 1927 they had founded four *kibbutzim* and in 1936 launched a left-wing socialist political party. The party played a major role in supporting the struggle to form a Jewish community in Palestine. From this influential elite came some of the future leaders of the state of Israel. Their distinct proletarian dress code was defined by four characteristics. There was a triple color scheme: proletarian blue, pure ascetic white, and frugal khaki (which signified the desert). There was a restricted repertoire of items, including buttoned working shirts worn over long or short trousers, usually made of coarse thick cotton twill. The footwear was also characteristic: restricted to dark-colored working shoes and Khugistic sandals with socks during work, and bare feet after work, a reminder of the footwear of their ancestors. Nathan Joseph remarks that organized groups often adopt the reconstructed dress of the past to express their political, cultural, and romantic ideals (Joseph 1986, 16). The only variety in this dress code was in headgear: the popular conic stitched fabric *tembel* hat, the straw hat, and the kerchief (the latter exclusively feminine, used to gather the hair). This dress code was first institutionalized in the *kibbutzim* and passed along to agricultural villages and other sectors of the Jewish population and was identified with the socialist message. The iconic image of the *chalutz* was present in many artistic expressions of the time; see Figure 5.2 (Ofrat 1983, 180–97).

Notwithstanding the complete exposure of the legs and feet that comes with shorts and sandals, this dress code was regarded by its adherents as austere and not at all erotic, by its adherents. It was especially embraced by self-aware intellectual Zionist women, manifesting their contempt for European gender-specific clothing. These women had envisioned in the Zionist project an opportunity to alter gender values by taking an equal part in the actual construction of the 'New Hebrew' society.[11] Wilson argues that dress reform was easily identified with feminism (Wilson 1985, 209). The wearing of trousers figured in two of the major dress reforms of the nineteenth century: the French *sans culottes,* the long male trousers that had replaced the aristocratic short breeches, and the bloomers that launched modern feminine trousers. Hebrew shorts could have been considered a dress

Figure 5.2   Kibbutz members working in the stone quarry of Kibbutz Ein Harod, 1941. Photographer: Kluger Zoltan. Courtesy of Israeli Government Press Office.

reform, although this could have been the result of a functional solution for the European pioneers who suffered from both a shortage of resources and the sweltering climate. Bare legs naturally promoted bare feet in sandals. Nevertheless, the unisex concept of the *chalutz* dress code was actually manifest only in headdress and footwear; shirts and trousers were gender-specific in cut, buttoning, and detail.[12] Yet it was the restricted color scheme that contributed to an impression of uniformity, thus enabling the dress code to be regarded as a sartorial sign of gender equality.

It should be emphasized that the *chalutz* dress code was the exclusive property of the socialist elite, who lived in *kibbutzim* or *moshavim* (agricultural villages) and their followers. The rest of the secular Jewish population in Palestine led an urban life, primarily in the burgeoning city of Tel Aviv. They did not renounce their *petit bourgeois* clothes. These two human spheres were set apart geographically and mentally, and their occasional meetings naturally produced a certain amount of dissonance. Henya Pekelman reports on such a weird encounter in the late 1920s:

> Friday after work I had left for Tel-Aviv.... I went to the ball... wearing a burlap dress that my mother had embroidered, and sandals without socks.... He introduced me to his other guests. There were present twelve young men, all smartly dressed; and five young women clothed with silk dresses and red lipsticks. Everybody in the room stared at me in bewilderment. (Pekelman 2007, 158)

The two spheres lived side by side until the late 1930s. There is no indication of when the name Khugistic Sandals was changed. One thing that might have brought this about was the 1944 opening of a flourishing footwear business called "Nimrod" on Dizengoff Street, then a deserted Tel Aviv byway, which in the 1960s and 1970s became a fashionable urban shopping district. In the late 1920s the workshop of Zvi and Kalman Rosenblitt in The Netherlands manufactured footwear bearing the biblical name "Nimrod," intended to identify the strapped sandal with ancient times. Immigration to Israel converted the German *Jesuslatchen* to the Hebraicized Biblical Sandals.

UNIFORMED SOCIETY

The appearance of Biblical Sandals in the urban arena coincided with major historical events in the late 1940s and early 1950s, which contributed to the popularity of Biblical Sandals among city dwellers. After the 1917 collapse of the Ottoman Empire, which had controlled the area since the sixteenth century, Palestine came under the rule of Great Britain. The British Mandate in Palestine lasted from 1920 until independence in 1948. The Zionist project in Palestine was threatened on two sides: the cultural challenge of British colonial rule and the enmity of native Arabs. The *yishuv* (Jewish community) leaders organized unofficial armies within their circles. Their members naturally adopted the ready-made *chalutz* dress code as a uniform. However, a uniformed society already clothed in *chalutz* style made it possible for military agents to easily and anonymously mingle with civilians. The meaning of the military uniform, says Joseph, is its role as a signal between adversaries (Joseph 1986, 10). In 1940s Palestine no member of the Palmach[13] could be identified by their dress. Their clothing masked their military identity, and Biblical Sandals served as an ideal accessory.

This choice of dress is a significant marker of the informal, straightforward, and courageous personality of the idealized Sabra Palmach fighter, exemplified in the personage of an officer nicknamed Ra'anana, mentioned in a book published by the parents of one of his fellow Palmach fighters, "Jimmy," who died during the War of Independence:

> Ra'anana had appeared...His negligent appearance was similar to Jimmy's—the shirt over the pants, and even when it was stuck in his pants, one side of the belt was usually more lifted than the other and his blond *blorit* dropped on his forehead down to his eyes, but Jimmy walked barefoot and Ra'anana—in sandals and he was dressed like this when he first addressed us and said: "guys—I am your commander." About the sandals of Ra'anana people used to say that he did not leave them behind even when he later went to battle. (*Friends Speak of Jimmy* 1966, 58)

One can see the development of a significant concept in this passage. The New Man of the new land of Israel was imbued with eternal youth, with body and spirit strong and firm; his curly hair is full; his posture is alert, always on guard, ready for immediate action. These young people left their families ready to sacrifice themselves for the Zionist cause.

This idea is visually expressed by the monument to the defenders of Kibbutz Negba, designed by Nathan Rappoport in 1950 (Figure 5.3). The three standing figures are easily

Figure 5.3   Kibbutz Negba. Monument dedicated to
the memory of those who defended the kibbutz during
the War of Independence. Monument designed by
Nathan Rappoport, 1950. Photographer: Moshe Pridan,
1963. Courtesy of Israeli Government Press Office.

identified in light of their sartorial attributes: to the left stands the Sabra Palmach fighter,
with the male *chalutz* in the middle and the *chalutza,* the female pioneer, to the right. The
chalutz is in standard attire, while the *chalutza* wears a simple dress with a new version of
Biblical Sandals: the strap, usually across the instep, extends high and is crossed on her leg,
similar to ancient Roman style. Another key attribute to understanding the iconography
of these images is their headwear: the Palmach fighter has only his *blorit,* the *chalutz* wears
the contemporary *tembel* hat, while the *chalutza* wears an archaic kerchief, in the European
style, and is thus depicted in a gender-specific manner. The type of sandals she wears became fashionable in the late 1940s, and female youth movement members who wore them
were criticized as being fashionably vain (Naor 1989, 238–39). In its updated iconography
the Negba monument deprives the woman pioneer of her sartorial advancement. The female kibbutz member is symbolized as riding on the wheels of capitalist consumption, as
if Zionist dress reform had never occurred.

FASHIONING THE NATION

The Negba monument is a visual requiem to the nongendered image of the *chalutz,* who
represented the struggle for nationhood. The Israeli state was founded in 1948, and the

Palmach became part of its army. The evolution of the official Israeli army, *Tzahal* (IDF),[14] occurred gradually during the following decade. Its uniform was based on the British model, with gender-specific clothing. The sandals were not forgotten and became a female item. Photographs of women soldiers show several versions of strapped sandals, whereas the premilitary (*Gadna,* youth battalions) uniform included Biblical Sandals on male feet. However, the gendered status of the sandals in Tzahal did not affect their nongendered status within Israeli civil life. The Biblical Sandals manufactured by "Nimrod" became standard sartorial dress, worn by many Israelis, no matter their affiliation. They were actually considered an authentic symbol of Israeli-ness.

This idea was visually conveyed in 1951 by the caricaturist Kariel Gardosh (nicknamed Dosh), not a native Israeli, but a Hungarian Holocaust survivor. His specialty was creating typical images of "The Israeli." His main cartoon character was called Srulik, a diminutive of Israel. Srulik immediately became a national icon, and Dosh depicted him reacting to contemporary events (Dosh 1964). Srulik was a perennial young boy who never aged. His clothes were based on the *chalutz* dress code: a *tembel* hat with a *blorit,* an open white shirt worn over blue shorts,[15] and Biblical Sandals. Yet, apart from his clothes, his other characteristics are completely different from those of the mythological *chalutz.* Srulik never appears in the act of hard work, and he often uses his too big hands clumsily. He looks like a naughty and innocent kid with big wide-open eyes, and a smile that often beams with childlike amazement (Broshy 2007). During the next two decades Srulik became a cultural icon that appeared on many artifacts. In the caricature entitled "Bar Mitzva Wish," Srulik is seen standing, his hand in his mouth, directed toward two giant legs clothed in long pants and two strapped slippers. On each leg one phrase appears: "Big Aliyah" (Figure 5.4). On his thirteenth birthday Srulik is hoping for a massive Jewish immigration. The new immigrants who have not yet become Israelis wear slippers, while Srulik wears authentic Biblical Sandals.

In the 1960s, a new interest in Biblical Sandals arose, triggered by an archaeological excavation of a first-century cave in Qumran in the Judean desert. An ancient leather

Figure 5.4 "Bar Mitzva Wish," from Dosh (1964). Artist:
Kariel Gardosh. Courtesy of Daniella Gardosh.

sandal was found side by side with the Hebrew Scriptures. This discovery was earthshaking, as both artifacts proved the existence of ancient Jewish life in the land of Israel, a reaffirmation of the Zionist founding narrative. This contributed to Biblical Sandals being granted the status of ethnic footwear in the 1960s and 1970s. Yvonne J. Seng and Betty Wass argue that the creation of ethnic dress often involves an "invented tradition" that is adopted and reinterpreted by certain subgroups or communities. The perceived or invented tradition acquires validity by being acted out (Seng and Wass 1995, 229–31), and such action was taken in the 1970s by a new pioneering group, *Gush Emunim* (Block of the Faithful), a religious-political movement that sprang up after the conquests of the Six-Day War (1967). Their eagerness to settle and thus claim the land, which they considered theirs by right of the Bible, reminded old *pioneers of the Second* Aliyah. To strengthen this historical link, *Gush Emunim* settlers, through their youth movement Bnei Akiva, adopted Biblical Sandals. As religious Jews they could not bare their bodies with shorts and shirts. Yet new technological developments in the footwear industry led to the invention of an advanced heavy-duty version of Biblical Sandals. Whether these sandals were manufactured by an American firm, "Teva" (nature) (Roman 2003, 44–48), or its Israeli

Figure 5.5   Settler staking an Israeli flag on top of Artis Hill next to the settlement of Beth El in Samaria, 1995. Photographer: Avi Ohayon. Courtesy of Israeli Government Press Office.

competitor, "Shoresh" (source), the settlers were, and still are, wearing Velcro-strapped sandals with rubber soles. The concept of undressing the foot is thus retained, along with the visual mimicry of the original *chalutz* (Figure 5.5).

EPILOGUE

At first, writing about sandals seemed like a marginal scholarly activity. However, researching and contemplating this item of Israeli clothing has completely changed my initial response. It is in the paradoxical nature of this type of dress that it is perceived as minimal and yet at the same time so symbolic. This footwear, whose shape and identity have often been altered, is a significant clue to the Israeli psyche. An anonymous artifact with a shapeless form, it was the representative of the Second Aliyah. As Khugistic Sandals, with two horizontal straps and no buckle, they covered the feet of the mythological *chalutz* in the 1920s and metamorphosed into Biblical Sandals, which were the buckled attribute of the Palmach fighter. The settlers of modern Israel wear the new hi-tech American version.

In contemporary Israel young people have returned to shoe wearing, while the elders prefer sandals (Ben-Ezer 1996, 20–21). Which footwear is now the authentic expression of Israeli identity? Or was this question answered by the proposed Knesset dress code banning the wearing of sandals? Does this reflect the wish of Israeli society to no longer identify itself with the socialist dress ideals from the early beginnings of the state, or do Israelis wish to identify with the more formal dress code of the Western world?

NOTES

1. *Khugistic* means that which belongs to the *khug* (circle); an exclusive society defined itself as *khug*.
2. The literal meaning of *sabra* is the prickly pear cactus *opuntia*. The nickname refers to the native Israeli personality, which is prickly and tough on its surface and soft and sweet within. For a detailed discussion of the Sabra type see Almog 1997.
3. Schroer and Staubli mention 250 references in the Bible to feet and legs (2001, 181).
4. See also Roth 1992, 176.
5. For an extensive study on the Second Aliyah (immigration of Jews to Israel) see Peled (2002).
6. *Aliyah* in Hebrew means "ascending." In modern Hebrew it means immigration to the land of Israel. The Second Aliyah occurred between 1904 and 1914.
7. Eliezer Shokhat, *Ha'poel Ha'tzair*, 4 (1915), quoted in Bartal 1997, 289.
8. Apart from the socks, the actual difference of "after-work clothes" was their cleanness.
9. This information comes from a conversation with the historian Professor Alon Kadish, June 17, 2007.
10. The same buckled sandals are also seen on the feet of pioneer dolls from the 1930s, made by Edith Samuel.
11. Research proves that, in reality, any substantial change in values had not been achieved (Bernstein 1987, 10–15).

12. Apart from the buttoned fly, the long trousers were quite similar for both genders; feminine shorts were gathered in rubber bands on the thighs.
13. Palmach was the regular fighting force of the unofficial army of the Jewish community during the British Mandate of Palestine.
14. The Israeli Defence Force.
15. White and blue are the colors of the Israeli flag.

BIBLIOGRAPHY

Almog, Oz (1997), *The Sabra? A Profile* [in Hebrew], Tel Aviv: Am Oved. Also available in English as *The Sabra: The Creation of the New Jew,* trans. 2000 Haim Watzman. Berkeley: University of California Press.

Beit Alpha Kibbutz. 1981. "The personal boxes were thrown to the fire." In *Here on the Land,* [in Hebrew] ed. Muky Tzur, Tair Zevulun, and Khanina Porat, 206–7. Tel Aviv: Hakibbutz Hameukhad and Sifriyat Hapoalim.

Ben-Ezer, Ehud. 1996. "The summer, the sandals and the Zionist dream" [in Hebrew]. *Hed Hakhinukh* 70 (11–22): 20–21.

Ben-Tzvi, Rachel Yanayit, 1959. *We Are Ascending: Life Chapters* [in Hebrew], Tel Aviv: Am Oved.

Bernstein, Deborah. 1987. *The struggle for equality: Women workers in the Palestine "yishuv"* [in Hebrew]. Tel Aviv: Hakibbutz Hameukhad.

Broshy, Michal. 2007. *Dosh: Caricaturist 1921–2000* [in Hebrew]. Tel Aviv: Eretz Israel Museum and Yad Ben-Tzvi.

Buber, Martin. 1948. *Between a people and their land* [in Hebrew]. Tel Aviv: Schocken.

Cavallaro, Dani, and Alexandra Warwick. 1998. *Fashioning the frame: Boundaries, dress and body.* New York: Berg.

Dosh [Kariel Gardosh]. 1964. *What happened? In the years 1960–1963: Caricatures and cartoons.* Tel Aviv: Karni.

Even-Zohar, Itamar. 1990. "The emergence of a native Hebrew culture in Palestine, 1882–1948." *Poetics Today* 11 (1): 175–76.

Franco, Nitzkhiya. 1981. "Three points of 'fashion' to our credit" [in Hebrew]. In *Here on the land,* ed. Muky Tzur, Tair Zevulun, and Khanina Porat, 308. Tel Aviv: Hakibbutz Hameukhad and Sifriyat Hapoalim.

Friends Speak of Jimmy. [in Hebrew] 1966. Tel Aviv: Hakibbutz Hameukhad.

Joseph, Nathan. 1986. *Uniforms and nonuniforms: Communication through clothing.* New York: Greenwood Press.

Meranda, Amnon. 2007. "New dress code may ban leather from Knesset." *Israel News* (June 29, 2007), available at http://www.ynetnews.com/articles/0,7340,L-3417863,00.html

Naor, Mordechai. 1989. "To be a youth movement member, 1947–1955" [in Hebrew]. In *Youth movements 1920–1960,* ed. Mordechai Naor, 238–39. Jerusalem: Yad Yitzkhak Ben-Tzvi.

Ofrat, Gideon. 1983. "The ascent and descent of the pioneer in Israeli art" [in Hebrew]. In *Within a local context,* ed. Gideon Ofrat, 180–97, Tel Aviv: Hakibbutz Hameukhad.

Pekelman, Henya. 2007. *Life of working woman in the land of Israel: An autobiography* [in Hebrew]. Beer Sheba: Dvir and Ben-Gurion University Press.

Peled, Rina. 2002. *"The new man" of the Zionist revolution: Ha'shomer Ha'zair and his European roots* [in Hebrew]. Tel Aviv: Am Oved.

Perrot, Philippe. (1994), *Fashioning the Bourgeoisie: A History of Clothing in the Nineteenth Century,* Princeton: Princeton University Press.

Pinski, Herschel. 1981. "The *Execution,* the excommunication of clothes" [in Hebrew]. In *Here on the land,* ed. Muky Tzur, Tair Zevulun, and Khanina Porat, 208. Tel Aviv: Hakibbutz Hameukhad and Sifriyat Hapoalim.

Rand, Itzkhak. 1981. "Broken shoes" [in Hebrew]. In *Here on the land,* ed. Muky Tzur, Tair Zevulun, and Khanina Porat, 198. Tel Aviv: Hakibbutz Hameukhad and Sifriyat Hapoalim.

Roman, Yadin. 2003. "Abridged history of the sandal" [in Hebrew]. *Eretz Ve'teva* (July–August): 44–48.

Rosenthal, Ruvik. 2007. "The Linguistic Arena," Ma'ariv, 6 July 2007.

Roth, Ariel. 1992. "The definition and meaning of the term 'shoe' in Judaism" [in Hebrew]. *Nizanei Aretz* 8: 170–82.

Schroer, Silvia, and Thomas Staubli. 2001. *Body symbolism in the Bible.* Collegeville, MN: Liturgical Press.

Seng, Yvonne J., and Betty Wass. 1995. "Traditional Palestinian wedding dress as a symbol of nationalism." In *Dress and ethnicity: Change across space and time,* ed. Joanne B. Eicher, 229–31. Oxford: Berg.

Shakhar, Ilan. 2007. "Miniskirts, but no shorts? Knesset ethics committee debates MKs' attire" [in Hebrew]. *Ha'aretz* (June 26): n.p.

Shapira, Anita. 2004. "The Bible and Israeli identity." *AJS Review* 28 (1): 11–42.

Shavit, Yaacov. 1997. "Kozak and Bedouin: The new national imagery." In *The Second Aliyah* [in Hebrew], ed. Israel Bartal, 483–93. Jerusalem: Yad Ben-Tzvi.

Wilson, Elizabeth. 1985. *Adorned in dreams: Fashion and modernity.* New York: Tauris.

PART II: MEMORIES AND COMMEMORATION

6　THE SHTETL SHOE
HOW TO MAKE A SHOE

MAYER KIRSHENBLATT AND
BARBARA KIRSHENBLATT-GIMBLETT

Mayer Kirshenblatt was born in 1916, in Apt (Opatów in Polish), where he completed seven grades of Polish public school and apprenticed to an electrician and cobbler. His father was a leather merchant and supplied cobblers with everything they needed. In 1934, at the age of seventeen, he left Poland for Canada. In 1990, at the age of 73, he began to paint everything he could remember about his childhood in Apt. He remembers in detail precisely how to make a shoe and much else to do with shoemaking and shoemakers, and illustrates his account of the step-by-step process of making a shoe with detailed drawings and paintings. What Mayer conveys in this extraordinary account are not simple facts: the cobbler is no ordinary cobbler but one whose sons died at birth, except for the very last one. These are felt facts, for this is a world not only to be known, but also to be sensed. It is the affective charge that gives to Mayer's memories of shoes, boots, and cobblers its luminosity. Speaking in his own voice—assisted by his daughter, who has been interviewing him for over forty years—Mayer tells us not only how to make a shoe, but also much about the world of those who made and wore them.

"It is perhaps in the artisan that one must seek the most admirable evidences of the sagacity, the patience, and the resources of the mind," writes Jean Le Rond d'Alembert in his "Preliminary Discourse to the Encyclopedia of Diderot," which appeared in 1751.[1] Like the plates of the Encyclopédie, Mayer's painting of the cobbler's workshop offers a tableau of the total scene, and like the step-by-step illustrations in the Encyclopédie, Mayer's drawing shows each stage in making a shoe. Mayer learned less from apprenticeship than he did from close observation of the cobbler at work. Delight in how things work—"in the pleasure taken in observing process"—is what Neil Harris calls the operational aesthetic.[2] With the town as his classroom, Mayer pursued a self-designed curriculum of gestural knowledge, embodied intelligence and know-how connected to tools, materials, processes, and workspaces.[3] Yet when this inquisitive boy appears in the paintings, as he often does, it is always in his blue "uniform," a reminder of the hard mastery of the school classroom—even when he is playing hooky so he could watch the cobbler. Today, in the unique world created by his paintings, the boy in blue who holds the shoemaker's baby has also become a child witness to a remembered world.

Two pairs of shoes stand out in my memory. Sporty fellows like me had red ski boots with brass eyes and wide yellow shoelaces. My red ski boots were my favorite shoes. They were *sportowe,* sporty, but they were not made in Apt. We wore two pairs of white socks: knee socks and a second pair that folded over the shoe like a collar. We looked pretty smart with those nice shoes and knee high socks. Everyone got a new outfit for Passover. One Passover, my father had a shoemaker make a beautiful pair of patent-leather shoes for me. During *khalemoyd,* the intervening days of the holiday, there was a big soccer match on the *torgeviske.* (There was no special playing field in Apt, so the *torgeviske,* the place where the livestock market was held, was the main place for soccer.) All of a sudden, the ball came my way. I gave it a powerful kick and ripped away the sole of my new shoe from the tip to the heel. You can imagine what happened to me when I got home. The shoes were brand new. I had only worn them a few times. The shoemaker repaired the one I tore.

Soccer, or *fusbal,* as we called it, was the game of choice. Somewhere, I don't know how, we acquired an old soccer ball. On the outside it was sewn together with a leather thong. The ball kept tearing all the time at the seams. Every time it would tear, we would take the ball to the shoemaker, who would sew it up. There was a balloon inside. It was full of patches, so whenever there was a leak we'd put new patches on it. We took turns blowing it up since we didn't have an air pump. It kept on bursting, and we kept on repairing it. If you didn't have a ball like this you played with a rubber ball. If you didn't have a rubber ball you made a ball out of rags. One guy would come with something to kick around, and, before you knew it, there were two teams with maybe three to five people on each.

In winter we loved to skate. Skates with built-in shoes were a real prize. Yankl *kuptsu* had brought such a pair back from Canada after he was deported and forced to return to Poland after he was caught stealing. Among the things that Yankl brought back to Apt from Canada were the skates with built-in shoes. He later sold them to the blacksmith's son. Very few of my friends owned such skates, but hope springs eternal, and all of us got the shoemaker to attach metal plates to the heels of our shoes just in case we got the chance to put on someone else 's metal skates. The metal plate was in the shape of a diamond; it had a small hole, also the shape of a diamond, in the middle. To recess this metal plate so that it was flush with the heel, but leave a little space under the hole in the metal plate, the shoemaker carved out a little hole in the middle of the heel; he made the hole in the heel a bit deeper and larger in diameter than the hole in the metal plate. That way the little projection from the heel of the skate would go all the way through the hole in the metal plate and, with one twist, secure the heel of the shoe to the skate. To hold the front of the shoe in the skate, there were two clamps, one on each side of the toes. We would tighten the clamps with a key. Most of the time we had to make do with skates we made ourselves from wood, metal strapping and rope. If you had the money you got the shoemaker to make two leather straps with buckles for each skate.

Yosl *luptsok* had two daughters. Pintshe, my grandfather's nephew, fell in love with one of them. Pintshe used to visit Apt from Wierzbnik, his hometown. One time Pintshe was in Apt at the same time as my father's brother Arn Yosef, who had come to see us from Drildz, my father's hometown. In despair over his unrequited love, Pintshe got drunk. He came to our house, flopped down on the bed and fell sound asleep in his clothes and shoes.

Arn Yosef was something of a prankster. He inserted big wooden matches between the sole and upper part of each of Pintshe's shoes. We woke him up and, while he was still groggy, we lit the matches. He jumped up and started dancing. That's called a hot foot. The romance eventually petered out. Pintshe survived the war. Upon being liberated he returned to his hometown and was shot by Polish people he probably knew.

Before the Germans drove the Jews out of Apt in 1942, Mordkhe Wajcblum, my mother's cousin, had a shoemaker make him a special pair of shoes with hollow heels so that he could hide gold coins in them. But after a dispute with the shoemaker, the shoemaker betrayed him to the Germans. In October 1942, the Germans forced about six hundred Jews in Apt to walk to Sandomierz, which was 21 miles away. All the others, about six thousand Jews—the number was so big because Jews from the surrounding area were forced to concentrate in Apt—were sent straight to Treblinka. It was in Sandomierz, where there was a labor camp, that the Germans took the money from the heels of Mordkhe's shoes and shot him.

I don't ever remember a time when my father was not in the leather business. His little shop was small, about ten feet square, and didn't carry much merchandise, just hard and soft leather, findings and other shoemaking supplies. I vividly remember the shoemakers who used to come to my father's store. One man, a Polish veteran, leased his cigarette permit to someone else—cigarettes were a government monopoly and permits were issued to disabled veterans instead of pensions—because he could make a better living as a shoemaker. He had a leg shot off in the war. This guy didn't wear a wooden peg but rather a shoe and some kind of prosthesis. Every time he stepped on that leg it squeaked. He was an alcoholic. I went to his home to collect the money he owed my father every Wednesday at the end of market day. I had to catch him before he got drunk.

Father was away much of the time, buying leather in Kraków and other big cities, so Mother used to run the place. Father would buy big cow and horse hides (*fel*) for the soles of shoes; soft hides of calf (*krom*), thin and supple goat hide (*gimze*), patent leather (*lakier*) and *kep* for lining boots and shoes. *Kep* came from the heads of animals, so those skins had to be flattened out. They were baled in small bundles of about a dozen pieces and sold by weight. *Kep* was yellow. *Gimze,* which was very pliable and expensive, came in brown and black; black was the most popular. *Lakier,* an expensive, high-gloss black leather, was used for fancy shoes, especially for women.

When my father brought a shipment of leather to Apt he would not store it in the shop for fear of theft. He kept it at home under his bed or on top of the armoire; he only kept one hide of each kind in the shop. Father sold the sole leather by weight because this leather was of uneven thickness. It was thickest in the back and thinned out toward the flanks. On the shelves were a few packages of little steel "horseshoes" to protect heels, little nose caps for toes, metal tacks, wooden pegs, special sandpaper, hog bristle and wax for the twine, and lasts—in short, everything a shoemaker needed, including shoe polish.

Erdal shoe polish was the most popular brand in Poland. Every spring a salesman would come to town in a car loaded with cases of shoe polish, which he would sell to the local

Figure 6.1   *The Shoe-Polish Salesman and His Black Chauffeur,* February 1995. Acrylic on canvas, 24" × 30". Artist: Mayer Kirshenblatt.

stores. As an advertising attraction he had a black chauffeur. This man was really black. Having never seen a black person before, we used to follow him around. He was the biggest attraction in town. Although it was warm he would be fully dressed in a three-piece suit, white shirt and tie. He would sweat and was shiny. Not knowing any better we thought the salesman polished him up every morning to show off the shoe polish.

HOW TO MAKE A SHOE

Shoemaking proper consisted of two trades: the *shister* (cobbler) made the hard sole and assembled the shoe, and the *kamashn-makher* made the uppers from soft leather, the part that is called *kholefkes* in Yiddish. A third trade was the *latacz* (*latutnik* in Yiddish), which means 'patcher'. He did repairs, replaced heels and patched leather footwear of all kinds. The *kamashn-makher* had the highest status and the *latacz* the lowest. I apprenticed to a *kamashn-makher* for a short time. I was very interested in trades and used to watch the cobbler who lived next door to us by the hour. I watched him so closely I could probably make a pair of shoes, even now. All our shoes were custom made, although shoemakers did make ready-to-wear boots for farmers. I remember going to the cobbler to be fitted for shoes. The first thing he did was to take the measurements. Most of the shoemakers were illiterate. They had their own system of measuring. The shoemaker took a piece of paper about fifteen to eighteen inches long and folded it over three times to make a strip about an inch wide. First he measured the length of your sole and made one tear. Then he measured the instep and made another tear. The third tear indicated the width of the foot, the space between the big toe and the small toe. He knew exactly what those tears meant.

Once he had the measurements the shoemaker gave the order to the *kamashn-makher.* At the *kamashn-makher* you chose the style and color. There were not many styles for me to choose from: I could order either ankle boots or regular shoes, which we called Oxford shoes, or *latshn* in Yiddish. He made all kinds of fancy patterns. He would cut leather in various shapes, perforate it with holes large and small, which he made with a small punching machine, and apply the decorative piece to the upper. He also added extra stitching. The *kamashn-makher* would buy the leather from our store. The most expensive leather for uppers was *gimze;* the next best was *krom.* The *kamashn-makher* then prepared the upper, complete with its lining and tongue; he made little holes for the laces with a punch and used a little hand press to attach metal eyelets to the holes.

After the *kamashn-makher* had completed the uppers he delivered them to the cobbler. The cobbler would pick the last that was closest to his measurements. In Polish the word for last is *kopyto,* which is the same as the word for hoof; in Yiddish it is called *kopete.* Then he would build up the last wherever it was smaller than the person's foot. If, for example, a person had a bunion, the shoemaker would take small pieces of leather and attach them to the last where the bunion was. He used tacks and glue to fasten leather scraps to the wood and a rasp and sandpaper to shape the last so that it would conform to the person's foot.

The cobbler made twine by placing hog bristle into the lay of linen twine, together with wax, which helped secure the bristle. He would roll the twine between his palms to make it firm; he also waxed the twine to make it easier to thread through the leather. The sole was fashioned out of four pieces of leather—the first midsole, the second thin midsole, the hard outsole and the soft insole. First the cobbler put a thin midsole on the bottom of the last. Then he put the upper on the last and tugged the bottom edges of the upper down so it would tightly overlap the first midsole: the midsole was thus between the last and the edges of the upper. To hold everything in place, the cobbler threaded twine through holes he had made with an awl along the bottom edges of the upper. He threaded the twine through the upper from one side of the sole to the other in a crisscross fashion and pulled it tight. Because the soft upper leather would gather and bunch under the last, he had to pound the gathered leather flat before gluing the second midsole, maybe from *kep,* over it.

As he was doing all of this the hard outsole, which was less than a quarter-inch thick, was soaking for about twenty-four hours in a bucket of water. When it was ready he put the wet leather on a stone and beat it with a mallet. The outsole needed to be soft and flexible so that it would conform to the shape of the last, which was not flat, as there was an arch. Beating the wet leather also made the leather a little larger. The cobbler now placed the last on the beaten leather and drew an outline around the last. This outline served as a guide for cutting out the outsole, which he then tacked to the last.

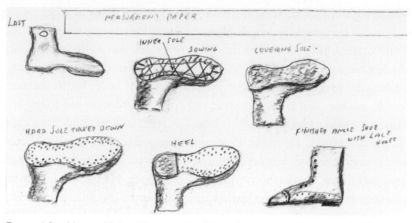

Figure 6.2   *How to Make a Shoe*, undated. Pencil on watercolor paper, 9.25" × 13.25". Artist: Mayer Kirshenblatt. How to make a shoe: * Measurement paper. * Last. Inner sole. * S[e]wing. * Covering sole. * Hard sole tacked down. * Heel. * Finished ankle shoe with lace holes.

Now he was ready to make the holes for the square pegs that would fasten the outsole to the upper. He made a light outline about an eighth of an inch from the edge of the outsole as a guide for the holes. The cobbler made round holes in the sole by driving his awl through the leather and into the last. Then he pounded square pegs into the round holes, spaced in two or three staggered rows to form a very nice design.

Only after this outsole was attached to the last did he trim it to fit the shoe with a special knife. This knife was small, sharp, and bent, so that it would cut the sole without damaging the upper. To finish the outer sole nicely, he used a rasp to make the pegs level with the sole and a piece of broken glass to shave the surface of the outsole. Finally, he licked the outsole with his tongue and slid the handle of the hammer over the moist leather again and again to give it a very nice shiny smooth surface. The outsole became a light brown and the pegs stayed white: the pattern stood out beautifully thanks to the contrast of the light pegs against the darkened leather sole.

For added effect he might make a decorative indentation with a little chisel along the outside edges of the outsole. For men's shoes the heels were made of layers of leather. Before attaching a heel the cobbler would apply a special liquid polish, either a dark brown or black, to the edges of the sole and to the heel. He used a small brush with a wire handle; the bristle was embedded in the twisted wire, similar to a bottle brush. He nailed the heel to the sole and used wooden pegs to attach the final layer of the heel. On request he would attach steel horseshoes to the heels and thin nose caps to the toes. The horseshoes had countersunk holes in them for nails. The nose caps came with sharp little triangular wedges that had been pressed out of the nose cap: when tapped into the sole, those sharp little wedges held the nose cap in place. Horseshoes and nose caps helped to prevent the heel and tip of the sole from wearing out as quickly; we also liked the way capped shoes would sound. I remember a fad for shoes that squeaked. The shoemaker knew how to do this too.

For ladies' shoes my father sold all kinds of wooden heels. The best lady's shoemaker in town was the brother of Świderśka, the prostitute. He, his wife and Świderśka lived in a tiny room, which doubled as his workshop. In a corner of the room he had a little table and a stool. In the summer the door was open and I could see inside. He would shape the wooden heels for ladies' high-heel shoes; he would sculpt them. His shoes were a work of art. Unfortunately he would rather sit at the tavern with his buddies than work.

To remove the last from the shoe the shoemaker inserted a hook into a hole that went through the top of the last, just above the ankle, and pulled the last out of the shoe. The hook was about a foot long, with a T handle; it had to be long enough to retrieve the last from a boot. He would then rasp the inside of the shoe to level all the protruding wooden tacks and make the surface smooth before gluing the insole over the tacks. With a little bit of shoe polish and a few strokes with a brush, the cobbler finished the shoe.

There is one cobbler I will never forget, our neighbor *der shvartser* Khiel, Khiel the Brunet, and I've painted him. Although he was a redhead and all his children were redheads, they called him Khiel the Brunet. To confuse matters further they nicknamed a brunet Khiel in town *der geyler* Khiel, Khiel the Redhead. One day my mother sent me to *der shvartser* Khiel in the early morning on an errand. It was before they had a chance to rise. When

Figure 6.3   *Boy in the White Pajamas,* 1992. 24" × 30". Artist: Mayer Kirshenblatt.

I walked into that room, there were people sleeping everywhere, wall-to-wall, at the head and foot of the beds, on benches and tables, and on the floor. The whole family lived and worked in two rooms. I remember even before my father left for Canada seeing how the cobblers lived. In my painting you can see all the action. The drinking water was in a barrel on the floor. The wooden bucket on the cabinet contained water for soaking the leather to make it flexible. You can see all the tools and each step in the process of making a shoe.

Der shvartser Khiel was so poor he could not pay his income tax (*dochodowy* in Polish). When he knew the tax collector was about to arrive he would hide anything of value. The tax collector, seeing that *der shvartser* Khiel couldn't come up with the money, would take his tools and anything else he could find, put them out onto the street and auction them off right in front of the cobbler's workshop. Meanwhile, *der shvartser* Khiel had arranged for a neighbor to place a low bid: "Moyshe, you bid. I'll pay you back." It was a put-up deal. Everyone knew, so no one else would bid. The tax collector settled for the pittance he got from the auction and wrote off the rest. After the tax collector was gone, *der shvartser* Khiel repaid his neighbor, which was considerably less than he would have paid in taxes, and got all his tools back. The poverty was unbelievable.

Der shvartser Khiel had seven daughters. Every time a male child was born something happened and the child died. Every Jew wants to have a son so that there will be someone to say kaddish, the prayer for the deceased, for him after his demise. In desperation *der shvartser* Khiel went to the rabbi and implored him: "Am I to die without a male heir?" Who will say the kaddish after I'm gone? I have seven daughters. Can I afford another one? Where will I find dowries and grooms for them all?" The rabbi thought for a while, then came up with a solution. He said, "Go home. When your wife gets pregnant and it's a baby boy, do exactly what I tell you." First he gave Khiel an amulet and told him to make the boy wear it all the time: it would ward off evil spirits. Second the child must always be dressed in white: the white clothes would fool the Angel of Death, the *malekh-hamuves,* into thinking the boy was already dead and not taking him, since Jews always bury their dead in white burial shrouds. A boy was born. *Der shvartser* Khiel followed the rabbi's instructions, and the boy survived. When I left Opatów in 1934 the boy was eight years old. I was told that even as a teenager he still wore the white pajamas. He was dressed in white in 1942 when the Jews of Apt were expelled, never to return.

I also remember an incident with a *kamashn-makher* in town. His name was Beyrl Czereśny, which means cherry (*czereśnia*) in Polish. Beyrl had many children, and he was poor. When he complained to his friends about his problems, they told him about condoms. He said he would make one himself from goat leather, *gimze,* which was very soft. One day his wife got sick. The doctor came to see what was wrong. He found the leather condom inside Beyrl's wife and removed it. When her mother heard the news, she ran up the street wailing, "Oy, oy! The baby is not yet born and he's already made the uppers." I knew the guy. He used to buy leather from my father.

My father finally had to leave Poland secretly because his business failed. Until then he had eked out a fairly good living: we were never short of food, and everyone got a new suit of clothing and new shoes for Passover. All that changed when my father went bankrupt through no fault of his own. I was twelve years old at the time. One time father went away to Kraków to buy heavy leather for soles. He arranged for it to be sent to Apt. The way they shipped leather was in a huge bale about three feet across: they would fill two hoops of metal baling with leather hides that had been rolled up inside one another. The bale was quite heavy. This time someone held up the train and stole my father's leather.

As luck would have it the railroad company found the leather. Maybe it was my father's leather, maybe not. Who knows? It was the same weight, but it was cut up into little pieces. It had very little value once it was all cut up. With a whole hide my father could lay out the soles and heels to waste as little leather as possible: the shoemaker would come to him with the size soles he needed, and my father would cut him a piece of leather and charge him according to the weight. A whole cowhide might be eight feet long and five feet wide. Given its irregular shape and that it was thicker in the middle than at the edges, you lose a quarter inch here, a quarter inch there and even more at the edges. There were also two prices: the thicker pieces from the back of the hide cost more than the thinner pieces cut from the sides. But from the little pieces they found you could barely even make a pair of soles; the pieces were so small the only thing you could do with them was make heels. Why the thief cut up the leather I do not know. All I know is that they found bags and bags of little pieces of leather. In any case the government said, "This is your leather. This is what we found and it is yours. We don't owe you anything. You have no case." My father was devastated. He had issued a promissory note, a *veksl,* to pay for the leather, but he had no money in the bank to cover it. This was a very serious thing in Poland. It was not like here. You could not renege on a promissory note. You had to pay up or it was immediate bankruptcy.

Believe it or not, we had our own mafia in Apt. I don't know about the *gemiles-kheysed* (Jewish interest-free loan society), but there sure were loan sharks, and my father was deeply in debt. The head of the mafia was Khamu Itshe Mayers, a butcher by profession (in more ways than one) and loan shark. He was an intimidating presence thanks to his enormous size: he was more than six feet tall and must have weighed three hundred pounds. In the synagogue he occupied the space of three people. He used three lecterns: he would put his prayer book on the middle one and his big hands on the other two. So when my father needed to borrow money to make good on the promissory note he went to Mayers for a loan. Father figured that, by the time he had to pay off the loan, he would have settled with the government railway company, received money from the insurance company, and be in a position to repay the loan. He was negotiating with the government to reimburse him for the leather; after all, it was their railroad, and they were responsible.

To make a long story short, my father never received compensation for his loss, not from the government and not from the insurance company. Because he worked at such a small profit margin with such low investment capital, everything collapsed if there were the slightest hitch. As long as he bought on credit, sold the leather and paid the bills with what he just earned, the ball kept rolling. The moment the ball dropped he was dead. He survived from day to day, from *veksl* to *veksl.* It made no difference that the leather wholesaler to whom he owed the money was Jewish. Business in our small town was very precarious. Most of the businesses operated with American currency. The Polish zloty was convertible, but it was too volatile. It went up and down, so people did business in American dollars. This was the time of the Great Depression. It was a hand-to-mouth existence, even though we were not too badly off. However, once my father became so deeply in debt he had to escape.

At the time two of my father's younger brothers, Joe (Arn Yosef) and Sam (Shmiel), were in Canada. They were both upholsterers and making a nice living and wanted to bring their youngest brother, Duvid, who was single, to Canada. It was 1928. Immigration was difficult under the best of circumstances and pretty much impossible for a married man with children, like my father. Duvid did not want to go. He was running his mother's store in Drildz. He did not like the idea of leaving a relatively comfortable life in Poland to risk everything for a new life in Canada, where he would need to learn a new language and establish himself economically. In Drildz he ran the family business: he didn't work for somebody else. After preparing the papers for Duvid three times, Joe and Sam told him that this was his last chance. Duvid refused to go, and my father volunteered to go in his brother's stead, using his name and papers. In a very short time my father left.

My father had to depart in secret. He used to go out of town often, so when he left town this time nobody knew it was for good. If the loan shark had the slightest suspicion he would never have let my father leave in one piece. He would have killed him or, at the very least, maimed him. Only my mother knew that father would never return to Apt. My father first went to Drildz, so he could say good-bye to his parents. His father was already very ill with what I later surmised was hardening of the arteries. My mother then sent me on my own to Drildz by horse and wagon without telling me why she was sending me. I was happy to go. When I got to Drildz, my father was already there awaiting my arrival. That's when I found out that he would not return to Apt. Being the eldest I was the only one to be informed of my father's departure. I was strictly warned not to tell anybody. I had to keep my father's departure a secret. The next morning my father left for Canada. My grandfather lay on a chaise lounge in the kitchen, where he would rest all day. He rose with great difficulty, went to the front door, and with tears running down his face walked to my departing father, crying, 'Son, my son, my firstborn, I will never see you again'. The wagon took off with my father. I ran after it for a while and then stopped to see my father and the wagon disappear over the crest of a hill. I felt very sad. I used to write my father very nice letters.

At sixteen I realized I had no future whatsoever in Apt. Of course, you could always go through the four years' apprenticeship for tailoring or shoemaking, which was very un-pleasant, but even after such an apprenticeship, there was little work in Apt. Most of the time young people drifted into the big cities to work in sweatshops. With so few prospects in Apt we were always discussing when and how to leave Poland. The preferred place to im-migrate was Palestine, but the British Mandate authority issued few permits. To immigrate to the United States or Canada you needed not only a permit but also a blood relative who would help you financially, and even so there was a strict quota, so a lot of people were immigrating to Argentina, Mexico, Uruguay and Paraguay. I decided that, since everyone else was going, I might as well go too. I told my mother that I was going to apply to leave. By 1933 my father had been in Canada almost five years. My mother wrote to my father that he must do something to bring us all to Canada because if I, the oldest son, left, his other three sons would probably follow. My father wrote back that I should apprentice to a *kamashn-makher* and learn the trade. A cousin of my father's was a foreman in a shoe factory in Toronto; he told my father that if I learned this trade he would give me a job the moment I arrived in Canada.

A *kamashn-makher,* who made the upper part of the shoe, was a profession in Poland one step higher than a cobbler, which wasn't very high. Following the instructions in my father's letter my mother started to ask around. Sure enough, there was a *kamashn-makher* who required an apprentice. His workshop was in a room on the second floor of a building just up from the pharmacy on the marketplace. Apprenticeships usually lasted four years. I didn't expect to learn the whole trade, because we anticipated immigrating to Canada at any moment; I just hoped he would teach me to use the machines and give me an idea what the whole business was about.

I was shocked by what I encountered. Upon my arrival early in the morning the man had just finished urinating in the slop basin. He gave the high sign: I was expected to empty the basin through a window. Walking carefully so as not to spill the contents along the way, I had to check that there was nobody below before I whooshed the slop out the window. By that time the household had come to life. Two experienced employees arrived and sat at their sewing machines. Then the lady of the house came out, carrying a baby. The dwelling had two rooms: you entered the kitchen, which served as both the living area and workshop, and from the kitchen you went into a nursery bedroom, where they stored leather. The owner would cut the leather, and the two workers would stitch the uppers on sewing machines.

The lady was not so much fat as she was big: she had broad shoulders, wide hips and enormous breasts. Of course she was breastfeeding. With her size she could have suckled a platoon. She wore a dress that reached below the knees in the front and just below the buttocks at the back. Since she didn't wear underwear, every time she bent over you got a full view of the whole landscape. She had vaginal lips the size of cabbage leaves. I had never seen anything like it. At home we were four boys, and my mother was very careful. The lady gave me the baby to hold. When the man of the house needed me I handed the baby back to her. He sent me out to do different chores, deliver finished goods, pick up some supplies and sometimes shop for groceries. After work I had to sweep the place, clean up and chop some kindling wood for the next day. I worked twelve hours a day. After a few days I got tired of playing with the baby, so every time the lady gave me the baby I would pinch it and the poor baby would cry. She came and grabbed the baby, exclaiming, "I don't understand how come every time you hold the baby, the baby cries." I replied, "The truth is the baby doesn't like me, and I don't like the baby." After one week I told my mother that

Figure 6.4   *Apprenticing to the Kamashn-Makher*, September 1997. Acrylic on canvas, 24" × 36". Artist: Mayer Kirshenblatt.

I would quit because I wasn't learning anything except being a nursemaid, and we would probably leave for Canada soon anyway. One day I decided enough was enough, and I just quit. I was never paid a penny.

In Canada, I never did work in a shoe factory. I started out in a clothing sweatshop and then became a house painter, eventually opening my own paint and wallpaper store. I recently talked to a friend who remembers life in Poland—he was a shoemaker—and asked him if my description of how to make a shoe was correct. "From your description, I could make a shoe," he replied.[4]

NOTES

© Mayer Kirshenblatt and Barbara Kirshenblatt-Gimblett, 2007. Excerpted from *They Called Me Mayer July: Painted Memories of Jewish Childhood in Poland Before the Holocaust* by Mayer Kirshenblatt and Barbara Kirshenblatt-Gimblett, University of California Press, 2007. With permission of the University of California Press.

1. d'Alembert 1995: 42. See also Pannabecker (1994).
2. Harris 1973: 81.
3. Sibum 1995: 25–37.

4. Berger 1965: 91–94 supplements Sheskin 1965: 59–61. Warm thanks to Robert Rothstein for bringing these articles on the Yiddish terminology associated with shoemaking to my attention.

BIBLIOGRAPHY

d'Alembert, Jean Le Rond (1995), *Preliminary Discourse to the Encyclopedia of Diderot,* trans. Richard N. Schwab, Chicago: University of Chicago Press.

Berger, Yekusiel (1965), 'Nokh terminologye funem shteperfakh', *Yidishe shprakh* 25(3): 91–94.

Harris, Neil (1973), *Humbug: The Art of P. T. Barnum,* Boston: Little, Brown.

Pannabecker, John R. (1994), 'Diderot, the Mechanical Arts, and the *Encyclopédie:* In Search of the Heritage of Technology Education', *Journal of Technology Education* 6(1): 45–57. http://scholar.lib.vt.edu/ejournals/JTE/v6n1/pdf/pannabecker.pdf.

Sheskin, Khaim (1965), 'A bisl terminologye fun shteperfakh in Grodne', *Yidishe shprakh* 25(2): 59–61.

Sibum, H. Otto (1995), 'Working Experiments: A History of Gestural Knowledge', *Cambridge Review* 116(2325): 25–37.

7 THE FOLKLORISTIC SHOE

SHOES AND SHOEMAKERS IN YIDDISH LANGUAGE AND FOLKLORE

ROBERT A. ROTHSTEIN

This chapter explores the vocabulary and imagery of shoes and shoemakers in Yiddish, the traditional vernacular of Central and East European Jews (Ashkenazim) and of their descendants in the Ashkenazic Diaspora (the Americas, Western Europe, Australia, South Africa, Israel). Yiddish is a Germanic language that, like modern German, derives from the dialects that linguists call Middle High German (c. 1050–c. 1350). Unlike German, however, Yiddish bears witness in its grammar and vocabulary to influences from Semitic (Hebrew and Aramaic) and Slavic (especially Polish and Ukrainian) languages. These influences range from borrowing and imitation to the creation of words and constructions that would not be understandable to speakers of the sourcesw languages. Like other Jewish languages (Ladino or Judezmo, Judeo-Persian, Judeo-Arabic, etc.) Yiddish is written in an adaptation of the Hebrew alphabet, although examples here are given in the standard transcription of the YIVO Institute for Jewish Research.[1]

The best estimates are that on the eve of World War II there were some ten to eleven million speakers of Yiddish, who constituted the audience for a multitude of religious and secular publications and for a wide variety of cultural activities. As a consequence of the Holocaust, however, and of assimilatory pressures (both internal and external), Yiddish speakers today number fewer than two million. Yiddish is the primary language of some segments of the Hasidic and non-Hasidic Orthodox communities, and it is a living but secondary language for a relatively small number of (mostly secular) Yiddish activists.[2]

This chapter considers aspects of Yiddish vocabulary and of folklore in Yiddish, especially proverbs and proverbial expressions (such as proverbial comparisons). The American folklorist Archer Taylor (1890–1973), the author of a book on the proverb (Taylor 1931), wrote that "the definition of a proverb is too difficult to repay the undertaking," but there is a well-known (one might even say, proverbial) reworking of a breakfast-table definition by Lord John Russell (1792–1878): "A proverb is the wisdom of many and the wit of one." We understand this to mean that a proverb is born when an individual member of a speech community finds a expressive way to represent a recurring situation and the conclusions to be drawn from it. If that formulation strikes a chord with fellow members of the community, it enters the language and folklore of that community as shorthand for a piece of its accumulated wisdom. Yiddish proverbs in particular also provide an opportunity for language play and parody of canonical religious texts (see Rothstein 1995, 1998).

The English word *shoemaker* ought to mean someone who makes shoes, and that is what shoemakers used to do. Nowadays, however, if one can find a shoemaker, he (usually) or she is more likely to repair shoes that were made in a factory. English used to refer to a repairer of shoes as a cobbler, but that word now has an air of quaintness about it. In Britain those who still make shoes by hand prefer the term *cordwainer*, an anglicization of French *cordonnier*, which is derived from the name of the Spanish city of Cordoba, home to the fine leather known as cordovan.

Yiddish makes do with the single word *shuster* for someone who makes or repairs shoes (*shikh*, singular *shukh*). See Figure 7.1. Both *shuster* and *shukh* derive from the medieval German word for shoe, which ended in *-h* in some Middle High German dialects and in *-kh* in others. In his history of Yiddish, Max Weinreich (1980, 512–13) suggests that the two Yiddish words derive from different dialects, with *shuster* having lost the final *-h* of *shuh* when it was combined with what Weinreich surmises to be a contracted form of Latin *sartor* (sewer of clothes or shoes). In modern German neither term (*Schuster, Schuh*) comes from the dialect with a final *-kh* (Weinreich 1973, vol. 4, 236). Etymologists disagree as to whether the ultimate source for these words was an Indo-European root meaning "to walk" or one meaning "to cover."

Figure 7.1   A Jewish shoemaker at work (Poland, 1920s–1930s). Courtesy of YIVO Institute of Jewish Research, New York.

The Yiddish word *shuster* also has a second, colloquial meaning: a bungler, an incompetent person. It shares that meaning with its Russian counterpart *sapozhnik,* which one dictionary illustrates with the sentence *"On ne pianist, a sapozhnik"* (He is a shoemaker, not a pianist). In his *Blondzhendike shtern* (Wandering Stars), Sholem Aleichem describes an actor's awareness of having performed poorly: "Rafalesko aleyn ober hot gevust beser fun aleman, az er hot haynt geshpilt, vi a shuster" (Rafalesco himself knew better than anyone that today he had performed like a shoemaker).[3]

Yehude Elzet (1920, 15–16) relates an anecdote about a Jewish theater company that arrived in Yalta, Russia, around 1910, only to be ordered to leave town within twenty-four hours. An official explained to their manager that the only Jews permitted to be in Yalta were craftsmen; no "artists" were allowed. "These are supposed to be artists?" the manager exclaimed. "They are shoemakers!" (*"Dos zenen den epes artistn? Dos zenen dokh shusters!"*)

English *cobbler* also used to have the same negative meaning, an echo of which is found in the expression "to cobble something together." The neutral and colloquial meanings of *shuster* may have contributed to the joking proverb "Tsvishn ale shusters iz der bester shnayder yosl der stolyer" (Of all the shoemakers the best tailor is Yosl the carpenter). A longer version adds an explanation: "er makht a hitl, ligt es afn kop vi a hentshke" ([when] he makes a hat, it fits the head like a glove).

To the neighboring Russians and Poles, shoemakers are known for their irascibility: *rugat'-sia kak sapozhnik/kląć jak szewc* (to curse like a shoemaker), *szewska pasja* (cold fury, literally, the passion of a shoemaker). In Yiddish it is market women or fishmongers who curse: *shilten* (*sheltn*) *zikh vi a mark-yidene/vi afn fishmark* (to curse like a market woman/like at a fish market). The only trace in Yiddish of angry shoemakers is the odd comparison *zidn* (*kokhn*) *vi a shuster in bulbe-kashe* (to boil [with rage] like a shoemaker in mashed potatoes), which may well derive from another proverbial comparison, *bodn zikh vi a shuster in bulbe-kashe,* where *bodn zikh* means "to be swimming [in something]," that is, to have a lot of something.

This is not to say that the shoemaker is a model: one can describe someone who is intelligent but doesn't look the part by saying *"A kop vi a minister, hent vi a shuster"* (A head like a minister, hands like a shoemaker). If someone tries to set you aside, you can defend your position by saying *"Ikh bin oykh nit keyn shuster"* (I am also no shoemaker—perhaps comparable to the contemporary American expression "What am I, chopped liver?"). To say that something has reached the shoemakers' street (*iz arayngegangen in shustergas*) means that it has lost its exclusivity, has become commonplace. When a Jewish boy behaves according to the Jewish stereotype of a gentile, that is, misbehaves, does not want to study Torah and Talmud, the solution is to apprentice him to a shoemaker: *"Az men iz a sheygets, git men op far a shuster"* (If one is [like] a gentile boy, he is apprenticed to a shoemaker). On the other hand, nine rabbis do not constitute a *minyen*—the quorum of ten adult men needed for some prayers—but ten shoemakers do (*"Nayn rabonim kenen keyn minyen nit makhn, ober tsen shusters yo"*).

Shoemakers are often linked in proverbs with the other traditional Jewish craftsmen, tailors. One such proverb refers to the religious prohibition against not returning unused cloth or leather to the customer: *"Shnayder un shuster hobn geshvoyrn baym barg sini nit nemen yiter"* (At Mount Sinai tailors and shoemakers swore not to take leftover material). Another proverb, however, takes a more cynical look at reality: *"Der eyntsiker bal-malokhe vos nemt nit keyn yiter iz der moyel"* (The only craftsman who does not take leftover material is the *mohel* [ritual circumciser]). Tailors are generally more respected than shoemakers: *"Nit umzist zitst der shnayder hekher farn shuster"* (It is not for nothing that the tailor sits higher than the shoemaker), but neither profession is very profitable, as we see in the proverb *"Shnayderay toyg af kapores, shusteray ligt in d'rerd"* (Tailoring is good for nothing; shoemaking is dead and buried), and in the Yiddish version of an international proverb: *"Ale shuster geyen borves, un ale shnayder geyen naket"* (All shoemakers go barefoot, and all tailors go naked). The same economic reality is reflected in the folksong *"Bin ikh mir a shnayderl"* ("I Am a Tailor," Kipnis 1925, 34–35), in which the tailor explains that he eats only bread because butter is too expensive, and the shoemaker says that when he runs short of money, no-one will loan him any or guarantee a loan to him. He sums up his situation with the lines *"Ikh bin a shuster,/gey ikh taki borves"* (I am a shoemaker,/I really go barefoot).[4]

There is also a Yiddish imitation of a Polish proverb that is supposedly based on a historical anecdote: *"Shevtsi kravtsi nye ludzhi"* (Shoemakers, tailors are not people—in Polish: *"Szewcy, krawcy nie ludzie"*). The folklorist Shmuel Lehman (1935, 728) quotes an informant's explanation that when King Kazimierz the Great invited the Jews to come to Poland in the fourteenth century he gave them permission to engage in trade, but not in crafts, a condition that the Jews accepted. When he found out there was a Jew fixing shoes and another working on clothing, he reminded the Jews of the provision to which they had agreed. Their response was supposedly "Shoemakers, tailors are not people". The Polish paremiologist Julian Krzyżanowski (1960, vol. 1, 510) cites the Polish version, attributing it simply to the low esteem in which peasants held craftsmen. Compare also the pseudo-Talmudic proverb *"Madekh a shuster est nisht dray teg, starbt er, bifrat a mentsh"* (If a shoemaker does not eat for three days, he dies; all the more so a person).

There is at least one folkloric reference to a situation in which a shoemaker was seen as more valuable than a tailor. The expression *kulikover mishpet* (a Kulikov judgment—the reference is to the town of Kulikov, now Kulykiv near Lviv in Ukraine) refers to an anecdote about a town where the shoemaker committed a serious crime, but a tailor was hanged because in that town there were two tailors but only one shoemaker. There are similar expressions or proverbs in Polish and Ukrainian: *"Sprawa jak w Osieku: kowal zawinił, a ślusarza powiesili"* (It is a case like the one in Osiek: the blacksmith was guilty, but they hanged the locksmith), and *"Koval' zohrishyv, a shvetsia povisily"* (The blacksmith sinned, but they hanged the shoemaker). The original source may have been an ancient Greek expression about a dog making trouble and a pig being hanged (Krzyżanowski 1960, vol. 2, 239).

There were, to be sure, professions that were viewed as being less respectable than that of the shoemaker—innkeeping for one. A proverb states that *"Geven shoyn a shuster a tane, ober es vet nit zayn a shenker a tane"* (There was a shoemaker who was a *tane*, but no innkeeper will be a *tane*). The term *tane* refers to any of the teachers mentioned in the

Mishnah, the oldest part of the Talmud. The reference in the proverb is to the *tane* Rabbi Yoykhenen (Yochanan), known as *Hasandler* (the shoemaker).

Proverbs do recognize the fact that shoemaking is a profession. One way of saying that people talk about what they know best is *"Der shuster redt fun der kopete, der beker redt fun der lopete"* (The shoemaker talks about his last [foot-shaped form used to make or repair shoes]; the baker talks about his peel [wooden spade used to remove bread from the oven].) There is also a Yiddish version of "Shoemaker, stick to your last," the international proverb used to tell someone to stick to subjects he or she knows about: *"Shuster, blayb bay dayn melokhe/bay dayn kapul/bay dayn kopete"* (Shoemaker, stick to your profession/your last). The proverb is said to derive from an anecdote about the classical Greek painter Apelles, who was criticized by a shoemaker for his depiction of a sandal. When the painter revised his picture in accordance with the criticism, the shoemaker went on to criticize his depiction of the leg. According to the Latin writer Pliny the Elder, Apelles told the shoemaker not to make judgments on things above the sole.

One final proverb that refers to shoemakers is really a proverb parody, what Wolfgang Mieder (1982) called an anti-proverb: *"A mentsh iz geglikhn tsu a shuster: a shuster darf hobn a vayb, un a mentsh darf oykh hobn a vayb"* (A man is like a shoemaker: a shoemaker should have a wife, and a man should also have a wife). This anti-proverb also illustrates the fact that the supposedly gender-neutral term *mentsh* (man = human being) can be understood as gender-specific (man = male human being). The use of *shuster* here is arbitrary, as we see from the parallel anti-proverb *"Der mentsh iz geglikhn tsu a shnayder: der shnayder lebt un lebt un shtarbt, un a mentsh oykh dos eygene"* (Man is like a tailor: a tailor lives and dies, and a man does likewise).

Shoemakers do not play a large role in Yiddish folksongs. Where they appear, it is usually alongside other craftsmen. A song published in two variants in Ginzburg and Marek's collection (1901/1991, ##312–13), for example, paints a negative picture of various craftsmen as husbands, starting with shoemakers:

> Mir hobn gehert, mir hobn gezen,
> a shuster a man nit tsu nemen:
> a shuster a man—a sharlatan,
> der tayvl zol im nemen!
> Shustershe vayber hobn gezogt:
> mir darfn drotves makhn;
> beser tsu nemen a shnayder a man,
> veln mir hobn ale zakhn.
>
> (We have heard, we have seen,
> Not to take a shoemaker as a husband:
> A shoemaker husband—a charlatan,
> May the devil take him!

Shoemakers' wives said:
We have to make shoemaker's twine;
It's better to marry a tailor,
We will have everything.)

In turn the tailors' wives recommend soldiers; soldiers' wives, coachmen; coachmen's wives, students, students' wives, ritual slaughterers; slaughterers' wives, tavern-keepers; and tavern-keepers' wives say that it is better to remain *an alte mad* (an old maid).[5] The other version published by Ginzburg and Marek has more potential husbands recommended and rejected but concludes on a positive note, suggesting that it is good to be a *rebitsn* (rabbi's wife). In some variations on this theme of different potential husbands, the context is a dialogue between mother (or father) and daughter.[6] In all of them the shoemaker is rejected, but for a variety of reasons. In "Neyn mame, neyn muter" (Kipnis 1925: 106–9) the daughter says:

Neyn mame, neyn muter [miter],
a shuster yung iz zeyer biter.
Er tsit di dratve mit di tseyn
un kukt oyf meydlekh mole kheyn…

(No, mama, no, mother,
A shoemaker's apprentice is very bitter.
He pulls the twine with his teeth
And looks at attractive girls…)

In "Vos zhe gebn dir, mayn tayeres kind?" (Pipe 1971, 171–73) the answer is

Oy, tate, neyn!
A shnayder-yingele neyt a late,
vert dos vaybele azoy vi a shmate,
oy, tate, neyn!

(Oh, father, no!
A shoemaker's apprentice sews a patch,
His wife becomes like a rag,
Oh, father, no!)

In another song from the Ginzburg-Marek collection (#244), now usually known as "Yome, Yome" (Mlotek 1977, 22–23), a mother tries to figure out what her daughter wants:

—Mame, vu geystu?
—Tokhter, vos vilstu?
Vilstu nit a por shikhelekh hobn?
Ikh vel geyn dem shuster zogn!
—Neyn, mame, neyn!

Heyst a shlekhte mame ikh hob:
Zi veys nit, vos ikh meyn!

(Mama, where are you going?
Daughter, what do you want?
Don't you want a pair of shoes?
I'll go tell the shoemaker!
No, mama, no!
That means I have a bad mother:
She doesn't know, what I have in mind!)

The mother gets similar reactions to her suggestion of sending for the seamstress or the milliner. Finally she guesses correctly that her daughter wants a groom and that she should send for the matchmaker.

A shoemaker is one of three craftsmen—the other two being a carpenter and a tailor—who are the subject of a song by the folk poet Zelik Barditshever (1898–1937).[7] The title of the song, "Melokhe-melukhe" (Mlotek and Mlotek 1989, 92–94), derives from the punning proverb *A melokhe iz a melukhe* (A trade is a treasure [literally, a kingdom]). The shoemaker in this song is the merriest of the three. The carpenter's hands and feet grow heavy; the tailor brings joy to the rich man's son for whom he makes a garment while his own son is an expert in being hungry. The shoemaker on the other hand does not seem to mind that he has only an apron instead of a coat, that he lives in a small room instead of an apartment. He is happy that he does not have to go out in the rain and mud:

Voyl iz dem vos iz a shuster
in aza pogode.
Mont dos vayb bay mir oyf pite,
Kh'makh zikh kileyode.

(It is good to be a shoemaker
In such weather.
[When] my wife asks for money for bread,
I play dumb.)

The shoemaker of "Tsum hemerl" (To the Hammer), a poem by Avrom Reyzen (1875–1953) that became a popular song, effectively a folksong, when set to music by A. M. Bernstein (1865–1932), is a much more tragic figure. There is no bread in the house, only endless troubles and suffering. It is already midnight, the shoemaker's eyes are closing, but he must stay awake to finish a pair of shoes for a rich customer's daughter. The song ends:

O, hemerl, hemerl, klap!
Nit glitsh fun mayn hant zikh aroys!
Mayn eyntsiker shpayzer bistu,
Fun hunger on dir gey ikh oys! (Mlotek 1977, 78–79).

(Oh, hammer, hammer, strike.
Don't slip out of my hand.
You are my only provider;
Without you I shall die of hunger.)

An even more tragic case is described in a street ballad published in Odessa in 1896; two variants were recorded by the Soviet ethnomusicologist Moshe Beregovski and published by him in 1934 (Slobin 1982, 138–41, 221–22, 273). The ballad recounts the death of a young *zagotovshchik* (the word is borrowed from Russian), a worker whose job it was to cut the leather, or in this case rubber, out of which shoes were to be made. The young worker accidentally stabbed himself and bled to death before his comrades could get him to the Jewish hospital.

When we shift our attention from shoemakers to their products, the first thing to note is the extensive Yiddish vocabulary related to shoes and shoemaking. In his *Thesaurus of the Yiddish Language,* Nahum Stutchkoff lists nearly five hundred nouns and some sixty-five verbs in §527, the section on *shusteray, bashukhung* (shoemaking, footwear; 1950, 588–91). Among them are terms for types and styles of shoes, tools used in making them, external and internal parts of shoes, and so on. They also include a few examples of shoemaker's slang, for example, shoes were referred to as *khales* (the plural of *khale* [challah], the traditional Sabbath and holiday bread), and a shoemaker's shop or a shoe store was called a *tare-bretl,* the traditional name for the table used to wash a corpse. Since Stutchkoff's work is a thesaurus and not a dictionary, one has to look elsewhere for explanations of the terminology (e.g., Berger 1965; Izra 1928; Sheskin 1965). Sheskin and Berger were nominally writing about the terminology of *kamashn-shteper,* the craftsmen who cut and assemble the upper part of a shoe (known as *oybns* or *verkhes* or *kholyevkes* or *kholivkes*), but in fact deal with various aspects of the shoemaking trade. (*Kamashn,* from Polish *kamasze,* which in turn is from German *Gamasche* or French *gamache,* can refer to leggings or gaiters or spats or a kind of boot with soft sides.)

Yiddish proverbs refer both to shoes (*shikh*) and boots (*shtivl,* same form for singular and plural). The Yiddish word for boots, like its German cognate *Stiefel,* derives from older Italian *estivale* (summer shoes, from the Latin adjective referring to summer, *aestivus*). It is not clear how the meaning "summer shoes" changed to "boots," but the same change affected the modern Italian word for boots, *stivale.*

Proverbs are usually meant to be understood figuratively, and that is generally the case with references to shoes and boots in Yiddish proverbs. One proverb that refers literally to shoes is *"Az du vilst fargesn in ale tsores, tu on a por enge shikh"* (If you want to forget about all your troubles, put on a pair of tight shoes). Another is the parodic commentary on a Talmudic maxim: *"Oznaim lakoysl—a shtivl hot oykh oyern"* (The walls have ears—a boot also has ears). The "ear" of the walls are figurative; the "ears" of the boot are the loops at the top that one can use to pull the boot on (bootstraps in English).

Some of the figurative or metaphoric Yiddish shoe proverbs are versions of internationally known texts. For example *"Keyner veyst nit, vemen der shukh kvetsht, nor der, vos geyt in im"* (No one knows whose shoe is pinching except for the person wearing it) and *"Keyner veyst nisht, vu mikh der shukh drikt"* (No one knows where my shoe pinches) are variants of a proverb that can be found in *The Canterbury Tales* (in "The Merchant's Tale") in the form "But I woot best where wryngeth me my sho." Its earliest recorded version is in Plutarch's account of a prominent Roman whose friends tried to dissuade him from divorcing his wife. According to Plutarch the husband's response was to hold out his shoe and ask his friends, "Is it not new and well-made? Yet none of you can tell where it pinches me."

The proverb *"Koyfst shikh far zikh, to mest zey nit af fremde fis"* ([When] you are buying shoes for yourself, do not measure them on someone else's feet) has an English parallel dating from at least the sixteenth century: "Every shoe fits not every foot" or "You can't put the same shoe on every foot." Another sixteenth-century English proverb, "He that waits for dead men's shoes may go a long time barefoot," also has a Yiddish counterpart, *"Az men kukt aroys afn shvers shtivl, geyt men borves"* (When you look forward to [getting] your father-in-law's boots, you go around barefoot). There is nothing particularly Jewish about *"Az men zitst in der heym, tserayst men nit keyn shtivl"* (If you stay at home, you won't tear/wear out your boots), but one has to know about Jewish custom to understand the proverb *"Koym putst zikh eyner op di shtivl, ruft men im shoyn oyf maftir"* (No sooner does one polish his boots, than he is called up for *maftir*). Polishing your boots or dressing up means that you have become well-to-do, and therefore deserving of the honors given to prominent community members, such as being invited to recite the blessing before the reading of the final Torah portion (*maftir*) on a given sabbath or holiday.

Two final proverbs are similar in structure but have contrasting meanings. *"Zay mir nit keyn feter un koyf/ney mir nit keyn shikh"* (literally, Don't be an uncle to me and don't buy/sew me any shoes) means don't be too friendly (too familiar) and don't do me any favors. *"Zay mir nit keyn feter, un tserays mir nit di shtivl"* (literally, Don't be an uncle to me and don't wear out [literally, tear up] my boots) means don't use the fact that you're my relative and don't ask me for any favors.

Worn-out shoes play a role in Yiddish songs as well. A dance song recorded by the late singer and musicologist Ruth Rubin from her mother (Rubin 1973, 193) begins

Hot zikh mir di zip tsezipt,
hot zikh mir tsebrokhn.
Hot zikh mir di shikh tserisn,
Tants ikh in di hoyle zokn.

(My sieve is all worn out,
It's all broken.
My shoes are all torn,
[So] I dance in my stocking feet.]

This may have inspired an anonymous song (with a different melody) written in the Vilna ghetto that begins with the third line of the above song, "Hot zikh mir di shikh tserisn"

(Kaczerginski 1948, 205). Torn boots are one of the complaints of the yeshivah student in Avrom Reyzen's popular "May-ko mashme-lon" (What Is the Meaning, Mlotek and Mlotek 1989, 116–18):

> Un di shtivl iz tserisn,
>
> un se vert in gas a blote;
>
> bald vet oykh der vinter kumen—
>
> kh'hob keyn vareme kapote.

> (And my boots are torn
>
> And the streets are turning muddy;
>
> Soon the winter will come
>
> [And] I don't have a warm coat.)

Two children's folksongs of literary origin have a more positive attitude toward shoes. In Moyshe Korman's "In an orem shtibele" (In a Poor Little House) the little boy is promised shoes and socks: "Tate't koyfn shikhelekh, / Mame't shtrikn zeklekh" (Papa will buy [you] little shoes, Mama will knit [you] little socks; Mlotek and Mlotek 1989, 9–11). In Yisroel Goykhberg's "Dray yingelekh" (Three Little Boys, *Lomir kinder zingen* 1970, 56–57) the reference to shoes is based on a pun: the verb *heysn* can mean "to be called," but it can also mean "to ask someone to do something," so the three boys are introduced as follows:

> Hot eyns geheysn Berele,
>
> dos tsveyte—Khayim-Shmerele,
>
> dos drite hot geheysn—
>
> men zol im koyfn shikh.

> (One was called Berele,
>
> The second—Khayim-Shmerele,
>
> The third—asked
>
> To be bought shoes.)

Perhaps the last folkloric word on shoes and boots can be left to Haman and the chorus in the folk retelling of the book of Esther in the *Purim-shpil* (Purim play) called the *Akhashverosh-shpil* (The Play of Ahasuerus, Beregovski 2001, 223). As he mounts the gallows that he had built for Mordechai, Haman asks the chorus "Vu vel ikh hengen mayne shtivl-shporn?" (Where will I hang my boots and spurs?), and they reply, "Oyfn galgn iz fran a dorn, z'fran a dorn, / dort vestu hengen dayne shtivl-shporn" (On the gallows is a thorn, there's a thorn;/there you will hang your boots and spurs).

NOTES

1. The YIVO transcription is an English-alphabet based system for representing the pronunciation of Yiddish words. Words not of Semitic origin are transliterated (an English letter or

combination of letters for each Yiddish letter). Since Yiddish words of Semitic origin are spelled in their traditional form, which does not directly represent pronunciation, the transcription of such words provides an English letter or combination of letters for each sound in the Yiddish word. The vowel letters *a, e, i, o, u* in the transcription have the general European values, that is, they represent approximately the sounds in English *ah, ebb, eat, ought, food,* respectively. The combinations *ay* and *ey* represent the diphthongs in *pie* and *pay,* respectively; *kh* represents the final consonant in German *doch* or Scottish *loch; tsh* represents the initial consonant in *chill; zh* represents the middle consonant in *fusion,* and *dzh* represents the initial consonant in *job.* Other letters have approximately their English values. Russian and Ukrainian examples are given in the Library of Congress transliteration, and Polish examples are given in normal Polish orthography.

2. An excellent and nontechnical account of Yiddish and its history by William F. Weigel can be found on the Jewish Language Research Web site at http://www.jewish-languages.org/yiddish. html.

3. Part 1, chapter 53.

4. In his memoirs of Jewish life in Lithuania before World War II, Hirsh Abramowicz points out that the remuneration for tailor's work was "very low" and describes the village shoemaker as living "in even greater poverty than the other village craftsmen. He was frequently out of work, and the occasional small jobs that he did get brought him very little income.... During the summer, the village shoemaker had no work at all, because everyone went barefoot" (Abramowicz 1999, 42–43).

5. *Mad* is an archaism; the more common form is *moyd.*

6. On these songs and the "Yome, Yome" type discussed in the next paragraph, see Rothstein 1989.

7. The song by Barditshever and others by known authors mentioned later should probably be characterized, following the terminology of many Slavic musicologists, as folksongs of literary origin.

BIBLIOGRAPHY

Abramowicz, H. 1999. *Profiles of a lost world: Memoirs of East European Jewish life before World War II,* trans. E. Z. Dobkin. Detroit, MI: Wayne State University Press [originally published 1958 as *Farshvundene geshtaltn: zikhroynes un siluetn.* Buenos Aires: Tsentral Farband fun Poylishe Yidn in Argentine].

Beregovski, M. [M. Ia. Beregovskii]. 2001. *Purim shpil: Evreiskie narodnye muzykal'no-teatral'nye predstavleniia.* Kiev: Dukh i Litera.

Berger, Y. 1965. "Nokh terminologye fun shteperfakh." *Yidishe shprakh* 25: 91–94.

Elzet, Y. 1920. *Melokhes un bal-melokhes: folkstimlikhe redensarten, glaykhvertlekh un anekdoten.* Warsaw: Y. Elzet (separate publication of part of his *Der vunder-oytser fun der yidisher shprakh*).

Ginzburg, S. M., and P. S. Marek. 1901. *Evreiskie narodnye pesni v Rossii.* Saint Petersburg: Voskhod [reprinted 1991. Ramat Gan: Bar-Ilan University Press].

Izra, E. 1928. *Shikh un kaloshn: fun vos un vi azoy vern zey oysgearbet.* Kiev: Kultur-lige.

Kaczerginski, Sh. 1948. *Lider fun di getos un lagern.* New York: CYCO.

Kipnis, M. 1925. *80 folks-lider.* Warsaw: A. Gitlin.

Krzyżanowski, J. 1960. Mądrej głowie dość dwie słowie: Trzy centurie przysłów polskich, 1–2, Warsaw: PIW.

Lehman, Sh. 1935. "Sotsialer moment inem yidishn shprikhvort." *Literarishe bleter* 45 (600): 728.

Lomir kinder zingen/Let's Sing a Yiddish Song. 1970. New York: Kinderbuch Publications.

Mieder, W. 1982. *Antisprichwörter.* Wiesbaden: Verlag für deutsche Sprache. (Also vol. 2, 1985, and vol. 3, 1989.)

Mlotek, E. G. 1977. *Mir trogn a gezang!,* 2nd ed. New York: Workmen's Circle Education Department.

Mlotek, E. G., and J. Mlotek. 1989. *Pearls of Yiddish song.* New York: Workmen's Circle Education Department.

Pipe, Sh. Z. 1971. "Yiddish folksongs from Galicia." In *Folklore Research Center Studies,* ed. D. Noy and M. Noy. Vol. 2, 97–332. Jerusalem: The Hebrew University of Jerusalem.

Rothstein, R. A. 1989. "The mother–daughter dialogue in the Yiddish folk song: Wandering motifs in time and space." *New York Folklore* 15: 51–65.

Rothstein, R. A. 1995. "Language play in the Yiddish proverb." In *Harvard studies in Slavic linguistics,* ed. O. T. Yokoyama. Vol. 3, 143–47. Cambridge, MA: Harvard University Slavic Department.

Rothstein, R. A. 1998. "The metalinguistic function as an organizing principle of the Yiddish folklore text." In *American contributions to the Twelfth International Congress of Slavists,* ed. R. A. Maguire and A. Timberlake, 479–87. Bloomington, IN: Slavica.

Rubin, R. 1973. *Voices of a people: The story of Yiddish folksong,* 2nd ed. New York: McGraw-Hill.

Sheskin, H. 1965. "A bisl terminologye fun shteperfakh in grodne." *Yidishe shprakh* 25: 59–60.

Slobin, M., ed. 1982. *Old Jewish folk music: The collections and writings of Moshe Beregovski.* Philadelphia: University of Pennsylvania Press.

Stutchkoff, N. 1950. *Der oytser fun der yidisher shprakh.* New York: YIVO.

Taylor, A. 1931. *The proverb.* Cambridge, MA: Harvard University Press.

Weinreich, M. 1973. *Geshikhte fun der yidisher shprakh. Bagrifn, faktn, metodn.* Vols. 1–4. New York: YIVO.

Weinreich, M. 1980. *History of the Yiddish language.* Chicago and London: University of Chicago Press.

8   THE HOLOCAUST SHOE

UNTYING MEMORY: SHOES AS HOLOCAUST MEMORIAL EXPERIENCE

JEFFREY FELDMAN

When visitors attend Holocaust museums, one of the most memorable experiences is standing before huge piles of personal objects left behind in Nazi concentration camps by the murder victims—mounds of relics displayed so as to evoke the horrific scale of the genocide committed. As seen from our era, so saturated by plastic soda bottles and plasma screens, these piles resonate with viewers because they are collections of enticing objects and evidence of mass murder, attractive and repulsive. We feel this tension in ourselves just by looking at them. I recall one instance when this tension emerged during a trip to the Auschwitz Museum and Memorial in Poland in the 1990s when I was a graduate student. After a tour through a storage room filled with the discarded objects taken from Jews who had been murdered in the camp, a friend turned to me and said: "I find these objects fascinating, but the fact that I do makes me very nervous." Indeed, we were all nervous on the study tour through Auschwitz that our expertise on Holocaust relics would lead us to develop a morally reprobate kind of fetishism—a fascination that is acceptable when focused on antique lamps and baseball cards, but highly suspect when it involves the goods left behind in mounds next to Nazi gas chambers. (See Figure 8.1.)

And yet, for contemporary visitors to Holocaust memorial sites and museums, the objects are filled with such tension because they are familiar, but assembled in ways that lead to painful and embodied impressions of the past. They are the kinds of intimate objects that most people rarely see discarded in such a way so as to form large piles: gold-rimmed eyeglasses, toothbrushes, empty suitcases, prostheses. And always there are the shoes. Half-rotten, half-preserved, leather shoes are almost always found in these Holocaust museum displays of relics. Of all the actual piles in museums and memorials of Holocaust objects, as well as the films of piles and still photographs of piles, shoes are the original sin of the species. Since a child's shoe taken from a pile at the Treblinka extermination camp was first introduced as evidence during the 1961 trial of Adolf Eichmann (1906–1962), shoes have been central to almost every attempt to use objects to relay the visceral brutality of Holocaust history by turning the memory of the concentration camps into things. More than a half century after the atrocities of the Holocaust, shoes play a variety of roles in Holocaust discourses, including historical evidence, memorial icon, and metaphor.

Figure 8.1   A warehouse full of shoes, Auschwitz (1945). Courtesy of YIVO Institute of Jewish Research, New York.

With the Holocaust shoe as a focus, and with its multiple emotional and cultural roles in mind, this chapter examines a number of interrelated issues that often elude historians and social scientists. These issues pertain not just to the physical quality of things, such as shoes, but to the nexus of memory and bodily feelings evoked by those things, and the importance of those embodied recollections for people who experience them. These topics often linger just off the page of Holocaust studies but are never fully articulated. Moreover, while specific to one focused episode of modern history, the experiential aspect of twentieth-century war relics has much in common with the experience of other kinds of relics in more distant periods of history, particularly the sacred church objects that have circulated in people's lives all over Europe for centuries (Geary 1986, 169). When and how did shoes become a central icon in Holocaust discourse? How do shoes signify meaning about the Holocaust in the social and symbolic context of the museum? What is the difference in terms of meaning and feeling between mounds of shoes, individual shoes, and shoe reproductions? What are the difficulties in describing the full sensory experience of shoes in Holocaust memorials, and how do these attempts at description impact our understanding of the past? These are questions that encourage us to consider sensory experiences in front of objects as essential to discussions of Holocaust history, to enter into the smell of rotting leather that emanates from Holocaust shoe displays and follow it back to the experience of violence and genocide.

SHOES FIRST

The first time I encountered Holocaust shoes in a museum setting was in a display of thousands of leather shoes piled in room-sized cages at the United States Holocaust Memorial Museum in Washington, D.C. The shoes had been brought there from a former extermination camp in Poland. My impression, although uniquely my own, was remarkably similar to a story in *Chicken Soup for the Jewish Soul* about the writer's pilgrimage to the Nazi extermination camps in Poland:

> When I walked into the first barracks at Majdanek and saw the floors covered with cages of shoes, the sheer numbers overwhelmed me. As I covered my mouth with my hand, I felt myself gasp. Then I walked into the next barracks and there were more shoes—over eight hundred thousand pairs altogether—on display in front of my eyes. Children's shoes thrown together with adults' shoes. As I reached over to touch them some of the dirt came off on my hand. I felt the leather; I smelled the leather and the strong scent that overtook the room. On the following day we were at Auschwitz, and I entered another room displaying shoes. I had seen so many shoes at Majdanek that I could not imagine there being any more. But here there were more—many more. This time they were behind glass walls, so I could not touch them. Like the shoes at Majdanek they were filthy and worn. All of these shoes had been lived in and each pair told the story of a different life once lived. The graceful sandal of a woman who stayed at home to raise her children. The heavy boots of a working class man lying on top of the dress shoes that another man wore to his office. The play shoes of a child who once ran in the park. In life these people were all unique. The young were different from the old. Their shoes their stories—not only of life before the war, but also of the long, hard walk from the train station in the center of town to Majdanek or of the death march from Auschwitz to Birkenau. (Greenbaum 2001, 276–78)

The story is familiar and begins with the visitor remembering the history itself. Upon arrival by train, prisoners were forced to drop their belongings and disrobe. In some instances heads were shaved and the prisoners were given striped uniforms, while in other instances they were immediately walked to the gas chambers to be killed. Once inside the camp the prisoners' objects were left behind, whereupon they were sorted into piles by other prisoners or local forced labor working as orderlies. The goal of the sorting was to turn a general mass of prisoner belongings into organized piles of goods split for two general purposes: disposal, and redistribution back into the general population. Amidst this recollection of the tragic events that led to the creation of the piles, the shoes and hair are singled out as the most resonant and most effective at turning the abstract idea of the Holocaust into a visual reexperiencing of the lives lost in the Nazi camps.

My experience in the Holocaust Museum in Washington was eerily similar to the quoted story. While visually overpowering, what caught me by the throat was not just the quantity of shoes, although the quantity was in some sense overwhelming. It was the smell, a deep-down stench of mildew mixed with rotting leather that made me feel sick to my stomach.

Because I was in a museum, I did not feel it was appropriate to reach out and touch the shoes, but I could feel the dirty sensation on my fingers, as if I had touched them just the same. The sense of the shoes literally filled the giant space of the museum gallery, pushing its way into my nose, my mouth, my skin. While it was true that each pair of shoes told a different story, the big story was the stench they gave off, and they all told it together.

The odor could have come from the moldy leather, the decomposing rubber, or even embedded human sweat. I turned to the accompanying text for more information, but there was none. As a result, the smell rendered the visual message of the memorial disconcerting and ambiguous. From a distance the shoes all looked the same, but one can hardly imagine the different particulars that led each into this pile. And while the size of the pile made a powerful statement, the experience of the people being forced to remove their shoes had been disregarded, and as such the crucial link between German colonialism and the relics of the Holocaust was missing.

Subsequently I learned that the shoes on display in Washington were collected not just from a pile of shoes in Majdanek, but from a similar memorial display in the Majdanek museum. As was the case in other concentration camps, the piles of shoes left by Holocaust victims were turned into museum memorial displays long before the opening of the memorial museum in Washington. As the status of Poland switched from German- to Soviet-occupied territory, the concentration camps themselves became museums, warning of the dangers of fascism. The shoes, together with piles of hair, suitcases, and eyeglasses, became powerful installations viewed by millions of people in the Soviet memorials that predated the term *Holocaust* or any global historical recognition that Nazism came close to complete genocide of European Jewry. In many ways the pile of shoes is about traces of the body.

Multiple levels of embodied experience had been lost in the shoe display. Not only was any attempt to include or recapture the physical distress soaked into the shoes missing from the display, but also missing were the decades of sensory encounter with the very same display of shoes. Gone was the history of the smell of genocide, and gone was its embodied record of Jewish and Polish experiences under successive waves of violent European expansion. Jews were present as both visitors and museum workers. But the lost bodies of the children who had worn the shoes were still present and disconcerting.

SUPPORTING EVIDENCE

Shoes left behind by people murdered in Nazi camps were first thrust into public view during the war crimes trial of Adolf Eichmann, which took place in Jerusalem in 1961. A former Nazi and SS *Obersturmbannführer*, Eichmann was the man charged with the logistics of shipping European Jews to and from the Nazi ghettos and on to the extermination camps during the Holocaust. Following a lead discovered by Nazi-hunter Simon Wiesenthal that after the war Eichmann had made his way to Argentina, Israeli agents captured him in 1960, whereupon he was tried during televised proceedings that captivated the world. Years after the war crimes trials in Nuremberg the prosecutors in Jerusalem skillfully transformed the trial into the first widely viewed public display of the horrors of the Holocaust, introducing evidence in testimony with the specific goal of connecting to the courtroom and the general public on a much deeper level than with typical courtroom exhibits. It was in the context of that trial that shoes of Nazi concentration camp victims became such powerful objects, which led to their subsequent exhibition in museums and their emergence among the most potent symbols of the Holocaust.

In a now-famous moment from that trial a witness stood on the stand and testified to having seen the Treblinka concentration camp covered in bones, skulls, and shoes after liberation (Cole 2000, 61), at which point Israeli Attorney General Gideon Hausner unwrapped a package containing a single worn pair of children's shoes to corroborate the testimony:

> For seemingly endless seconds, we were gripped by the spell cast by this symbol of all that was left of a million children. Time stood still, while each in his own way tried to fit the flesh to the shoes, multiply by a million and spin the reel back from death, terror and tears to the music and gay laughter and the animated joy of youngsters in European city and village before the Nazis marched in. (Pearlman 1963, 304)

This moment when "time stood still" was the origin point for a new way of understanding the Holocaust, in which the cold and impersonal archivist's document gave way to an object that, while abandoned in the process of murder, somehow retained a living quality. In that moment in the courtroom the viewer felt as if the life of the child had been pressed from skin to shoe leather, whereupon it was preserved across time. This initial desire to reclaim the contact between skin and shoe is a key aspect of what allowed shoes from the Nazi concentration camps to become memorable "contact points" (Feldman 2006, 263). As an image forged out of violent genocidal acts, the shoes bear impressions of the people who wore them, contain sensory links to the earth and to the fluids of the body, and symbolize—both individually and in large quantities—the pain and rupture of the murder that took place in the camps. Although individuals walked around in the shoes, on display in museums and memorials decades later they stand for the mechanized, factory-like system of extermination that ripped the physical body from personal belongings.

Ultimately the shoes raise a question that seems new in memorial discourse. For example, does Holocaust memory have a distinct smell? The experience of being near Holocaust shoes suggests that the Holocaust has the smell of rotting leather for many people who visit museums. This is not to suggest a singular smell can evoke all Holocaust memory or experience. Nazi camp survivors have testified to a wide range of smells resulting from the breakdown of the human body. In fact, the smell of leather shoes is not just a lingering reference to the point at which the camps ended a life, and then many lives, but a testimony to the diverse, often morally confusing experience of the camps by people whose lives were forced into them:

> Keeping himself clean and polishing his shoes helped Primo Levi maintain his self-respect, but the same was true for Levi's guards. As Fania Fénelon, a member of Alma Rose's orchestra, says, "I don't know whether this concern for appearance was part of

Nazi ideology but it certainly occupied a key position in their lives. Furthermore, their shoes and boots always shone and smelled; I shall never forget the smell of German leather." (Todorov 1996, 69)

Thus the question emerges as to whether or not the Holocaust is best understood as a process of destroying Jews through violence or as an industrialized encounter between multiple social actors, which produced a broad range of contact points. The smell of the shoes is a much more complex reference than even the most sophisticated footage, photographs, or narrative. Through the smell of leather we travel to the moment of tension between Jews stripped of their humanity in the process of extermination—sometimes prolonged, sometimes instantaneous—and the process of German soldiers seeking to maintain what they viewed as the register of their humanity. The smell of leather becomes the richest and most painful memorial nexus.

SHOE REPAIR

After the Eichmann trial two children's shoes found in the ruins of a Nazi camp became a symbol for all the children killed during the Holocaust when they became part of the main museum display in Israel's central Holocaust memorial and research center, Yad Vashem (Cole 2000, 62). Since Yad Vashem first displayed them, children's shoes have become contact points within a standardized set of global museum routines. As such the shoes have taken on a narrative focus beyond their original display purpose. In recent attempts to repair the Auschwitz Museum and Memorial from decades of decay, the eighty thousand shoes in the museum's collection became a focal point for a kind of experience that could not have been foreseen:

> Time itself is the enemy, eroding the site and its contents. "Conservationists are like doctors: we can extend life, but not for eternity," said Cywinski, who opposes any suggestion that decaying original artifacts should be replaced by copies. Faded and frail, two tons of hair shorn from victims is piled up in one cell block: once blonde plaits, black ponytails and auburn curls, it is gradually decaying and now looks like grey wire wool. The museum has had more luck with its 80,000 shoes, mostly odd. Chief conservationist Rafal Pioro and his staff of 38 invited school children to help clean and polish some of them. But there are so many, most still have to be stored in a warehouse without air-conditioning. Slowly, most are falling apart. "The work is endless and painstaking and can be heartrending," said Pioro. "When we were working on the children's shoes, some of us were crying all the time." (Johnson and Baczynska 2007, 8)

The conflict between life and death in the quote is evident. By arresting the decay of clipped hair and shoes on display at the Auschwitz museum the conservationists are holding off the annihilation of life, even though the objects would not exist as such were it not for the murders that created them. Here we are in the semiotic puzzle that defines much of early twenty-first-century Holocaust memorial representation: the limits of representing the absences created by genocide. But the shoes introduce a level of understanding beyond representation to embodiment. It is difficult to distinguish, for example, between tears cried for the shoes, for the children who once wore the shoes, and for the process whereby the shoes were violently transformed into evidence of murder. For some observers, the thought of museum conservationists crying for a pair of shoes in addition to the murdered child who once wore the shoes may be a sign of commodity fetishism in the memorial.

Tim Cole, for example, has argued provocatively that display cases "filled with piles of suitcases, shoes, glasses and women's hair" have transformed Auschwitz into a Holocaust version of Elvis's Graceland (Cole 2000, 98). Once a site of mass murder, Auschwitz has become a tourist destination that sells representations of mass murder to heritage pilgrims. Holocaust museums worldwide have become so obsessed by the fetish of concentration camp relics that camps rich in relics, but poor in operating resources, have even brokered loans of shoes in exchange for assistance in setting up and paying for museum functions (Cole 2000, 160). Nonetheless, while Cole's critique points to an important level of political economy to have emerged in the world of Holocaust memorials and museums, the emphasis on the fetish of the relic misses the complexity of the encounter. Shoes and hair are no longer just evocative references to the camps, as they once were intended in the Eichmann trial, but have become experiences of memory in and of themselves. The struggle to maintain the objects of memory is itself resonant for those involved, having given rise to a struggle to prevent the shoes and hair from dying. One weeps at the loss of a loved one, but also at the loss of the photograph or object that stood as a reminder of a loved one over so many years.

As James Young has argued, the history of the Holocaust is now overlaid with a history of Holocaust commemoration. As a result, the encounter with these large piles of relics is part of the memory evoked for visitors to Holocaust memorials and museums. Young argues that the power of the camp artifacts lies in their quality as "dismembered fragments," not commodities (Young 1993, 132–33). The shoes, in other words, contain traces, not of the physical bodies that once wore them, but of the social bodies that gave them meaning. The ability of the shoes to make a person cry, for example, lies in their power to conjure images of community and the murder victim's involvement in it, as well as their inability to reanimate that community, if only in passing. Still, Young counsels caution about this process as too much emphasis on "dismembered fragments," which has the potential to become a problem for Holocaust commemoration precisely because it could displace the active performance of memory work with the passive encounter.

By bringing to light the role of the social body in the life of Holocaust memory, Young engages a critical aspect of contemporary Holocaust museums and memorials overlooked by a singular focus on political economy. Still, to a large extent Young's suggestive description of Holocaust objects as "dismemberment" is not rooted in a full concept of embodiment, but limited to mostly visual assumptions about the encounter with museum displays. It does not take into account, for instance, the common experience of sensing Holocaust shoes or hair primarily through smell. Considering Holocaust artifacts as disarticulated social bodies alone does not fully reference the many levels of sensory experience intersecting the objects. The problem, however, is less one of critical perspective than of the difficulty in finding ways to describe what objects like Holocaust shoes are relative to other objects both in and out of museum display cases. What makes pieces created out of genocidal encounters distinct is not just the fact that they exist in large quantities, but that they exude a discernable record of the body's experience of murder decades after the event. Moreover, once discovered, they accumulate the emotional resonance that sensations such as smell and touch elicit. These qualities bring the objects into a way of talking and thinking separate from mundane objects, one more familiar to sacred relics. Indeed, the interregnum between the death of the person who originally owned or used the Holocaust objects and memorial rediscovery of the object can be seen as a critical period during which ordinary objects take on the sensory qualities of sacred objects. Even if this reliquary aspect of Holocaust does not appear in museum documentation or gallery signs read by visitors; it remains an important aspect of the experience of Holocaust memory beyond the visual focus of most museum displays.

Considering Holocaust shoes as sacred objects rather than mundane objects allows for the multiple histories and experiences involving the shoes to come to light. The core of these experiences involved the violent processing of the body in industrialized extermination camps. Thus relics such as shoes, hair, and eyeglasses are impregnated with the bodily byproducts that resulted from the radical experience of violence on shoe leather, the stain of human fluid in cloth, and the rim of a prison cap worn shiny by constant pressing against the forehead. But relics also contain those traces of the whole bodies that were removed, incarcerated and incinerated—traces of scissors against the scalp that left only a cut of hair, the sudden rip of glasses from a face that left only the thin gold wire frames, and the piercing of skin by the tattoo pen that, despite millions of repetitions, left few living bodies to recount the experience.

Thus while it is crucial to delineate the economics and social rupture in Holocaust objects, the significance of the relics cannot be reduced to their roles as visual signpost to the past or tourist destination in the present. They are vestiges of the violent act of biological racism layered onto history and a material journey from personal belonging to museum piece. The shoes, eyeglasses, or hair that one observes in Holocaust museums never appeared "in real life" as they appear in Holocaust exhibits. They are not mere images of the past but are products of the brutal genocidal encounter as well as accumulated records of our attempts to come to grips with the experience of extreme violence.

FIELD OF SHOES

Beyond the critical literature on museums and memory, another factor that makes it difficult to understand the sensory aspect of Holocaust objects is the use of shoes in other examples of memorial representation. In the wake of the 2003 U.S. invasion and occupation of Iraq, for example, several groups have used shoes as the central focus of their efforts to memorialize the deaths of soldiers and civilians in Iraq. One such example is the Eyes

Wide Open exhibit first organized by the American Friends Service Committee in 2004, an exhibition about the human cost of war. Each time the exhibition is mounted, local organizers arrange thousands of pairs of black leather military boots on an open field: one pair for every soldier killed in the conflict. When the exhibition was first launched, it included 504 pairs of boots, which has subsequently increased to more than 3,000 along with the rising body count. While the organizers of the exhibition sought to use the shoe as a symbol specifically to emphasize the quantity of military deaths in Iraq, they chose not to pile them up but to arrange them evenly spaced in a manner reminiscent of the rows of headstones in Arlington National Cemetery. Whether arranged outdoors or indoors, the exhibition thus created a memorial conceived as a traveling "field of shoes," allowing members of the public to experience the display in a manner very similar to how they would interact with a field of headstones:

> As the exhibit makes its appearances across the country, families and friends come to grieve for lost loved ones and strangers honor those who gave their lives to a cause far from home. At each stop, person after person leaves notes of commemoration, photographs of lost soldiers, identification tags, flowers, and American flags to accompany the boots on their journey. (McNish 2004)

The "field of shoes" approach to memorials differs in several key ways from the mound of shoes in Holocaust memorials. Most importantly, the field is not imitating an accumulation of objects created by a process of murder, but seeks instead to recreate the very symbolic ritual space of a cemetery. Also significant is the fact that the individual shoes that make up the field do not have any direct link to the events surrounding the deaths of the soldiers. The field is not, in other words, a field of the shoes taken from the bodies of the fallen, but generic military boots either purchased or loaned specifically for the exhibit. This does not diminish the significance of the field relative to Holocaust objects, but helps to distinguish between the experience of interacting with the two.

The sensory aspect of the boots themselves does not enter into the "field of shoes," but habits and practices surrounding sacred objects and memorial pilgrimage sites do. As a result of the symbolic framing of the arrangement, the field of shoes transforms individual pairs of boots into a coherent memorial site, functioning along lines very similar to other veterans' memorials, in particular Maya Lin's Vietnam Veterans Memorial Wall in Washington. Similar to the Vietnam wall, the field of shoes transforms the act of commemorating fallen soldiers into a ritual pilgrimage site, complete with the leaving of written messages and the personal effects of fallen soldiers. What ensues is a blurring of the distinction between the memorial as a living thing imbued with the memory of a lost friend or relative and the actual life lost.

Perhaps the best way to understand the difference between the boots in Eyes Wide Open and Holocaust shoes is the manner in which visitors talk about the tears the shoes brought forth. For the shoes at the Auschwitz camp, tears were a product of tactile interaction with the leather, the feel of grit on the fingers. For the boots in Eyes Wide Open, tears result less from the full sensory experience of the shoes than from the sight of them, a dynamic exemplified by recent visitor reactions to the exhibit:

> He was against the war, but he had come to see the display to show his support. He was talking with a reporter when he was surprised that he was more emotional than he had expected to be. Seeing the ages of many of the soldiers and feeling like he could be one of them brought the exhibit to a level that both saddened and shocked him. (Eyes Wide Open 2004)

The emotion that follows seeing the boots is the common thread in visitor reactions. While these emotions often overwhelmed visitors, they omit any reference to the feel or smell of the boots.

Memorial interaction with shoes qua relics forged out of a moment of homicidal violence is thus noticeably different from memorial interaction with shoes that symbolize violence without having any direct connection to a given moment. Both instances provide links to a set of strong emotions that the visitor seems to have trouble reaching or sustaining without the object as a conduit or starting point, but the relic makes full use of the body's senses, whereas the symbol seems to draw primarily on the eyes. Spending time in the presence of the boots thus elicits talk about past experience, while being near the relics saturates the mind and body with a range of experiences not easily described, classified, or even understood. The visitor who sees a field filled with military boots reacts by speaking with others about war. The visitor to a gallery filled with Holocaust shoes becomes silent with nausea.

CONCLUSION: THE MORAL UNIVERSE

What struck me as a dissonance between the putrid sensory qualities of Holocaust shoes and the presentation of them in Holocaust exhibitions thus opens onto a range of observations and conclusions. Rather than ignoring the sensory qualities of Holocaust relics, for example, Holocaust museum displays can be updated to account for them, using basic museum display elements to engage the visitor in a critical experience of those qualities— elements such as revised display labels, accompanying museum texts, and catalogues. In this respect Holocaust shoes and relics of equal resonance can become a point of departure for a new approach to Holocaust museum and memorial displays, where objects are treated not just as visual evidence but as sensory contact points between past and present, thereby bringing questions of physical experience and discomfort to the forefront of an arena hitherto dominated by a concern for historical authenticity (Feldman 2006, 263).

Beyond museums, the shoes suggest that Holocaust objects evoke what anthropologists have described as the "three bodies" at work simultaneously in certain experiences: the individual body, the social body, and the body politic (Csordas 1993, 136–37; Scheper-Hughes and Lock 1984, 7–8). As visitor reactions to the military boots of Eyes Wide Open suggested, Holocaust shoes step beyond dual representation of the social body and reference to political narratives, shuttling viewers to the experiential level of objects and memory more akin to radical empiricism. We feel the shoes in a way that eludes explanation, and so we respond with descriptions of our own bodies. When considered from this experiential perspective, Holocaust shoes suggest a new way of understanding why people are driven to visit sites and installations containing relics widely perceived as unpleasant or putrid. While a typical understanding of museums and memorials emphasizes the visitor's encounter with evidence so as to remember, encounters with shoes suggest that visitors are seeking the complex experiences of the body. Even though so much of Holocaust discourse focuses on the means to remember the past so as not to forget and inadvertently reproduce past violent genocide in a similar manner, the visitor who seeks out sites of Holocaust crimes may be doing so to keep something far more elemental alive in their own lives: enduring pain, and discomfort with the unimaginable.

Holocaust shoes, therefore, are not fundamentally about counting bodies or reducing genocide to quantifiable statistics in the service of law or history, but points of departure for recovering embodied experience of anguish while contemplating the crimes against humanity committed within recent memory. Piles of shoes are not about representation so much as an aid to help us pay attention. As Primo Levi learned in his post-Auschwitz encounter with the Greek survivor Mordo Nahoum, shoes in war are not just protection for the feet or warmth from the cold, but the protective boundary between hunger and death (Levi 1965, 35–57). Accordingly, Holocaust shoes as relics of this boundary offer individuals much more than a confirmation that a series of violent events actually happened. They are doorways into the moral universe of the Holocaust and the individuals whose countless experiences make up that universe (Cannon 2001, 2–3). Curiously, while a concern for decay of the shoes might lead many to fear for the vanishing of crucial evidence, an experiential focus suggests a very different result. As the smell of decaying leather grows stronger, so does our sense of history and morality.

BIBLIOGRAPHY

Cannon, JoAnn. 2001. "Storytelling and the picaresque in Levi's 'La tregua.'" *Modern Language Studies* 31: 1–10.
Cole, Tim. 2000. *Selling the Holocaust: From Auschwitz to Schindler, how history is bought, packaged, and sold.* New York: Routledge.
Csordas, Thomas. 1993. "Somatic modes of attention." *Cultural Anthropology* 8: 135–56.
Eyes Wide Open. 2004. "Eyes Wide Open: The human cost of war in Iraq." Available at: http://peacechicago.blogspot.com/2004_9_01_archive.html. Accessed August 1, 2007.
Feldman, Jeffrey. 2006. "Contact points: Museums and the lost body problem." In *Sensible objects: Colonialism, museums and material culture,* ed. E. Edwards, C. Gosden, and R. Philips, 245–67. Oxford: Berg.
Geary, Patrick. 1986. "Sacred commodities: The circulation of medieval relics." In *The social life of things,* ed. Arjun Appadurai, 169–91. Cambridge: Cambridge University Press.
Johnson, Chris, and Gabriela Baczynska. 2007. "Auschwitz succumbs to the ravages of time." *Cape Times* (February 14): 1: 8.
Levi, Primo. 1965. *The reawakening.* London: Bodley Head.

McNish, Mary Ellen. 2004. "Eyes Wide Open: About the exhibition." Available at: http://www.afsc.org/eyes/about-the-exhibit-htm. Accessed July 15, 2007.

Pearlman, Moshe. 1963. *The capture and trial of Adolf Eichmann.* New York: Simon & Schuster.

Scheper-Hughes, Nancy, and Margaret Lock. 1984. "The mindful body: A prolegomenon to future work in medical anthropology." *Medical Anthropology Quarterly* 1: 6–41.

Todorov, Tzvetan. 1996. *Facing the extreme: Morality and heroism in Auschwitz and the Gulag.* New York: Henry Holt.

Young, James. 1993. *The texture of memory: Holocaust memorials and meaning.* New Haven, CT: Yale University Press.

PART III: IDEOLOGY AND ECONOMICS

9 THE WANDERER'S SHOE

THE COBBLER'S PENALTY: THE WANDERING JEW IN SEARCH OF SALVATION

SHELLY ZER-ZION

> Paul von Eitzen, Doctor in the Holy Scripture, and Bishop of Schleswig, who is respected by all, and considered to be a teller of the truth, told this to me and to other students very often: Once, during my student days in the winter of 1542, I went to visit my parents at Hamburg. I saw the next Sunday in church during the sermon a very tall man standing opposite the pulpit; he was barefoot, and his hair hung down over his shoulders. The man listened to the sermon with such attention that he stood there perfectly still and stiff, but every time the name Jesus Christ was mentioned, he bowed, beat his breast, and gave a deep sigh. In conversation which I had with the man later, he informed me that he had been in Jerusalem at the time of Christ, had helped towards His condemnation, and on His last sorrowful journey had repulsed him from his house with rough words. Thereupon Jesus had looked hard at him, and said: "I shall stand here and rest, but you shall wander forth and be everlastingly restless." Then he saw Jesus die on the Cross, but could not possibly return to his people in the town of Jerusalem; ever since he had been a wanderer on the face of the earth, and longed for death. (König 1986, 12–13)[1]

This is an edited quote from a pamphlet titled *Kurtze Beschreibung und Erzehlung von einem Juden mit Namen Ahasverus* [a short description and story of a Jew with the name of Ahasverus]. The pamphlet, whose author is unknown, was published in 1602. Based on the legend of the Wandering Jew, it reflected the growing popularity of the story at the end of the sixteenth century. By then it already possessed a long tradition, dating back to the early Middle Ages. The myth of the Wandering Jew was rekindled during the Reformation and would become a prominent anti-Semitic image during the nineteenth century.

Along with its popularity in Christian host societies, the character of the Wandering Jew entered the discourse of European Jewry in the seventeenth century. With the advent of modern Zionism in the late nineteenth and early twentieth centuries it was adopted as a popular Zionist symbol (Idalovichi 2005, 3–26). Zionist leaders such as Leon Pinsker (1821–1891) and Theodor Herzl (1860–1904) as well as artists, poets, and theatre people such as Nathan Birnbaum (1864–1937), Alfred Nossig (1864–1943), and Abraham Goldfaden (1840–1908) appropriated the mythological figure and adapted it to the Zionist discourse, constructing the Wandering Jew for negative comparison with the Zionist "New Jew." The Wandering Jew turned into a *realm of memory,* which constructed the Jewish exile as a dystopia of "no-place" and the Diaspora Jew as a "no-body" entity. The artists and thinkers secularized the Christian motifs of the legend and transformed the Wandering Jew into an icon of modern Jewish revolution, with its declared nihilist negation of the prerevolutionary past along with the yearning for salvation.[2]

* * *

In 1602, with the publication and distribution of the pamphlet *Kurtze Beschreibung und Erzehlung von einem Juden mit Namen Ahasverus,* the legend of the Wandering Jew gained unification and canonization. However, the legend can be traced back to the early Middle Ages. The first versions appeared in monks' chronicles from the sixth century and in the chronicle *Leimonarion* by the monk Johannes Moschos of Cyprus. Other versions appeared in a chronicle of pilgrims from Bologna in 1223, in *Flores Historiarum* in England in 1228, and in *Chronica Majora,* by an English monk, Matthew Paris, in 1243 (Körte 2000, 3–28). The figure of the Wandering Jew captured the imagination of plastic artists, with the earliest visual renditions dating back to 1236 and 1240 (Amishai-Maisels 2006, 59–82). He featured in many folktales throughout Europe, from Italy and France to Sweden and Finland, and was known as The Wandering Jew in English, *Le Juif errant* in French, and *Der ewige Jude* (the eternal Jew) in German. Notwithstanding its different names, the figure manifested the same characteristics.[3] The name *Ahasverus* was one of the innovations of the 1602 pamphlet, echoing the influence of local Jewish *Purimshpil* traditions (Daube 1986; Schaffer 1986). These *Purim Plays* were comic folk performances held on Purim, often based on the book of Esther. The Persian King Ahasverus was a main character in these plays.

The 1602 pamphlet was tremendously popular and was soon translated into numerous European languages, signaling its entry into the world of canonic literature (Bengt of Klintberg 1986; Anderson 1986; Glanz 1986; Hasan-Rokem 1986). Johann Wolfgang von Goethe intended to devote an entire epos to the Wandering Jew, although he relinquished the project, producing only a fragment that describes the narrative of the cobbler from Jerusalem in a rhythmic and humorous manner (Goethe 1950, 373–83). The figure left its imprints on Richard Wagner's operas *The Ring of the Niebelungen* and *The Flying Dutchman.* The Wandering Jew was the protagonist of German plays and novels, such as Johann Nestroy's *Zwei ewigen Juden und keiner: Burleske* (1846), Wilhelm Hauff's *Memoiren des Satan* (1825), and Fritz Mauthner's *Der neue Ahasver: Roman aus Jung-Berlin* (1882). It captured the imagination of Percy Bysshe Shelley and his circle. Furthermore, the Wandering Jew featured in Eugene Sue's immensely popular novel *Le juif errant* (1844–1845) and its subsequent stage adaptations. Sue's story takes place in post-Napoleonic Europe of the 1830s. Joseph, the eternal Jew, who witnesses the international intrigues of the era, finally finds eternal peace. Extending beyond the boundaries of the original legend, this archetypal Jew was also reincarnated in new and complex characters. With the neoclassicism of the late eighteenth century, the Wandering Jew was often depicted as a history teacher or a geographer, and in the late nineteenth century he was also portrayed as a traveling journalist, as an archivist who documents the dying civilization, or as a rich capitalist who addresses new markets (Anderson 1948: 199–213; Idalovichi 2005; Körte 1992: 39–62; Körte 2000: 3–28).

In many ways the Wandering Jew was like a vampire; he could not die and therefore could not really live (Körte 1992: 3–28). Unlike the vampire, however, the Wandering Jew was not portrayed as an elegant nobleman, but rather as a poor passer-by, his shoes serving as a metonym for his earthly existence. According to the medieval tale, during his earthly life the Jew was a cobbler in his shop on the Via Dolorosa, busy mending and making footwear for Israelites. His craft reflected the infrastructure of a complex society. The cobbler made footwear for men, women, and children, city dwellers and peasants, the wealthy and the poor. When he was cursed, he lost his ability to work and live in society. Thus shoemaking served as a metonym for his and his people's earthly existence.

In many traditional interpretations the cobbler of Jerusalem appears barefoot.[4] He is doomed to wander throughout the world as silent proof of the power of Christ, yet he is not permitted to leave a single footprint on the face of the earth. His existence is a constant repentance for his sin and a yearning for Christ's second coming. Other interpretations have him wearing tattered shoes that attest to endless walking and characterize him as a nomad. In still others, the Wandering Jew wears sandals. This type of footwear, which is associated with the ancient Mediterranean region, labels the Jew with the locus and age of his sin. The sandals, however, contain a more complex meaning, because they refer to the golden age of the Jew in his homeland in the days preceding his sin (Brichetto 2006, 22–37). All of these types of footwear depict the body of the Jew as a walking imprint of the power of Christ.[5]

The myth of the Wandering Jew, a legend born out of Christian theology, did not die out during the age of secularism. Rather, it gained new life with the emergence of modern secular anti-Semitism. An 1858 woodcut titled *Le Juif Errant* ('The Wandering Jew), created by the French illustrator Gustave Doré, captures many of the anti-Semitic traits that have been incarnated in modern interpretations of this figure (Figure 9.1). In the woodcut he appears as an old and grotesque figure. His hair is unkempt, his beard is wild, and his large nose signals his Semitic origins. His physical proportions are deformed; his limbs are too long in relation to his torso, and his excessively large bare feet support thin, stick-like legs with no musculature. He takes long strides, leaning on his walking stick, and swings his big hand backward. His limbs occupy the entire frame, creating the impression of a huge spider. His forehead is emblazoned with the sign of the cross: like Cain, he can neither escape nor alter his destiny.[6] The woodcut is reminiscent of the image in *The Elders of Zion*, the anti-Semitic czarist fabrication that accused Jews of conspiring to take over the world by extending their long limbs around the globe and usurping possessions and power.

Cultural historian Dietrich Schwanitz argues that the image of the Wandering Jew is one of the fundamental archetypes constituting modern anti-Semitic imagination and that it stigmatizes Jews as eternal foreigners, estranged from the nations in whose midst they reside.[7] Philosopher Arthur Schopenhauer fully identified Ahasverus with the Jewish

Der wandernde Ewige Jude
Farbiger Holzschnitt von Gustave Doré. 1852

Figure 9.1   A 1858 woodcut titled *Le Juif Errant* [The Wandering Jew], attributed to the French illustrator Gustave Doré, captures many of the anti-Semitic traits that accompany modern interpretations of this figure.

people, whom, he wrote, should have died out long ago, like the Wandering Jew. Yet unlike the great nations of antiquity—the Assyrians, Egyptians, or Persians—the Jews have refused to die, clinging instead to life and becoming the living dead, unable to participate in the creative world of existing nations, and unable to die in peace. Estranged from life, they became nomads with no place of their own on this earth (Schopenhauer 1988, 278). Composer Richard Wagner went one step further by calling for the redemption of the Germans from the curse of Ahasver—a redemption that could be accomplished only by annihilation (Wagner 1888, 70–71). Houston Stewart Chamberlain, Wagner's English-born anti-Semitic son-in-law, stressed the barefoot status of the Jew, contrasting it with modern technological vehicles such as ships and trains, which, he said, proved national superiority and expressed imperialistic claims that he favored (Presner 2003, 269–96). These types of anti-Semitic accusations, stereotypes, and pathologies were used in the notorious 1940 Nazi propaganda film, *Der ewige Jude* (The Eternal Jew), a pseudo-documentary directed by Fritz Hippler and closely supervised by Hitler and Göbbels. The film focused on the history of the Jews as a deformed race and "exposed" their eternal conspiracy to control the world.

By the end of the nineteenth century the Wandering Jew had penetrated the scientific discourse of Jewish pathology. Henry Meige described the preoccupation of psychiatric discourse with the myth of the Wandering Jew during an analysis of three case studies in fin-de-siècle France. Jan Goldstein analyzed the discourse and argued that the psychiatrists were fascinated by the newly emerging social sciences, which sought to define group identities. Almost without noticing, they abandoned the liberal belief affirming each patient to be an individual in his own right. The myth of the Wandering Jew penetrated the discourse of the profession. Psychiatrists argued that Jewish patients hospitalized in mental institutions suffered from restlessness and the craving to wander inherent in the Jewish race and embodied in the myth of the Wandering Jew (Goldstein 1985, 521–52; Meige 1986, 190–94).

Sander Gilman describes another Jewish pathology, this time in the field of orthopedics. German and Austrian physicians such as H. Nordmann and Dr. Elias Auerbach concurred that flatfootedness was a common Jewish deformation. Because flatfooted Jews were deemed unsuitable for military service, this assumption carried deep ideological implications as it served as a test case for appropriate civil conduct. While physicians ascribed the deformation of Jewish feet to the protracted oppression of ghetto life, this putative deformation prevented Jews from becoming decent citizens and from enjoying equal civil rights (Gilman 1991, 38–59). Jewish flatfootedness can be understood as another imprint of the Wandering Jew upon the shaping of the modern Jewish body. The Wandering Jew became a cultural test case for defining the Jew as the Other. In modern times, this image shifted from the field of theology to the field of pathology. However, its function remained unchanged: to mark the Jew as an outsider vis-à-vis the religious and bourgeois social order (Geller 1992, 243–82).

* * *

The Wandering Jew gained access to Jewish discourse as Jews began to integrate into their non-Jewish surrounding. Art historian Ziva Amishai-Naisels describes a Jewish adaptation of this figure in the mid-seventeenth century. The Amsterdam rabbi and publisher, Menasseh Ben-Israel, used the figure as his icon and interpreted it as the image of a devoted pilgrim (Amishai-Maisels 2006). Yiddish playwright Abraham Goldfaden, known as the "Father of the Yiddish Theater," employed this figure in his operetta, "Dr. Almasada, oder di yidn in Palermo" (Dr. Almasada, or the Jews of Palermo), written at the end of the nineteenth century (Goldfaden, 1893).[8] According to the libretto, the Christian authorities are planning to expel the Jews from Palermo. The governor's daughter is gravely ill. Her physician, Alonzo, stands helplessly by her bedside. There is only one person who can save her: his mentor—the Jewish physician, Dr. Almasada, who is smuggled into the governor's palace. However, while attending to his patient, his only child, the beautiful Miriam, is kidnapped. Almasada is immediately suspected of murdering his daughter and is thrown into jail, where he laments his destiny and sings the song of the eternal Jew:

> Lamenting, blaming / Chased away from home / … The missing child of God / He cannot stay long / In one single place / Only walk without getting tired / This is why / His father, God / Gave him the name Jew / In order to save his skin, he begs / Sometimes

weeps, sometimes cries *Oy vey* / No one opens the door, no one lets him in / This is who you are / Walk further, walk. (Goldfaden 1893, 34)[9]

The play ends happily: Miriam escapes her kidnapers, her father is released from jail, and the governor's daughter is saved. Grateful to Almasada, she demands that the Jews be permitted to dwell in the town. The young Christian physician Alonzo discovers his Jewish roots and marries Miriam. By means of the image of the Wandering Jew, Goldfaden lamented the misery of the Jewish people and evoked the modern experience of loss and migration that was so central to his audience. He expressed a unified Jewish fate, although it was not translated explicitly into a pro-Zionist perception.[10]

Zionist interpretations of the Wandering Jew did not attempt to endorse this figure, but rather sought to reshape and thus redeem it. We can find an excellent example of this in the sculpture, *Der ewige Jude* (The Eternal Jew), by Alfred Nossig, a Lemberg Zionist activist and artist (Figure 9.2). The sculpture depicts the Eternal Jew, his garment ruffled by the wind, his thick beard and headdress in disarray. Yet he stands firm, holding his walking stick forcefully and placing it securely in the earth. His other hand embraces the Torah scrolls and clutches them to his heart. The Star of David is imprinted on the Torah, marking the Jewish identity of the figure. He wears sandals that indicate his ancient history and connection to a prewandering Golden Age. No earthly obstacle can shift him from his path.

A photograph of the sculpture was published in the prominent German Jewish journal, *Ost und West* (East and West),[11] and almost immediately became a Zionist icon of Jewish heroism (Schmidt 2003, 200–16). Robert Jaffe argued that Nossig appropriated the sublime art of the Italian Renaissance for the purpose of bringing about a contemporary Jewish and Zionist revival (Jaffe 1901, 191–94). *The Eternal Jew* is a Moses-like figure that

Figure 9.2   Sculpture, *Der ewige Jude* [The Eternal Jew], by Alfred Nossig, a Zionist activist.

stands for the eternal Jewish spirit leading his people to salvation in the Promised Land (Bodenheimer 2002, 7–28).

Another interpretation of the Wandering Jew can be found in the midst of the early Zionist canon. This figure was transformed into a leitmotif in *Auto-Emancipation,* the seminal essay written in 1882 by the Russian physician, Leon Pinsker, in the aftermath of the horrendous pogroms that ravaged the Russian Pale of Settlement. The essay inspired the establishment of the "Khibat Zion" (Love of Zion) movement that preceded Herzl's political Zionism. In his essay Pinsker analyzed the plight of Russian Jews and expressed his deep disillusionment with the Russian promise for enlightenment and emancipation. Jews, he wrote, would not be rescued by outside forces and should emancipate themselves and establish their own national territory. The metaphor of the Wandering Jew serves as a leitmotif in the essay:

> Among the living nations of the earth, the Jews are as a nation long since dead.... The world saw in this people the uncanny form of one of the dead walking among the living. The ghostlike apparition of a living corpse, of a people without unity or organization, without land or other bonds of unity, no longer alive, and yet walking among the living—this spectral form without precedence in history, unlike anything that preceded or followed it, could but strangely affect the imagination of the nations. And if the fear of ghosts is something inborn, and has a certain justification in the psychic life of mankind, why be surprised at the effect produced by this dead but still living nation.... This way have Judaism and Anti-Semitism passed for centuries through history as inseparable companions. Like the Jewish people, the real Wandering Jew, Anti-Semitism, too, seems as if it would never die. (Pinsker 1948, 5–8)

The metaphor of the Wandering Jew shaped an allegorical stratum. The Wandering Jew, who exists in a twilight zone between the living and the dead, is a metaphor of the Jewish people, which is incorporeal, constantly on the edge of extinction. At first, Pinsker writes, it seemed that the spirit of European enlightenment and civil emancipation promised to extricate the Jews from their precarious existence and stand them on their feet, but their legs were too weak to support their bodies. They were either swept into total assimilation and annihilation or driven back into their former wretched situation. Thus, emancipation and enlightenment proved to be bitter disappointments because they failed to serve as the right "shoes" that would march the Jewish people back into the history of the living nations. The appropriate metaphorical shoes could only be found within the Jewish national enterprise and the claim for auto-emancipation. Only they could stand the Jew on his own feet (Pinsker 1948).

Under the harrowing impact of the Russian pogroms, the Polish-Jewish artist, Samuel Hirszenberg (1865–1908), created the 1899 painting, *The Wandering Jew* (Figure 9.3). The picture depicts the devastation of a pogrom: a frantic, elderly Jew escapes barefoot and naked from a field full of corpses and large threatening crosses—the eternal victim of the

Figure 9.3   *The Wandering Jew* (1899), by Samuel Hirszenberg
(1865–1908), which depicts the devastation of a pogrom.

Christian world. A positive account of this figure can be seen in the allegorical works of
the Zionist artist, Ephraim Moses Lilien.[12] In a postcard titled *Von Ghetto nach Zion* (From
the Ghetto to Zion), which publicized the fifth Zionist Congress (1901), Lilien depicts an
old Jew surrounded by thorns. An angel guides him to a vision of himself marching upright
behind a plough and two oxen, tilling the earth. His feet tread on the fresh lumps of earth.

The Wandering Jew was also a popular motif in the writings of poets and authors in
Hebrew (Idalovichi 2005). Chaim Nachman Bialik, the poet laureate of Hebrew Zionist
culture, addressed this motif in his momentous poem, "Be'ir Ha'harega" (In the City of
Slaughter), which was written in response to the infamous Kishinev pogrom (1903) and
in which the poet bitterly berated the Jews for passively accepting their fate as slaughtered
and murdered victims (Bialik 2004, 253–62).

Why did the Wandering Jew, a legendary figure saturated with anti-Jewish theology and
anti-Semitism, appeal to Zionist thinkers and artists in Eastern and Central Europe? What
was its function in Zionist discourse?

Historian and cultural critic Amnon Raz-Krakotzkin argued that Zionist thinking can be read as a secular assimilation in the dominant nineteenth-century European political theology. European nationalist political theology derived from the dominant premodern Christian theology, according to which the world was in the age of grace that followed the first revelation of Christ. The world would be redeemed upon the return of Christ. European secularism translated this concept into political theology: the age of nationalism was perceived as the age of grace and salvation. As opposed to the Christian world, the concept of return was alien to religious Jewish thinking, which, instead, stressed the concept of exile. The world was created by the process of exile: the exile of God from his creation and the exile of his Chosen People from their land. Exile was perceived as an existential human and theological condition that necessitates unique moral sensitivity and religious conduct. Rebelling against this traditional Jewish concept, Zionist thinkers borrowed the Christian theological concept of return in its political sense and appropriated it for the understanding of Jewish nationality. They called for a return to the biblical homeland, a return as a nation into the pages of history. By embracing the concept of return and its national implications, they "converted" into the dominant European national discourse and perceived nationalism as salvation (Raz-Krakotzkin 1993, 23–56; 1995, 113–32; 1999, 249–76).

Literary scholar Michael Gluzman argues that Zionist ideology left its mark on the male Jewish body. Zionist artists, thinkers, and authors sought to reshape it, thereby constructing a solid Hebrew nationality symbolized by this very body (Gluzman 2007, 11–33). The figure of the Wandering Jew incorporates the encounter between Zionist political theology and bodily image. It translates Zionist political theology into the popular *realm of memory,* which constructed the Zionist notion (Nora 1996, 1–20). In the age of assimilation the figure of the Wandering Jew accentuated a unified premodern Jewish identity. It depicted Jewish existence as semi-death, thereby highlighting the power of national renaissance. Moreover, the figure of the Wandering Jew encapsulated the memory not only of past persecution, but also of modern anti-Semitism, and the profound disappointment caused by emancipation. It incorporated a dystopia that possessed the seeds for rebirth, for national physicality and territory, and for the postrevolutionary utopia.

Both Theodor Herzl and Max Nordau dealt with the image of the Wandering Jew. Their interpretation of the figure and its allegorical meaning sought to exclude it from the exclusive anti-Semitic discourse and to endow it with positive Zionist meanings. Herzl examined the issue in an article titled "The Wandering Jew," which was first published in 1897 in the British newspaper, *The Daily Chronicle.* Herzl appealed to British Jewry and enumerated the reasons for the mass migration of Eastern European Jews to Great Britain (Herzl 1934, 233–40). He explained that the development of modern transportation magnified the problem of the Wandering Jew because it facilitated the westward movement of masses of Jewish migrants who consequently became a collective reincarnation of the Wandering Jew. Modern transportation thus served as the "shoes" of the Wandering Jew: although it intensified his distress, it contained a promise of salvation. Herzl embraced Chamberlain's perception of technological transportation and cultural superiority, arguing that the very use of technology enabled the Eastern European Jewish wanderers to claim their own territorial state.

Max Nordau reacted to the discourse on Jewish pathology. He accepted the assumption that Jews suffered from orthopedic and psychological problems that prevented them from becoming useful citizens. Thus he developed the concept of *Muscle Jewry* and advocated the establishment of sports clubs in Jewish society. It was not the right shoes that would redeem the Wandering Jew but rather well-shaped and highly trained legs and feet. Powerful legs can carry a healthy body and host a peaceful mind. Thus Nordau perceived sporting activity as a fundamental tool for the civil improvement of the Jews (Nordau 1909, 379).

We can find an interesting interpretation of the Wandering Jew discussed in a cycle of seven poems about Ahasver by Zionist thinker Nathan Birnbaum, who was among the outstanding figures in the pre-Herzl Zionist movement in Vienna. In 1882 he founded *Kadima,* the first Zionist organization in Vienna, and it was he who coined the term *Zionism* in 1890. After Herzl rose to power, Birnbaum was gradually cut off from Zionist activity and developed an autonomist ideology. The poems were first published anonymously in the journal, *Ost und West,* in 1902, and only in 1910 did they appear in an edition of Birnbaum's collected writings (Gelber 2000, 125–60).

The cycle of poems examines different aspects of the fate of the mythical Ahasver (Birnbaum 1910, 315–16, 317–18, 319–20, 321–22, 323–24, 325–26, 327–28). All the poems express the tension embodied in the figure of Ahasver—the tension between vitality and decline and death, between hope and love and pessimism and vengefulness. Ahasver, the speaker in most of the poems, is the embodiment of a turbulent Jewish memory of deep religiosity, intimacy with God, persecution, and oppression. At the same time, he is the reflection of the confused existence of modern Jews, who are torn between the desire to belong to the modern world and the deep frustration engendered by anti-Semitism. The poem *Ahasver und Acher* (Ahasver and Akher) exposes a deep and intimate connection between Birnbaum the speaker and Ahasver the archetype. The Wandering Jew carries the burden of his memory, yet rediscovers his youthful physicality and a promise for the future.

> I look inside and see my image— / But no, not mine! / Certainly these are the same eyes, / Full of questions and misery deep down, / The same mouth, a seal of great silence, / The same young expression / Over the long white beard— / And yet different!...I am not this! / I am not me! / Different is my reflection, / I am myself different— / I am Akher, / Elisha ben Abuya / I am Ahasver and Akher, / We are two in one.... / And I, I did not know that! (Birnbaum 1910, 325–26)[13]

Birnbaum's cycle of poems examines the figure of the Wandering Jew beyond Zionism. The Wandering Jew turns into a symbol of unresolved Jewish existence that shifts constantly between anger, fear, and the yearning for redemption. Zionism is not represented in the cycle. Rather, the Wandering Jew turns into a spiritual, Jesus-like figure that redeems the world by his exile as he bestows the gift of love on his haters and opponents. Unlike other

Zionist interpretations, this spiritual Wandering Jew lacks a body. The body remains nothing more than a vision.

A Jewish version of The Wandering Jew also appears in a Talmudic legend. On the day the Temple in Jerusalem was destroyed, the Messiah was born. This was the eternal Jew who would lead the people of Israel back to their land (Bialik and Ravnitzki 1965, 149, par. 20).[14] The Hebrew-language *Habima* theatre troupe, one of the primary cultural institutions of the Zionist movement and Israel's national theater today, made the eternal Jew its symbol with the production of *Ha'yehudi Ha'nitz'khi* (The Eternal Jew) in 1919 and in its renewed interpretation in 1923. Both stage adaptations were based on a one-act play written by Dovid Pinski in 1906, its plot inspired by the Talmudic legend. The leading role is that of the prophet who wanders throughout the world in search of the Messiah (Kaynar 1998, 1–20), and it was played by Nahum Zemach, the leader of the troupe. A photograph of the performance shows him dressed in a long, heavy robe, leaning on his walking stick and carrying two tattered bundles (Figure 9.4). His hair and beard are scraggly. His legs are wrapped in shabby cloth that eases the pain of the constant walking. The Habima production evoked former versions of the Wandering Jew and planted them in an explicitly Zionist context, with both actors and the Jewish audience perceiving it as a Zionist allegory. Poet Chaim Nachman Bialik, who collaborated with the theater and was personally invested in it, portrayed the Habima actors as modern Hebrew prophets who traveled around the world and spread the message of Hebrew renaissance (Bialik 1933, 3–12),

Figure 9.4   Nahum Zemach in the role of the prophet *(The Eternal Jew).*

thereby embodying the revolutionary role of the Wandering Jew not only onstage but also in their very beings. The actors themselves became a *realm of memory* that captured the transitory phase between the ancient mythical figure and its Zionist regeneration.

The Wandering Jew was thus a revolutionary icon, a figure that reflected the estheticization of the revolution and its translation into an accessible cultural metaphor that participated in the shaping of popular public opinion. This image vividly describes the prerevolutionary dystopia and delineates the seeds of the desired utopia. For that reason, medieval pilgrims believed that they met the Wandering Jew while undertaking the dangerous journey to Jerusalem. For that reason, he was revived in the age of the Lutheran religious wars. For that reason, he was adopted by modern anti-Semites, who sought to establish a racist-ethnic national identity and to mark the Jews as the Other. There were Jewish interpretations of the Wandering Jew that preceded and extended beyond Zionism (Shahar 2003, 35–54). The cultural function of this figure was similar to its Zionist role. It symbolized the distorted existence of the Jews and stressed the yearning for utopia. Many of these Jewish artists sought to construct their utopia beyond nationalism; they went on a personal moral, philosophical, and aesthetic quest.

The revolutionary impulse embodied in the figure of the Wandering Jew explains the flood of interpretations that it underwent in early Zionist culture. The figure reflected the oppressed prerevolutionary Jewish existence by capturing the dystopia of Jewish life in the Diaspora and condemning Jewish religious spiritualism. But the Wandering Jew expressed an inherent ambivalence with regard to the Zionist context, because this very figure also possessed the seeds for regeneration and redemption. The Zionist interpretation of the figure dealt with the Wandering Jew's yearning for one land, for a lively and youthful (national) body. The real and metaphorical shoes were structured as a metonym for corporeal existence. As a result of Jesus's curse, the cobbler of Jerusalem lost his shoes and started his eternal wandering. Zionist interpretations of this figure tried to reshape the Jew's shoes, thereby bringing him back to life. Artist Samuel Hirszenberg depicted the barefoot Jew as escaping from death on Christian soil. Alfred Nossig and Ephraim Moses Lilien pictured the Jew as a prophet who could find his path on earth. Herzl constructed modern transportation as the metaphorical shoes that would support the Jewish claim for a homeland. Physicians Max Nordau and Leon Pinsker tried to heal the deformed body of the Jew through political and physical practice. Abraham Goldfaden depicted the establishment of a new family as a tool for regeneration. Nathan Birnbaum led his Ahasver back into the domains of spirituality while initiating the search for a Jewish renaissance beyond Zionism. The Habima actors constructed themselves as prophet-like Wandering Jews: they carried in themselves the eternal Jewish spirit while evoking the promise of national renaissance.

NOTES

1. Aharon Schafer compared the changes between the different editions of "The Ahasver-Volksbuch of 1602" (1986, 27–35). Original text in German is: *Kurtze Beschreibung vnd Erzehlung von einem Juden/mit Namen Ahaßverus* (1602, Bautzen: Wolffgang Suchnach), available online

at http://de.wikisource.org/wiki/Kurtze_Beschreibung_vnd_Erzehlung_von_einem_Juden_mit_Namen_Aha%C3%9Fverus.

2. On the dualist structure of the nihilist revolutions see Ohana 1993, 5–78. On revolutionary patterns in Zionist culture see Peled 2002, 2–29.

3. See for example Edelmann 1986, 1–10; König 1986, 36–8; Bagatti 1986, 39–49; Jaccod 1986, 50–67; Champfleury 1986, 68–75; Anderson 1986, 76–104; Glanz 1986, 105–18; Hasan-Rokem 1986, 119–53; Bengt of Klintberg 1986, 154–68; and Blind 1986, 169–89.

4. Amishai-Maisels argues that in most medieval interpretations of the character he appears barefoot. This image exists also in some of the literary and folktale adaptations of the myth. See Amishai-Maisels 2006; König 1986; Jaccod 1986.

5. On the relationship between Christ and the Wandering Jew see Isaac-Edersheim 1986, 195–210; and Hurwitz 1986, 211–26.

6. Joanna L. Brichetto discusses the visual characteristics of the Wandering Jew (2006, 22–37).

7. On the secularization of the myth and its adaptation into anti-Semitic discourse see Leschnitzer 1986, 227–35; Maccoby 1986, 236–60; and Schwanitz 1997, 3–28.

8. Nahma Sandrow argues that the publication of the plays was infrequent and quite long after their first performances (1996, 70–90).

9. My translation.

10. The Yiddish scholar Seth Wolitz argues that one can spot Zionist sentiments in his mature plays (2003, 87–106).

11. This journal was extremely important in the shaping of Jewish culture in early twentieth-century German Jewish culture. See Brenner 1998.

12. On the allegorical works of Lilien see Mishory 2000, 15–42; and Schmidt 2003, 151–89.

13. My translation.

14. Based upon Jerusalem Talmud, Berakhot 2:4, 5a; Eicha Rabbah 1:51; and Midrash Panim Akherim.

BIBLIOGRAPHY

Amishai-Maisels, Ziva. 2006. "Menasseh Ben Israel and the 'Wandering Jew.'" *Ars Judaica* 2: 59–82.

Anderson, George K. 1948. "The neo-classical chronicle of the Wandering Jew." *PMLA* 63 (1): 199–213.

Anderson, George K. 1986. "Popular Survivals of the Wandering Jew in England." In *The Wandering Jew: Essays in the interpretation of a Christian legend*, ed. Galit Hasan-Rokem and Alan Dundes, 76–104. Bloomington: Indiana University Press.

Bagatti, P. B. 1986. "The legend of the Wandering Jew: A Franciscan headache." In *The Wandering Jew: Essays in the interpretation of a Christian legend*, ed. Galit Hasan-Rokem and Alan Dundes, 39–49. Bloomington: Indiana University Press.

Bengt of Klintberg. 1986. "The Swedish wanderings of the Eternal Jew." In *The Wandering Jew: Essays in the interpretation of a Christian legend*, ed. Galit Hasan-Rokem and Alan Dundes, 154–68. Bloomington: Indiana University Press.

Bialik, Chaim Nachman. 1933. "The ways of the Hebrew theatre" [in Hebrew]. *Bamah* 2: 3–12.

Bialik, Chaim Nachman. 2004. "In the City of Slaughter" [in Hebrew]. In *Chaim Nachman Bialik: The Poems,* ed. Avner Holtzman, 253–62. Tel Aviv: Dvir.

Bialik, Chaim Nachman, and Yehoshua Khana Ravnitzki, eds. 1965. *The book of legends* [in Hebrew]. Tel Aviv: Dvir.

Birnbaum, Nathan [Mathias Acher]. 1910. *Ausgewählte Schriften zur jüdischen Frage.* Czernowitz: Verlag der Buchhandlung Dr Birnbaum und Dr Kohut.

Blind, Karl. 1986. "Wodan, the wild huntsman and the Wandering Jew." In *The Wandering Jew: Essays in the interpretation of a Christian legend,* ed. Galit Hasan-Rokem and Alan Dundes, 169–89. Bloomington: Indiana University Press.

Bodenheimer, Alfred. 2002. *Wandernde Schatten.* Göttingen: Wallstein.

Brenner, David A. 1998. *Marketing identities: The invention of Jewish ethnicity in Ost und West.* Detroit, MI: Wayne State University Press.

Brichetto, Joanna L. 2006. *The wandering image: Converting the Wandering Jew.* PhD dissertation. Nashville, TN: Vanderbilt University.

Champfleury (Jules François Felix Fleury-Husson). 1986. "French images of the Wandering Jew." In *The Wandering Jew: Essays in the interpretation of a Christian legend,* ed. Galit Hasan-Rokem and Alan Dundes, 68–75. Bloomington: Indiana University Press.

Daube, David. 1986. "Ahasver." In *The Wandering Jew: Essays in the interpretation of a Christian legend,* ed. Galit Hasan-Rokem and Alan Dundes, 36–38. Bloomington: Indiana University Press.

Der ewige Jude. 1940. Directed by Fritz Hippler, Germany: DFG, videocassette.

Edelmann, R. 1986. "Ahasuerus, the Wandering Jew: Origin and background." In *The Wandering Jew: Essays in the interpretation of a Christian legend,* ed. Galit Hasan-Rokem and Alan Dundes, 1–10. Bloomington: Indiana University Press.

Gelber, Mark H. 2000. *Melancholy pride: Nation, race, and gender in the German literature of cultural Zionism.* Tübingen: Max Niemeyer.

Geller, Jay. 1992. "(G)nos(e)ology: The cultural construction of the Other." In *People of the body: Jews and Judaism from an embodied perspective,* ed. Howard Eilberg-Schwatz, 243–82. Albany: State University of New York Press.

Gilman, Sander. 1991. *The Jew's body.* New York and London: Routledge.

Glanz, Rudolf. 1986. "The Wandering Jew in America." In *The Wandering Jew: Essays in the interpretation of a Christian legend,* ed. Galit Hasan-Rokem and Alan Dundes, 105–18. Bloomington: Indiana University Press.

Gluzman, Michael. 2007. *The Zionist body: Nationality, gender and sexuality in new Hebrew literature* [in Hebrew]. Tel Aviv: Hakibbutz Hameukhad.

Goethe, Johann Wolfgang. 1950. "Der ewige Jude." In *Goethes poetische Werke: West-Östlicher Divan und Epen,* ed. Liselotte Lohrer, 373–83. Stuttgart: J. G. Cotta'sche Buchhandlung Nachfolger.

Goldfaden, Abraham. 1893. *Doktor Almasada oder di yidn in Palermo* [in Yiddish]. New York: Jacob Sapirshtein.

Goldstein, Jan. 1985. "The Wandering Jew and the problem of psychiatric anti-Semitism in fin-de-siècle France." *Journal of Contemporary History* 20 (4): 521–52.

Hasan-Rokem, Galit. 1986. "The cobbler of Jerusalem in Finnish folklore." In *The Wandering Jew: Essays in the interpretation of a Christian legend,* ed. Galit Hasan-Rokem and Alan Dundes, 119–53. Bloomington: Indiana University Press.

Herzl, Theodor. 1934. "Der ewige Jude." In *Theodor Herzl: Zionistische Schriften*. Vol. 1, 233–40. Tel Aviv: Hoza'a Ivrit.

Hurwitz, S. 1986. "Ahasver the eternal wanderer: Psychological aspects." In *The Wandering Jew: Essays in the interpretation of a Christian legend*, ed. Galit Hasan-Rokem and Alan Dundes, 211–26. Bloomington: Indiana University Press.

Idalovichi, Israel. 2005. "Creating national identity through a legend: The case of the Wandering Jew." *Journal for the Study of Religions and Ideologies* 12: 3–26.

Isaac-Edersheim, E. 1986. "Ahasver: A mythic image of the Jew." In *The Wandering Jew: Essays in the interpretation of a Christian legend*, ed. Galit Hasan-Rokem and Alan Dundes, 195–219. Bloomington: Indiana University Press.

Jaccod, Louis. 1986. "The three apples of Easter: A legend of the valley of Aosta." In *The Wandering Jew: Essays in the interpretation of a Christian legend*, ed. Galit Hasan-Rokem and Alan Dundes, 50–67. Bloomington: Indiana University Press.

Jaffe, Robert. 1901. "Alfred Nossig Skulpturen." *Ost und West* 3: 191–94.

Kaynar, Gad. 1998. "National theatre as colonized theatre: The paradox of Habima." *Theatre Journal* 50 (1): 1–20.

König, Eduard. 1986. "The Wandering Jew: Legend or myth?" In *The Wandering Jew: Essays in the interpretation of a Christian legend*, ed. Galit Hasan-Rokem and Alan Dundes, 11–26. Bloomington: Indiana University Press.

Körte, Mona. 1992. " 'Wir, die wir die Helden des Märchens sind, wir wissen es selbst nicht': Ahasver-Dichtungen in der Literatur des 19. Jahrhunderts." *Jahrbuch für Antisemitismusforschung* 4: 39–62.

Körte, Mona. 2000. *Die Uneinholbarkeit des Verforlgten: Der Ewige Jude in der literarischen Phantastik*. Frankfurt and New York: Campus.

Kurtze Beschreibung vnd Erzehlung von einem Juden/mit Namen Ahaßverus. 1602. Bautzen: Wolffgang Suchnach.

Leschnitzer, Adolf L. 1986. "The Wandering Jew: The alienation of the Jewish image in Christian consciousness. In *The Wandering Jew: Essays in the interpretation of a Christian legend*, ed. Galit Hasan-Rokem and Alan Dundes, 227–35. Bloomington: Indiana University Press.

Maccoby, Hyam. 1986. "The Wandering Jew as sacred executioner." In *The Wandering Jew: Essays in the interpretation of a Christian legend*, ed. Galit Hasan-Rokem and Alan Dundes, 236–60. Bloomington: Indiana University Press.

Meige, Henry. 1986. "The Wandering Jew in the clinic: A study on neurotic pathology." In *The Wandering Jew: Essays in the interpretation of a Christian legend*, ed. Galit Hasan-Rokem and Alan Dundes, 190–94. Bloomington: Indiana University Press.

Mishory, Alec. 2000. *Watch ahead: Pioneer icons and visual symbols in Israeli culture* [in Hebrew]. Tel Aviv: Am Oved.

Nora, Pierre. 1996. "Between memory and history." In *Realms of memory: Rethinking the French past*, ed. Pierre Nora, trans. Arthur Goldhammer. Vol. 1, 1–20. New York: Columbia University Press.

Nordau, Max. 1909. "Muskeljudentum." In *Max Nordau's Zionistische Schriften*, ed. Die Zionistische Aktionkomitee, 397. Köln und Leipzig: Jüdischer Verlag.

Ohana, David. 1993. *The nihilist order: The birth of political culture in Europe 1870–1930* [in Hebrew]. Jerusalem: Mosad Bialik.

Peled, Rina. 2002. *The new man of the Zionist revolution: Hashomer Hatza'ir and its European roots* [in Hebrew]. Tel Aviv: Am Oved.

Pinsker, Leon. 1948. *Auto-Emancipation,* trans. D. S. Blondheim. New York: Zionist Organization of America.

Presner, Todd Samuel. 2003. "'Clear heads, solid stomachs, and hard muscles': Max Nordau and the aesthetics of Jewish regeneration." *Modernism/Modernity* 10 (2): 269–96.

Raz-Krakotzkin, Amnon. 1993. "Exile in sovereignty: For the critique of the exile negation in Israeli culture, part 1" [in Hebrew]. *Te'orya u-bikoret* 4: 23–56.

Raz-Krakotzkin, Amnon. 1995. "Exile in sovereignty: For the critique of the exile negation in Israeli Culture, part 2" [in Hebrew]. *Te'orya u-bikoret* 5: 113–32.

Raz-Krakotzkin, Amnon. 1999. "The return to the history of redemption or: What is the history to which one returns in the phrase 'The Return to History'" [in Hebrew]. In *Zionism and the return to history: A reevaluation,* ed. Shmuel Noah Eisenstast and Moshe Lissak, 249–76. Jerusalem: Yad Ben-Zvi.

Sandrow, Nahma. 1996. *Vagabond stars: A world history of Yiddish theater.* Syracuse, NY: Syracuse University Press.

Schaffer, Aaron. 1986. "The Ahasver-Volksbuch of 1602." In *The Wandering Jew: Essays in the interpretation of a Christian legend,* ed. Galit Hasan-Rokem and Alan Dundes, 27–35. Bloomington: Indiana University Press.

Schmidt, Gilya Gerda. 2003. *The art and artists of the Fifth Zionist Congress, 1901.* Syracuse, NY: Syracuse University Press.

Schopenhauer, Arthur. 1988. *Arthur Schopenhauer: Sämtliche Werke,* ed. Julius Frauenstädt and Arthur Hübscher. Vol. 2. Mannheim: Brockhaus.Schwanitz, Dietrich. 1997. *Das Shylock Syndrom oder die Dramaturgie der Barbarei.* Frankfurt am Main: Eichborn.

Shahar, Galili. 2003. "Theater Avantgarde in Deutschald. Jüdische Wanderer-Figuren: Stereotypen, Humor und Selbstinszenierung." *Forum Modernes Theater* 18 (1): 35–54.

Wagner, Richard. 1888. "Das judentum in der Musik." In *Gesammelte Schriften und Dichtungen.* Vol. 5, 70–71. Leipzig: Frissch.

Wolitz, Seth L. 2003. "Shulamis and Bar Kokhva: Renewed Jewish role models in Goldfaden and Halkin." In *Yiddish theater: New approaches,* ed. Joel Berkowitz, 87–106. Oxford: Littman Library.

10 THE EQUALIZING SHOE

SHOES AS A SYMBOL OF EQUALITY IN THE JEWISH SOCIETY IN PALESTINE DURING THE FIRST HALF OF THE TWENTIETH CENTURY

AYALA RAZ

Fashion is a social force that functions effectively not only as an economic engine but as a semiotic system that transmits social and political messages by means of a nonverbal language rich in signs, symbols, and iconography. This essay focuses on the communicative role of footwear during the first half of the twentieth century, a formative period of modern Israel, when socialist Zionism set the values and goals for the emergent nation.

SHOES AS A SYMBOL OF ZIONIST EQUALITY

Socialist Zionism was a revolutionary ideology that merged national and cosmopolitan left-wing ideals. It wished to create not merely a new Jewish nation in the Jewish ancestral homeland, but a model society organized along principles of equality and social justice. Seeking to revolutionize Jewish life, it embraced the stereotypical ideal of the "New Jew" as the antithesis of the exilic "Old Jew," who was disparaged for excessive intellectualism and physical weakness. The new Zionist Jew was defined by physical and moral rather than intellectual abilities: young and healthy, able to defend himself against his enemies, and engaged in physical labor in the field or factory, earning his living by the sweat of his brow. This utopian model reflected to a large extent the Nietszchean ideal of the *Ubermensch,* who is engaged in the willful process of continual self-overcoming.

The young radical pioneers—known in Hebrew as *chalutzim*—arrived in Palestine in the years 1904–1914 within the framework of the Second Aliyah (the second wave of immigration), which brought some 35,000 new immigrants to the land. Most of the *chalutzim* were young, single, children of traditional Jewish families who lived within the czarist Pale of Settlement. They belonged to a generation that turned its back on religion and rebelled against the mores of the Eastern European Jewish lifestyle. Greatly influenced by Russian radicalism, they possessed a strong political consciousness that would guide them in their struggle for national and social redemption in their new land. It was they who were the founders of the ethos that dominated the *yishuv* (Jewish community in prestate Palestine) and the state of Israel in its early years.

The *chalutzim* discarded ornamental clothing and adopted symbolic marks of identity were inspired by an ideology of ascetic minimalism and their rejection of anything that smacked of "the bourgeoisie." They ate little, lived in extremely uncomfortable conditions, wore shabby clothes and worn-out shoes, and espoused a puritanical ethos that advocated renouncement of private property and personal belongings.

Their antagonism to luxury clothing and their adherence to extremely austere substitutes not only reflected the *chalutzim's* extremely scarce resources but also served as public ideological codes. In his book *Fashion, Culture and Identity,* Fred Davis argues that the anti-fashion of a counterculture is instrumental in shaping a distinctive identity for a self-defined subcultural group. Counterculturists, he writes, seek to distance themselves from, diminish, and even scandalize society's dominant cultural groups (Davis 1992, 183). Indeed, the Marxist anticapitalist stance espoused by the *chalutzim* of the Second Aliyah found expression in their austere clothing. Worn-out shoes became both a banner and a slogan conveying the message of an idealized society based on equality and social justice.

By ignoring conventional fashion and its social significance, the *chalutzim* intended to point out that it was irrelevant to their revolutionary way of life, rejecting European urban clothing and replacing it with utilitarian laborers' outfits and heavy-duty shoes. Yet ironically they transformed what they considered as anti-fashion into a leading dress code. Modesty and austerity, historically associated with socialism, seem to contradict the very nature of fashion, but the phenomenon of anti-fashion becoming the leading mode is well known to sociologists and culture theorists. Davis argues that anti-fashion is another face of fashion and is motivated by such sentiments as opposition, rejection, studied neglect, and parody. It is important to point out that the oppositional nature of anti-fashion distinguishes it from nonfashion, which simply reflects indifference. The indifferent stay out of the fashion dialogue, while the anti-fashionists sustain and nurture fashion. In his argument Davis cites George Simmel, who noted, "indeed, it occasionally happens that it becomes fashionable in whole bodies of a large class to depart altogether from the standards set by fashion" (Simmel 1983, quoted in Davis 1992, 159).

While wishing to disassociate themselves from the Diaspora "Old Jew," the *chalutzim* were dreaming of a renewed bond with the ancient roots of biblical Judaism. They regarded their immigration to Palestine as a full departure from the Jewish experience in the Diaspora, whose norms and traditions they rejected, and they embraced the Bible and glorified tales of ancient Jewish heroism. This ideology was also inspired by romantic movements that flourished in Europe at the end of the nineteenth century, which looked back to the ancient Orient as a source of innocence and purity.

It was not uncommon for the *chalutzim,* both men and women, to walk barefoot to a point where the soles of their feet were so hard they felt neither heat nor cold. This was described by Alexander Zaid (1886–1938), one of the iconic figures of the Second Aliyah. A native of Siberia, he came to Palestine in 1904 and was instrumental in the establishment of Jewish settlements in the Galilee and in the foundation of *Ha'Shomer,* the near-mythological defense organization. In his memoirs he described the general meetings of the left-wing *Po'ale Zion* (Workers of Zion) party, which usually took place in Jaffa, and noted, "we went there barefoot, over the rocks. Never mind! Our feet didn't hurt because they were hardened like the Jerusalem rocks" (Zaid 1981, 86).

The popular poet Rachel (Bluwstein) (1890–1931), who came to Palestine at the age of nineteen and lived first in Kinneret, a settlement near the Sea of Galilee, and later in Degania, then a small agricultural kibbutz, portrayed women's bare feet and roughened skin as a symbol of equality and dedication: "Blistered hands, bare sunburned legs, scratches, strong faces, hearts burning…they swung their hoes up and down ceaselessly. Stop for a minute, wipe the sweat from your brow with your *keffiya* [traditional Palestinian man's headdress] cast a glance at the sea, how wonderful it is—blue, blue, blue" (Milstein 1985, 36).

The *chalutzot* (pioneer women) strove to be like men in task and appearance. They insisted on sharing the agricultural work and wore coarse clothes and high workers' boots. At Sejera (now Ilaniya), a communal settlement established in 1902 in the Lower Galilee, where the young David Green, later known as David Ben-Gurion, Israel's first prime minister, spent eighteen months working as a farm laborer, the young women wore men's trousers, deemed more practical for agricultural work. To complete the utilitarian and androgynous look, they also cropped their long hair and strapped on pistol belts (Zaid 1981, 86).

A new item of clothing that reflected the spirit of the Bible and the socialist heritage was a pair of improvised sandals the pioneers created for themselves. Idealistic members of the socialist communes—which would later develop into the kibbutz model—looked at these ascetic sandals as a source of inspiration that reflected noble principles. Rivka Shturman (1903–2001), a German-trained dancer who settled in Palestine in 1929 and who would become known as the mother of Israeli folk dancing, described her strong impression of Yitzhak Ben-Zvi—Israel's second president—by focusing on his footwear: "Ben-Zvi quite amazed me with his strange attire. On his feet he had tied soles, just like the monks of one of the Christian orders who live on Mount Carmel. His modest face expressed inspiration and seriousness.…I was overwhelmed, and at that moment the fate of my life in this

Figure 10.1 Shoes of boys and girls in front of the children's house at Kibbutz Hanita represent the equality between kibbutz members. Photographer: Moshe Fridan, 1958. Courtesy of the National Photo Collection, State of Israel.

country was settled" (Shturman 1981, 86). The improvised sandals described by Shturman functioned not only as footwear but also as a kind of advertisement for status, a comment on the wearer's ideological and social position. Indeed, quite often the higher-ups in leadership positions were the shabbiest-dressed members of the community.

Ben-Zvi's sandals were not simply a class badge but also a practical solution to genuine shortages encountered by the *chalutzim*. Since it was often necessary to share one pair of shoes among five people, home-made sandals were a logical solution. The decision to share the limited number of shoes among all members of the commune also had its ideological aspect, as shoes that were shared by all belonged to none, thus erasing personal singularity in favor of collective identity. Such rituals molded the collective into a unified entity in which the whole was much more important than its parts. The ideal of total sharing and the renunciation of private property were not merely applied to personal items. Even children were considered to belong to everyone: "They were not the children of a mother and father, or of their collective, but of everyone—Gideon from Degania was the son of the whole community" (Tabenkin 1981, 80). A commune that insisted on uncompromising equality criticized and rebuked those who chose not to toe this line: "I came from Czechoslovakia as a young woman, I believed in colors, in beauty, and I wore trousers with colorful stripes. For that reason I wasn't very popular in grim faced Degania," wrote Miriam Zinger, one of its founders (Miriam 1981, 207). In his classic novel, *The Day before Yesterday,* author Shmuel Yosef Agnon describes the change that occurred in the economic status of Rabinowitz, originally a Second Aliyah *chalutz,* as metaphorically marked by his shoes: "You love yourself in the polished shoes you wear now, and I love you because I remember your crooked sandals" (Agnon 1979, 87). We can see footwear functioning here as a metonym for personhood and values.

The Third Aliyah (1919–1923)—triggered by the October Revolution; pogroms in Russia, Poland, and Hungary; the British takeover of Palestine; and the Balfour Declaration—included many *chalutzim* among its 40,000 arrivals, who brought the number of the Jewish community in Palestine to 90,000. The new *chalutzim,* mostly young, idealistic, single, and penniless, found themselves in a largely desolate land with an underdeveloped economy that offered few jobs and insufficient budgets for construction of the many new communal settlements. A large number ended up working in public projects, mostly road construction. It was brutal physical labor, regarded as a test of endurance, sanctified as total selfless dedication to the creation of a Jewish homeland. Poverty was so extreme that many found they were unable to cope and left their communes; some took their own lives. The harsh conditions would be incorporated into the Zionist ethos and became a lifelong badge of honor for those who participated. In this state of virtual destitution, shoes and their absence became the ultimate symbol of the pioneering spirit. Memoirs of individuals written in this period attest to this:

> It's hard to describe the tremendous impression made on me by Richard's bare toes, as
> they poked out from his torn shoes. I had not yet met him face to face, but his reputation

as a young leader of the movement had reached me...and now I was looking at him, his legs in torn shoes. Is there anything nobler than torn shoes on the feet of a leader? That is the ultimate symbol of the pioneer. (Rand 1981, 207)

Avigdor Hameiri's hugely popular song, set to music by Joel Engel, captured the spirit of the time and the link between the iconic pioneer shoe and the Zionist idea:

Hey, Hey, Hey, shoes;
Shoes without soles;
And the rocks torch the feet;
Torch, torch, torch.
Never mind, never mind, never mind;
The *chalutz* will build, build, build Jerusalem!
Build, build, build, build, build.[1]

During the Third Aliyah, the principal formats of communal agricultural communities, most notably the kibbutz, took shape: the ideological cornerstone of the kibbutz was expressed in the Marxist slogan "From each according to his ability, to each according to his need." Since this utopian doctrine was rather abstract and hard to implement, the more realistic solution was an emphasis on equality. In the name of equality the kibbutz leadership could define the personal needs of the membership, including clothing and personal items. This manifested itself in modest uniform-like outfits, work shoes, and simple sandals. The fact that this policy was a temporary measure was gradually forgotten, and equality across the board became a cherished principle in itself. (See Figure 10.1.)

URBAN ISRAELI CULTURE

During the 1920s and 1930s the center of gravity of Jewish settlement in Palestine shifted to urban centers. Tel-Aviv, founded in 1909, grew quickly and by the end of the 1930s was the most prominent city of the *yishuv*. The fourth (1924–1928) and fifth (1929–1939) waves of immigration brought to the country an influx of many Central and Eastern European urban Jews who, unlike their predecessors, cherished the bourgeois lifestyle and were not committed to social revolution. Jewish urban life in Palestine at the time was difficult, largely due to bloody conflicts between Arabs and the Jewish community, which had reached 450,000 by 1940. As the situation of European Jewry worsened and draconian limits on immigration were instituted by the British, Palestine's Jews supported illegal Jewish immigration and helped the new immigrants in every way. The struggle nurtured national pride, which was expressed publicly by the blue/white flag and personally by dressing in khaki shirt and shorts, supplemented by modest footwear. In the 1930s and 1940s khaki was not merely a color—it was a demonstrative statement against British colonialism and in support of the establishment of an independent Jewish state and free Jewish immigration. The two notions became intertwined in the dominant slogan of the period, *"Medina Ivrit, Aliya Khofshit"* (Hebrew state, free immigration).

As a preliminary army for the Jewish state, the Palmach, a commando army force, was established in 1941. It was joined by the elite of Palestine's Jewish youth—among them future prime minister Yitshak Rabin and his wife Leah—and within its ranks the iconic stereotype of the *sabra,* the authentic native Israeli Jew, was shaped. Amos Elon delineates the appearance of the *sabra* as an "eager teenager in khaki shorts and open sandals" and explains that "the harsh starkness that marks '*sabra*' speech and manners stems from many years of deliberate educational efforts to produce a 'normal,' 'manly,' 'free' 'new Jew,' unsullied by the shameful weakness of exile" (Elon 1971, 322).

In his milestone study *The Sabra—A Profile,* sociologist Oz Almog analyzes the components of the *sabra* stereotype and describes its distinctive clothes. He points to the ascetic outfit and shabby shoes as status symbols, both for urban pioneers and kibbutz members: "the dull and common appearance symbolizes not only the proletarian status but also the seriousness that characterizes members of recruited society who are concerned in public missions rather than in their very own needs" (Almog 2001, 325).

A member of the Palmach was seen as the ultimate sabra: "tough from outside but sweet from inside," suffused with profound patriotic feelings and totally devoted to his comrades (Almog 2001, 325). Almog explains that the fighters' intense sense of comradeship was born out of the war, noting that "standing as one in front of death and fighting together towards a common enemy creates a special intimacy that feels like brothers in blood" (Almog 2001, 377). The *palmachniks'* (Palmach members') simple uniform symbolized not only their modest way of life but also their devotion to collective national aspirations. Khaki shorts and open sandals became their trademark. The sandals, designed in the most basic way, consisted of two straps across the foot, sometimes with a buckle, and another strap round the ankle. They were given various names, such as Biblical Sandals and Khugistic sandals.[2]

In his iconic poem "The Silver Platter," in which he equated Israel's 1948 Declaration of Independence with the revelation at Sinai, poet Nathan Alterman offered a collective paean to the young people who sacrificed their lives for the creation of the state. With bold brushstrokes he depicted their torn clothes and rough footwear as emblems of their heroic spirit (Alterman 1948, 366). The "heavy shoes" in Alterman's poem signify the enormous weight placed on the young generation and reflect the strong linkage between the earthy shoes and the soil of the land to which they were so vividly attached.

The establishment of the state in May 1948 was followed by enormous waves of Jewish immigration. During the first 44 months of statehood the original pre-1948 Jewish community of 650,000 absorbed some 700,000 new immigrants from Europe, Asia, and Africa, who came from places as diverse as Iraq, Rumania, Poland, Yemen, North Africa, Bulgaria, Turkey, Libya, Iran, Czechoslovakia, Hungary, Germany and Austria, Egypt, the Soviet Union, and Yugoslavia. Needless to say, the struggle of the newcomers to adjust to the new homeland was often complex and painful (Naor 1991, 130–34).

The new arrivals differed from the native *sabra.* Often displaced and alienated, many subsisted in the early years on governmental charity and low-paying public work programs.

Clothes were often the remnants of once fashionable outfits and looked shabby and neglected despite efforts to maintain minimal levels of hygiene in the substandard conditions of the *ma'abarot,* the transit camps where many immigrants were housed upon arrival. True, externally the mostly young *sabra* looked rough as well, with long unkempt hair, and careless outfits: khaki shirt, khaki shorts, "dummy cap" (*kova tembel*), a *keffiya* round the neck and Biblical Sandals or working shoes on their feet. But there was a fundamental difference: the *sabra* had chosen to dress like a proud member of the working class, while the new immigrants had to wear whatever they could get their hands on.

THE AUSTERITY REGIME AS A MELTING POT

With the establishment of statehood the frail Israeli economy faced massive difficulties. It had to support a great number of immigrants while lacking food, resources, and foreign currency, and at the same time having to meet the military expenses incurred by the War of Independence. In order to ensure equal and fair distribution of food and basic goods to all citizens, in April 1949 the government decided on an emergency austerity regime (known in Hebrew as the *tsena;* see Figure 10.2), supervised by a special Ministry of Supply and Rationing. At first the rationing covered only basic food items: every citizen was attached to a specific grocery shop where he or she received basic foodstuffs according to a fixed allocation based on

Figure 10.2 Window shopping during the time of austerity. The sign advertises "Buy Tsena," and its top line declares "Long Live Joseph," a reference to Dov Joseph, who headed the Ministry of Supply and Rationing. Photographer: Fritz Cohen, 1950. Courtesy of the National Photo Collection, State of Israel.

gender, age, and so on. People were issued a coupon book that allowed them to buy a specified limited amount. In August 1950 most consumer goods—including textiles, clothing,
and footwear—were added to this system. In addition to economic considerations, the *tsena*
regime was also motivated by the ideological stance of the ruling socialist party, which was
strongly committed to economic and class equality. In response to great popular dissatisfac-
tion, however, the Ministry of Supply and Rationing was disbanded by the end of 1950 and
tsena rules were gradually relaxed. The policy was officially terminated in 1959.

The brand name chosen for the *tsena* products was *lakol* (meaning "for everybody").
The quality of *lakol* apparel was poor and unappealing, but it had the advantage of modest pricing: lower by sixty percent than the free market equivalent. Though *lakol* apparel
was disappointing, the footwear was an unanticipated success (Raz 1996, 139). The first
lakol shoes were produced in fifty Israeli factories in fifteen diverse styles; within a year the
number of producers grew to 175, the variety of styles became more diverse, and the prices
dropped to thirty-five percent of free market value.

On October 10, 1949 the newspaper *Ha'aretz* reported, "the Israeli consumer has no
doubt that the production of '*lakol*' shoes has made a nice improvement lately. You can
find today *lakol*' shoes for fixed prices in almost every shop in large range and good quality." The styles were varied during the first year of rationing, but producers occasionally cut
corners. Dr Dov Joseph, Minister of Supply and Rationing, explained, "we found out that
when a certain quantity of leather was allocated to a shoemaker for producing a certain
number of shoes, he would sometimes change the confirmed style into a simpler one, in
order to produce additional pairs of shoes and sell them on the 'black market.' We did not
have a choice but to limit formally the variety of styles as to get the required shoes" (Segev
1984, 291).

The major problem in obtaining *lakol* shoes was the "points" required for their purchase,
as the tiny monthly allowance was not sufficient for the purchase of a single pair of shoes.
Here is how Joseph had to explain to dubious Knesset members how to manage buying
shoes for each family member within the annual points allocation:

> If the average family consists of four people and the father urgently needs a pair of shoes,
> which cost thirty-three "points," he can take all the family "points" and buy these shoes. The
> following month he will take half the family "points" and buy shoes for his wife and one of
> the children. In the third month he can buy shoes for the other child, and thus the whole
> family will have shoes by winter. (Knesset Proceedings, vol. 6, p. 2428, February 2, 1950)

As shoes of full leather required about fifty points, while sandals required only twenty-
five, more and more Israelis decided to wear sandals.

No wonder that the so-called Biblical Sandals became the most popular model. The
small quantity of leather required for their manufacture and their uncomplicated design
made their production simple, keeping their price low. The Biblical Sandals became so normative in Israel in the 1950s that they became an authenticating mark of the "real" *sabra*,
so much so that anyone who wished to appear like one felt impelled to put them on.

Figure 10.3   Rosie and Sam Cohen converted into "real sabras."
Caricaturist: Fridel Stern, 1958.

The caricaturist Friedl Stern drew humorous illustrations of the Israelization process whereby an American couple, Rosie and Sam Cohen, turned into *sabras* (see Figure 10.3), their transformation marked by a change of costume: they are wearing shorts and Biblical Sandals (Stern 1958).

This basic dress code institutionalized by the *tsena* austerity regime helped in creating a social melting pot, in which differences of origin and social status were blurred by the simple outfit of sandals and khaki clothes.

AFTERTHOUGHT

In her book, *The Chosen Body,* Meira Weiss argues that, although the fashion and lifestyles of today's individualistic society in Israel reflect to a large extent the global patterns of consumption, Israeli society still sees negative connotations with regard to individualism, while the notion of collectivism is perceived as positive (Weiss 2002, 19). I suggest that this attitude reflects the residue of the much-admired ethos of its now mythologized founders. For a short period of time it seemed as if socialist theories and government policy could indeed create full economic and class equality. However, in hindsight we realize that it was a superficial equality that could not endure. In the early 1950s, while the young state was struggling to survive, it was *bon ton* to wear khaki clothing and Biblical Sandals, but as the economic situation improved, the ideal of equality started to wear thin and finally collapsed in the aftermath of the 1967 war. From that moment on, the naïve Israeli who believed in equality and socialism gradually became a member of an increasingly capitalist society where one can express nostalgia for the idealistic *chalutzim,* yet where personal achievements are largely measured by financial success and the labels of designer clothes and footwear.

NOTES

1. This song is found on http://www.shiron.net/songView.aspx?song_id=6517&singer_id=8841& song_title=181f0.
2. From the Hebrew *Khug,* meaning a social circle.

BIBLIOGRAPHY

Agnon, S[hmuel] Y[osef]. 1979. *The day before yesterday* [in Hebrew]. Jerusalem: Shoken Publishers.

Almog, Oz. 2001. *The sabra—A profile* [in Hebrew]. Tel-Aviv: Am Oved Publishers. Also available in English as *The Sabra: The Creation of the New Jew,* trans. 2000 Haim Watzman. Berkeley: University of California Press.

Alterman, Natan. 1948. "The silver platter." In *The seventh column* [in Hebrew], 366–67. Tel-Aviv, Am Oved Publishers.

Davis, Fred. 1992. *Fashion, culture and identity.* Chicago: University of Chicago Press.

Elon, Amos. 1972. *The Israelis: Founders and sons.* Jerusalem: Shoken Publishers.

Knesset Proceedings [in Hebrew]. Available at http://www.knesset.gov.il. Accessed November 7, 2006.

Milstein, Uri, ed. 1985. *Rachel: Poems, letters, writings, biography* [in Hebrew]. Tel-Aviv: Zmora-Bitan.

Miriam (from kibbutz Deganya Aleph). 1981. "In trousers with multicolored stripes." In *Here on the land,* ed. Muky Tzur, Tair Zevulun, and Khanina Porat, 207. Tel Aviv: Hakibbutz Hameukhad and Sifriyat Hapoalim.

Naor, Mordechai. 1991. *The Aliyot book* [in Hebrew]. Tel-Aviv: Massada Publishers.

Rand, Yitzhak. 1981. "Torn shoes." In *Here on the land,* ed. Muky Tzur, Tair Zevulun, and Khanina Porat, 198. Tel Aviv: Hakibbutz Hameukhad and Sifriyat Hapoalim.

Raz, Ayala. 1996. *Changing of styles* [in Hebrew]. Tel-Aviv: Yediot Acharonot.

Segev, Tom. 1984. *1949—The first Israelis* [in Hebrew]. Jerusalem: Domino Press.

Shturman, Atara. 1981. "Like Monks." In *Here on the land,* ed. Muky Tzur, Tair Zevulun, and Khanina Porat, 86. Tel Aviv: Hakibbutz Hameukhad and Sifriyat Hapoalim.

Simmel, George. 1983. *Philosophische Kultur: Über das Abenteuer, die Geschlechter und die Krise der moderne.* Leipzig: Alfred Kröner Verlag.

Stern, Friedel. 1958. *In short—Israel* [in Hebrew]. Tel-Aviv: Hod Publications.

Tabenkin, Yitzhak. 1981. " 'Gideon of Deganya' was the Son of the Entire Country." in *Here on the land,* ed. Muky Tzur, Tair Zevulun, and Khanina Porat, 80. Tel Aviv: Hakibbutz Hameukhad and Sifriyat Hapoalim.

Weiss, Meira. 2002. *The chosen body.* Stanford, CA: Stanford University Press.

Zaid, Alexander. 1981. "Barefoot from Jerusalem to Jaffa." and "They sewed trousers for all the girls." In *Here on the land,* ed. Muky Tzur, Tair Zevulun, and Khanina Porat, 86. Tel Aviv: Hakibbutz Hameukhad and Sifriyat Hapoalim.

PART IV: THEATRE, ART, AND FILM

11 THE FETISHIST'S SHOE

"POEMS OF PEDAL ATROCITY": SEXUALITY, ETHNICITY, AND RELIGION IN THE ART OF BRUNO SCHULZ

ANDREW INGALL

Bruno Schulz (1892–1942) is one of Poland's most celebrated modern writers. Since the translation and publication of his stories into the English language, Schulz has been redis-covered by new generations of international authors (David Grossman, Cynthia Ozick, Philip Roth), filmmakers (The Quay Brothers), theater makers (Theatre de Complicité, Double Edge Theatre), and readers.[1]

Schulz is renowned not only for phantasmagorical stories based on his Jewish childhood, but also visual art saturated with fetishistic masochism. In numerous paintings, drawings, prints, and prose Schulz depicts shoes and feet as objects of beauty, power, and oppression. In another body of work exploring Jewish motifs, which appears to be thematically un-related, Schulz idealizes the intimate, all-male milieu of Hassidim who converse, study, and observe holidays. Schulz's graphic series *Encounter* unites two seemingly disparate motifs of erotic fantasy and religious tradition in a creative expression reflecting a modern artist's need to synthesize sexual, religious, and ethnic identities.

Schulz was born in the provincial Galician town of Drohobycz in the Austro-Hungarian Empire, a region rich in linguistic and ethnic diversity. Multicultural Galicia had approxi-mately eight million inhabitants at the turn of the century: 45 percent Polish, 43 per-cent Ruthenian (Ukrainian), and 11 percent Jewish. In 1939, just prior to the Holocaust, Drohobycz's Jewish population, a community representing a wide spectrum of accultura-tion and religious practice, would peak at 40 percent, totaling 15,000. Bruno was the youngest son of Jakub Schulz, a textile merchant who encouraged his son's early artistic development. After completing gymnasium, Schulz entered the architecture program at LVOV (Lemberg) Polytechnical College. However, the outbreak of World War I and a bout of illness interrupted his studies. During the war Schulz concentrated on improving his drawing and painting skills with support from *Kalleia* (Beautiful Things), a local art society whose membership consisted mainly of Jewish artists and intellectuals. The fruits of Schulz's labor resulted in *The Book of Idolatry* (1920–1922, republished 1988), an erotic cycle of graphics comparable in subversiveness to the work of Francisco Goya and in deca-dence to that of Félicien Rops.[2] He employed *cliché verre,* a nineteenth-century technique in which etched glass serves as a photographic negative to produce multiple prints.

Numerous images from *The Book of Idolatry* feature monstrous, dwarfish men crouching and gazing at women's shoes and feet. In *Beasts* a woman wearing a slip holds a whip between her naked legs, poised to lash her demented lover should he dare fondle her shoe (Figure 11.1). Similarly, in "The Age of Genius," a short story in his 1937 autobiographical collection *Sanatorium under the Sign of the Hourglass,* Schulz introduces Shloma, a 40-year-old brute who could easily stand in for the lascivious male beast depicted in *The Book of Idolatry.* Shloma, recently released from prison, enjoys a stroll through the streets of a Central European town that approximates Schulz's native Drohobycz. Spying Shloma from the window, a young boy named Joseph (Schulz's youthful alter ego) invites the ex-con up to see his drawings. In a chest of drawers Shloma catches sight of a pair of high-heeled shoes belonging to the household servant Adela (Schulz 1978, 15–26).

> And lifting up with awe Adela's slim shoe, he spoke as if seduced by the lustrous eloquence of that empty shell of patent leather: Do you understand that horrible cynicism of this symbol on a woman's foot, the provocation of her licentious walk on such elaborate heels? How can I leave you under the sway of that symbol? God forbid that I should do it. . . . (Schulz 1978, 25)

With nimble fingers, Shloma stuffs Adela's shoes and other belongings into his pocket and exits the door, leaving Joseph bewildered.

Adela, a dominatrix-domestic who wields tremendous power in Schulz's fictional household, reappears in the story "Treatise on Tailors' Dummies, or the Second Book of Genesis,"

Figure 11.1   *Beasts* (1920–1922), cliché-verre, 22.3 × 17 cm. Adam Mickiewicz Museum of Literature, ML. Bibl. II 14606/5. Courtesy of the Estate of Bruno Schulz.

an erotic reinvention of the golem myth (Schulz 1977, 59–63). Joseph describes a scene in which his father Jakub, a textile merchant with a deluded sense of grandeur, lectures Adela and his seamstresses Polda and Pauline on mankind's need to reclaim creativity from God and pronounces his desire to create man a second time in the form of a tailor's mannequin.

Fatigued by Jakub's oration, Adela and the seamstresses silence and disempower the master of the house with a simple gesture:

> Adela looked at her wristwatch and exchanged a knowing look with Polda. She then moved her chair forward and, without getting up from it lifted her dress to reveal her foot tightly covered in black silk, and then stretched it out stiffly like a serpent's head. (Schulz 1977, 62–63)

Embarrassed and humbled, Jakub stops in mid-speech, casts his eyes to the ground, and falls to his knees like an automaton.

The two women strolling in *The Enchanted City II* (Figure 11.2), another print from *The Book of Idolatry*, also have the power and charm to transform men into beasts and bring them to their knees. Wearing crisscrossed ankle-strap pumps, the ladies keep five men in check with a whip cradled in their hands. On the left, Schulz portrays his own likeness as a half-man, half-animal restrained by a studded neck collar. He crawls on all fours, looks up at his mistresses, and appears to beg for domestication. On the right, Schulz appears again

Figure 11.2   *The Enchanted City II* (1920–1922), cliché-verre, 16.3 × 22.1 cm. Adam Mickiewicz Museum of Literature, ML. E. 903/1. Courtesy of the Estate of Bruno Schulz.

in fetal position, staring at a pair of exquisite shoes. With noses turned up and eyes averted, the haughty women appear indifferent to their coterie of idol worshippers.

Several years after completing *The Book of Idolatry,* Schulz secured employment as a full-time drawing teacher at a Drohobycz gymnasium. According to biographer Jerzy Ficowski, Schulz's curious students happened to come across their mentor's erotic prints. When asked about them, the anxious art professor replied falsely that the prints were illustrations to *Venus in Furs,* the Galician writer Leopold von Sacher-Masoch's erotic novel. Although Schulz avoided direct discussions of masochistic themes in his work, his contemporaries were eager to offer their insights. His friend and colleague, writer and artist Stanislaw Ignacy Witkiewicz, interpreted Schulz's interest in shoes and feet as a tool for self-abasement. In a 1935 introduction to an interview with Schulz, Witkiewicz explains "To him, the instrument of oppression is the leg.... It is with their legs that Schulz's women tease, trample, drive to sullen, helpless madness his dwarfish men-freaks, cowed as they are by erotic torture, degraded and finding supreme painful relish in their degradation. His graphics are poems of pedal atrocity" (Ficowski 1988, 109).

Witkiewicz's concept of Schulz's fetishistic and masochistic tendencies reflects commonly held medical viewpoints during the early twentieth century. In *Psychopathia Sexualis* (1890), the classic collection of "medico-forensic" studies on deviant sexual behavior, psychiatrist Richard von Krafft-Ebing coined the term masochism based on the literature of Sacher-Masoch. Krafft-Ebing defined it as a perversion "in which the individual affected, in sexual feeling and thought, is controlled by the idea of being completely and unconditionally subject to the will of a person of the opposite sex; of being treated by this person as by a master, humiliated and abused" (von Krafft-Ebing 1922, 131).

Krafft-Ebing believed that practically all shoe fetishists are masochists. To the masochist-fetishist, shoes symbolize the desire to be trod upon and function as necessary props for sexual arousal. A century later Gilles Deleuze took the study of masochism beyond the psychiatric clinic and returned it to its philosophical and literary sources. In his essay *Coldness and Cruelty,* Deleuze suggests that, although the masochist suffers abuse, he is not merely a passive participant in his relationships. He derives pleasure from his ability to transform a compassionate partner into someone cold and callous. Thus, for example, in Sacher-Masoch's *Venus in Furs,* the protagonist Severin von Kusiemski is by no means a victim. By negotiating and executing a contract with his lover Wanda, Severin is an active participant in a relationship that he is the one to ultimately dissolve (Deleuze 1991, 75).

While scholars and critics recognize the influence of Sacher-Masoch's erotica on Schulz, none acknowledge the possible resonance of Sacher-Masoch's more obscure body of work: Jewish folktales. Like his late nineteenth-century contemporaries Karl Emil Franzos and Leopold Kompert, the non-Jewish author Sacher-Masoch wrote *Ghettogeschichten,* stories characterized by nostalgia, sympathy, and criticism toward traditional Eastern European Jewry.[3] While on the one hand *Ghettogeschichten* writers wanted to humanize religious Jews, they simultaneously disparaged their parochialism. Staying true to his erotic inclinations, Sacher-Masoch imbues his *Ghettogeschichten* with sensual touches. He emphasizes the romantic lives of Eastern European Jewish women whom he portrays as domineering and exotic *belles juives*. Historian David Biale argues that Sacher-Masoch was a "philosemite in furs," a writer who attempted to portray Jews in all aspects of their humanity, including their sexuality (Biale 1982, 318).

Like Sacher-Masoch, Schulz used Jewish themes as a vehicle for his erotic fantasies. *Temptresses and Boys from the Talmudic School* (Figure 11.3) is a pencil drawing first published in the short-lived Jewish journal *Cusztajer,* whose title is based on a Yiddish word *tsushtayer,* meaning "contribution," in Polish transliteration. Like much of Schulz's oeuvre, the original is lost. *Temptresses and Boys* echoes masochistic themes in *The Book of Idolatry* but reverses gender roles. The gnome-like foot fetishists that appear in *The Book of Idolatry* are absent. The center of the composition, usually occupied in the *Encounter* series by seductive women, features two young Hassidic males. Walking shoulder to shoulder, the androgynous pair appears to be engaged in an intimate conversation, completely unaware of two scantily clad women exposing their long legs and pointed shoes.

The Hassidic men in *Temptresses* reflect what Talmud scholar Daniel Boyarin calls "rabbinic homosociality," a gentle, all-male culture in which the boundaries between the social and the sexual are blurry (Boyarin 1997, 133). The delicate yeshiva boys in *Temptresses* may stand in for Schulz who, despite his minimal religious practice, had affinities for a

Figure 11.3   *Encounter: Temptresses and Boys from the Talmudic School* (c. 1920), pencil on paper. Original lost. Courtesy of the Estate of Bruno Schulz.

religious world in which men were free from traditional sexual and gender roles practiced by non-Jews.

The most famous work from the *Encounter* series is Schulz's one extant oil painting from 1920 (Figure 11.4). In this version of a Drohobycz street scene, a slightly bowed Hassid in a long, black caftan lowers his face toward the high-heeled shoes of two fashionable flappers. His eyes look up shyly to meet the gaze of one *flaneuse* while the other woman turns to stare at the viewer. The ladies in this painting, compared with females depicted in *The Book of Idolatry* and *Temptresses,* appear less contemptuous and more accessible to male attentions. Unlike the sideshow freaks in *The Book of Idolatry,* the Jewish man in the painting is tall, dignified, and, like the yeshiva boys in *Temptresses,* decidedly androgynous.

In another version of *Encounter,* this one a pencil drawing, Schulz replaces the young Hassid with his own self-portrait. Wearing a long overcoat, Schulz appears anxious. His posture is bent slightly and his arm is raised in a protective gesture. Unlike the Hassid from the painting, Schulz's head in this drawing is turned up looking directly at the women. Schulz introduces another male figure on the lower right, whom Ficowski identifies as Stanislaw Weingarten, a friend of the artist and one-time owner of the painting *Encounter,* until the Nazis looted his art collection. The most notable aspect of this *Encounter* drawing is its Cubist cityscape. Schulz's transformation of the alleys and buildings of Drohobycz

Figure 11.4   *Encounter: A Young Jew and Two Women in an Alley* (1920), oil on cardboard, 53 × 70 cm. Adam Mickiewicz Museum of Literature, ML. K. 1420. Courtesy of the Estate of Bruno Schulz.

Figure 11.5 *Encounter* (c. 1920), pencil on paper, 39.5 × 58.5 cm. Lviv Museum of Art, G-V-345. Courtesy of the Estate of Bruno Schulz.

into modern geometric forms is perhaps a desire to break free from provincial life. In reality, Schulz's depression, anxiety, poverty, and familial responsibilities prevented him from living a cosmopolitan life outside of provincial Drohobycz (Figure 11. 5).

Like Sacher-Masoch and other *Ghettogeschichten* writers of the previous generation, Schulz expressed a tension between romantic and critical views of traditional Judaism. Schulz came from a moderately observant family who attended synagogue in Drohobycz. "Closer to secular literature than to the Hebrew scriptures, the family was more connected with the abacus of the store than the menorah of the synagogue" (Ficowski 2003, 35). However, Schulz never cut himself off from organized religion, and although his social milieu consisted of secular Jews, he attended Yom Kippur services regularly. Schulz's visual art and literature alternate between reverence and rebellion. He produced numerous sketches of Hassidic men, including an illustration (Figure 11.6) for the story *Night of the Great Season,* in which Schulz describes Jews in tall fur hats as "distinguished and solemn men, stroking their long well-groomed beards and holding sober and diplomatic discourse" (Schulz 1977, 135).

On November 19, 1942, a Gestapo officer shot Schulz on the street of the Drohobycz ghetto. During his brief life Schulz boldly experimented with sexual and religious expression in visual art and literature. Schulz describes his father in the story *Treatise on Tailors' Dummies* as a "heresiarch," a term that Ficowski and other scholars have applied to Schulz himself, an artist who departs from established beliefs or standards. His *Book of Idolatry*

Figure 11.6   The Hassidim/town elders, members of the Sanhedrin. Illustration for *Night of the Great Season* (before 1934), India ink on paper, 16 × 24 cm. Adam Mickiewicz Museum of Literature, ML. K. 216. Courtesy of the Estate of Bruno Schulz.

transgresses the second commandment prohibitions, both in terms of creating graven images and worshipping the false idols of women, shoes, and feet. At the same time Schulz's literature and visual art are equally reverent toward religious Jewish subjects, including the noble, gentle Hassidic men depicted in the *Encounter* series.

The shoe provides a locus for Schulz's fascination with traditional Judaism and fetishistic masochism. According to Sigmund Freud's theories of foot fetishism, the shoe substitutes for the woman's missing penis and functions as a man's talisman against castration (Freud 1961, 152–57). In her study of fetish and fashion, cultural historian Valerie Steele notes that the shoe, with its phallic heel/toe and orific insole, functions as weapons and wounds for sexual pleasure (Steele 1996, 101). The shoe, like the traditional all-male milieu of traditional Judaism, is an expression of fluid gender and sexuality. Androgynous yeshiva boys, high-heeled dominatrices, and their adoring worshippers converge in Schulz's inner fantasies and artistic actualities.

NOTES

1. In 1977 Celina Wieniewska's translation of *The Street of Crocodiles* appeared in the series *Writers from the Other Europe* (Philip Roth, general editor). She also translated the second and final work of Bruno Schulz, *Sanatorium under the Sign of the Hourglass*.

2. Erotic depictions of shoes and feet appear in Goya's "Bien tirada està" from *Los Caprichos* (1796–1797) and in Rops's *Pornokrates* (1878).

3. Collections in English translation include *Jewish Life: Tales from Nineteenth-Century Europe* and *A Light for Others and Other Jewish Tales from Galicia.*

BIBLIOGRAPHY

Biale, David. 1982. "Masochism and philosemitism: The strange case of Leopold von Sacher-Masoch." *Journal of Contemporary History* 17: 205–323.

Boyarin, Daniel. 1997. *Unheroic conduct: The rise of heterosexuality and the invention of the Jewish man.* Berkeley: University of California Press.

Deleuze, Gilles. 1991. *Masochism.* New York: Zone Books.

Drawings of Bruno Schulz. 1990. Jerusalem: The Israel Museum.

Ficowski, Jerzy, ed. 1988. *Letters and drawings of Bruno Schulz.* New York: Harper & Row.

Ficowski, Jerzy. 2003. *Regions of the great heresy and environs.* New York and London: W. W. Norton.

Freud, Sigmund. 1961. "Fetishism." In *The standard edition of the complete works of Sigmund Freud,* ed. James Strachey. Vol. 11, 152–57. London: Hogarth Press.

Krafft-Ebing, Richard von. 1922. *Psychopathia sexualis.* New York: Rebman Company.

Sacher-Masoch, Leopold von. 1994. *A light for others and other Jewish tales from Galicia.* Riverside: Ariadne Press.

Schulz, Bruno. 1977. *The street of crocodiles.* New York: Penguin Books.

Schulz, Bruno. 1978. *Sanatorium under the sign of the hourglass.* Boston and New York: Mariner Books.

Schulz, Bruno. 1988. *The book of idolatry.* Warsaw: Interpress Publishers.

Steele, Valerie. 1996. *Fetish: Fashion, sex and power.* New York and Oxford: Oxford University Press.

12   THE ARTIST'S SHOE
DIGGING INTO THE JEWISH ROOTS OF SHOE-FIELD

SONYA RAPOPORT

"Digging Into the Jewish Roots of Shoe-Field" is my reflection as a Jewish artist upon my ongoing artwork entitled *Shoe-Field*. This article is an assessment of what I consider to be the underlying Jewish roots that may have motivated me to create the many phases of my artwork about shoes. This project spanned sixteen years, included five interactive installations, produced four artists' books, and is still going strong. The Jewish roots that were exposed by digging into the roots of my shoe experiences and extending the shoe experiences to others confirm my conviction that my being Jewish influenced the work.

In keeping with the Jewish tradition of giving, participants received a personalized shoe-psyche reading after engaging in the interactive art events. Jew-psyche readings are used in the headings.

JEW-PSYCHE READING: *MISCHPOCHE*/FAMILY BONDS ARE DRAWN IN MUTUAL TRUST AND SUPPORT

I was nurtured in a footwear environment. Shoes were in my genes. Dad was in the shoe fabric business in Boston. The shoe business in itself formed a Jewish community. Instead of leather, fabric substituted for lining in women's shoes. Then it became fashionable for fabric to be used as the outer shell. Later, Dad introduced Lucite. It was a hot item. When he came home from work, he was usually carrying boxes of sample shoes to show the family and for me to try on. Fortunately they were my size. Lively discussions ensued while I self-consciously paraded in my new footwear across the living room floor. Each family member vociferously and critically analyzed the shoe on view. We focused mostly on the covering because Dad was responsible for that part of the shoe. Invariably we slipped in other remarks.

JEW-PSYCHE READING: *GALUT*/THE EXCHANGE OF CULTURAL CODES STIMULATES EXTENSIONS TO UNEXPECTED AREAS

Many years elapsed and my arcane shoe gene remained embedded in my soul/sole. In 1978, during my collaboration with archaeologist Dr Dorothy Washburn[1] at the University of California in Berkeley, I came upon an image of a ceramic foot effigy from a southwestern gravesite. It was wearing a displaced sandal style of Mexican origin, unique to its area of discovery. This find validated the historical conjecture that early trade relations between the United States and Mexico existed circa 1000 c.e. I immediately expanded my artwork to include American Indian sandal styles that were worn during the period of our study from 450 to 1350 c.e.

JEW-PSYCHE READING: *IN MITN DERINEN*/AN EGOISTIC SENSE OF SELF SHOWS ITSELF

I began to think about my own shoes and listed the forty-one pairs of shoes that remained in my closet. In preparation for computer analysis, the shoes were categorized by a system similar to that of Dr. Washburn for identifying American Indian pottery designs. The material for input data consisted of how my shoes were obtained, where and when acquired, how used, what color, and my shoe preference. The computer output, printed on continuous archival computer forms, overlaid with typed text, transferred xerox images, and drawings became the final art product.[2] I labeled the drawings of the shoes with their corresponding computer coded numbers. Viewers were able to correlate the shoe data embedded in the printout diagrams with the image of the actual shoe. I learned that I preferred red shoes and that my shoe collection was mostly acquired from gifts, naturally.

JEW-PSYCHE READING: *CHUTZPA*/A COMPETITIVE DRIVE CAN NURTURE INNOVATION

By satirizing the over-application of computer technology with a concept as quirky as one's choice of shoes, I began to probe into other people's feelings about their shoes. In 1982, I presented my first audience participation-performance. The following press report was released March 31, 1982, in *The Berkeley Gazette:*[3]

> On April 2 from 5:30 to 7:30 P.M. artist Sonya Rapoport will produce the audience participation-performance, *A Shoe-In,* at Berkeley Computer Systems. In conjunction with the event, the store window will display a computerized study of forty-one pairs of Rapoport's shoes along with the actual shoes involved in the study. An accompanying artwork, also expressed on computer output, describes Native American sandals from the ancient southwest.

Upon entry to the computer store, people put their best foot forward as Uri, the Israeli proprietor, handed out ticket numbers. The number was later used in the computer program to identify the shoe wearer. Seventy-six people of similar curiosity, and their shoes, stood in line to participate in what was then, in 1982, considered to be an unusual art event. Many engaged in conversation while they waited to take their first interactive step by reclining on a red leather cushion. The cushion was secured to the seat of a stool that resembled a small camel, a product of Israel. Participants were to select a setting in which their shoes were to be photographed.[4] A blue velvet pillow, an antique cobbler stand, and a plywood platform were the options upon which to rest at least one shoed foot.

During the instant photo session participants were asked to declare why they wore those shoes to that particular event on that rainy April evening. Recorded on audiotape were their responses, such as "To pass as a bureaucrat, I wear my tips," spoken by number 95. Number 48 replied, "I feel more macho…pointed toes to get into the stirrups. It's insertion, masculine."[5] The attendees completed their interaction by answering shoe questions to the shoe data collector, who was seated at a computer. Where the participants lived, where they purchased their shoes and why, and lastly, how they liked their shoes were entered with other qualitative shoe information.

JEW-PSYCHE READING: *GEMATRIA*/NUMERICAL ANALYSIS REVEALS SOCIOLOGICAL INSIGHTS

The influence that the participants had upon each other in their choices was indicated in the graphic output of the "force-field" computer program (Figure 12.1). Interpreted as a social field, people's interpersonal attractions and repulsions can be discerned in the plot's imprint by the specific graphic characters that were used and their spatial distances from each other.[6] The influence was most evident in the choice of where the shoe would reside for the photo shoot and, to a degree, the answers to shoe questions. While waiting to participate in each phase of the event, those persons near each other were shown in the

Figure 12.1   Shoe-Field Plot. A force-field plot derived from data calculation of seventy-six people's shoes. Photographer: Marie-José Sat.

plot to make similar selections. To quantify the qualitative data that were necessary for generating the force-field plot, a hierarchy of numerical values was created according to the extent of the individual's shoe participation, and an arbitrary evaluation was made of the given shoe information. Choice of footrest, position on the stool, and whether the right or left foot was extended for the photograph were factors that were calculated by simple addition and division. According to the numerical difference from the norm, five energy charge values were established. The charges were minus two, the least active; minus one; zero, the average; plus one; and plus two, the most active. A charge value was assigned to each participant. This number and the visitor's entry number into the gallery were the figures used in the computer computation to generate the force-field plot, *Shoe-Field,* by which the social interaction among the seventy-six people who participated in *A Shoe-In* could be determined.

JEW-PSYCHE READING: *CHOCKEM*/SERENDIPITY AWAKENS PRACTICALITY

Soon, thereafter I was invited to exhibit[7] a computer-assisted artwork at Foot Hill College in Los Altos Hills, California. There was no doubt that I would show the *Shoe-Field* plot to commemorate the college's name. For the exhibition the plot that had been originally printed on three continuous sheets (11 × 14 inches) of computer forms was photographically enlarged to 17' high × 6' wide. The shoe wearer's identities were represented by tildes, which were located in the center of each of five vertical columns in a sixteen-row grid. The array of coded ASCII characters that surrounded each tilde revealed the intensity of the participants' shoe feelings. The plot was ready for exhibition after transparencies of the Polaroid shoe photos taken at the onset of *A Shoe-In* were mounted directly on their associated tildes. A lone tilde, barren of an applied shoe transparency, was an indication that its owner was a less interactive person. The lack of photo participation would lessen the intensity of the energy's charge value.

JEW-PSYCHE READING: *ALEVAI*/PARSING THE WHOLE INTO ITS COMPONENTS ALLOWS FOR GREATER HUMAN UNDERSTANDING

The Shoe-Field map is an interactive plot in which the characters, that is, letters and numbers in the space surrounding each tilde/person comprise a unique configuration that is based on an influence from the charges of its neighboring tildes. Although the resultant interactive factors produced an attractive and meaningful graphic plot (see Figure 12.1), the single individual charge of each tilde/person remained undefined. To describe the noninteractive individual charge, the shoe-field plot was decoded into noninteractive single plots. The individual field plots that resulted from the parsing depict a graphic representation of each participant's individual shoe-psyche reading.

The *Shoe-Field* Exhibition Press Release (Figure 12.2):

> From 7 October through 1 November 1986 at the Media Gallery in San Francisco, Sonya Rapoport will present an installation of a floor show in "real time" interactivity.

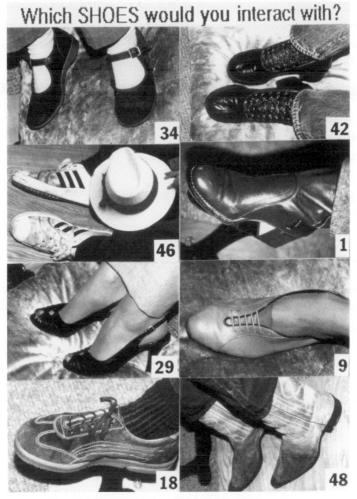

Figure 12.2   Shoe-Field Installation. Installation view.
Photographer: Marion Gray.

Participants will humanize the interactive shoe-field plot by reversing the procedure by which it had been originally computer generated. The *Shoe-Field* plot will be virtually decoded by the process of walking, talking, taking off and positioning shoes, and selecting shoe partners. Upon entrance to the site the visitors "tell" the computer about their shoes. The information will determine their shoe charge value. A hard copy of the charge's graphical representation, a shoe-psyche printout, is given to the participants. With this shoe-psyche reading in hand they will set out to find its matching mate, i.e. a pattern on one of the five field plots printed on floor tiles. There the participants will "take their stand." Covered with two-foot square black Sintra tiles the floor[8] "resembles a huge checkerboard or the set of a mythical TV game show."[9] The tiles are imprinted in white silk-screened characters that depict the individual non-interactive plots, i.e. the plots derived from decoding the large interactive *Shoe-Field* plot. The latter will be on view, stretched out upon a large wooden ramp near the entrance. Installed in the interactive area are "gossip" columns which are color-coded blueprints of the large *Shoe-Field* plot that have been wrapped around the building's structural pillars. The computer characters in the "gossip" columns have sketched over in Prisma[10] colors ranging from hot red to cool blue. The differentiation by color allows viewers to discern at a glance the shoe/social intensity of those who had participated in the former event *A Shoe-In*.

JEW-PSYCHE READING: *MEGILLA*/TENSIONS ARE RESTRAINED AND RELEASED DURING RITUAL EXPERIENCE

Sharon Simburg relates[11] her shoe participation experience in the *Shoe-Field* interactive installation of 1986:

> Computers freak me out. They confuse me and upset me. I feel I'm being controlled, manipulated, dehumanized and digitized. I feel like Alice looking at this monster Shoe-Field printout threatening to roll down on me. But at Sonya Rapoport's installation it was different. The computer was humanized. It's about people. It was fun. I came in sort of nervous, especially when I was told I had to take my shoes off. I placed them on a shoe rack. In return I was given for what was supposed to be our claim check, a black plastic gold embossed shoehorn with a shoelace through its hole to put around my neck. I started to wonder if I'd ever see my shoes again. Then I noticed people putting on those plastic foot bags. While donning mine I came to realize that I was preparing for some kind of ritual. With all those shoes lying around I began to feel like everyone was in mourning. Soon I was seated before the computer oracle where I punched in answers to shoe questions: how long have I had my shoes; why did I purchase them. This question provided possible responses to choose from: needed them, price, gift, comfort and finally how much did I like them. I was tense, waiting to see what the computer would reveal about my responses and the comparison to the average score. Out from the printer popped my "shoe-psyche" pattern. It looked to me like a podiatric Rorschach blot, only it had to do with my feet instead of my head. To be certain that the computer was diagnosing my personal psyche, the output confirmed my identity number, gave me a shoe charge of plus two and written directions as where to go next. I retrieved my shoes, was allowed to keep my shoehorn and sauntered among the other visitors into the field of "shoe-psyche" tiles, hoping to discover my future.
>
> Swinging our shoes by their laces we wandered around the floor field on a mystical journey looking for a tile embedded with a matching pattern on which to place them. It was as though the secrets of our shoe-psyches were hidden in the etched symbols of the patterns. I was reminded of the seashore where I would search for exotic seashells buried in the sand. When I found the tile with an image similar to the imprint on my personal

handout I dropped my shoes, aiming into the bull's eye. A photographer took an instant photo of my shoes reposed on their shoe-psyche turf. I was told that my plus two charge is the highest I could get, meaning I was a very interactive person and liked to be at the center of things. I began making my acquaintance with other participants who were also endowed with plus two charges. They were hovering around and dangling their shoes over my special tile. Some pairs were dropped on the spot and kept my shoes company, while others chose to reside in another domain of corresponding energy values. I heard a man and a woman arguing about what their charges meant. Everyone seemed to find their corresponding tile pattern locations where they surrendered their shoes.

There was a popular meeting place that appeared to be near a leaded glass window. It turned out to be a hanging shoe bag divided into transparent pockets. We were to place the shoe photos in the pocket labeled with our shoe charge number. At first everyone looked through the pocket of photos having their own charge. They wanted to see who their shoe colleagues were and to figure out what they had in common. Eventually all the participants dug vigorously into all the pockets to view their contents. Around the corner in the inner sanctum of an Aladdin-like cave was a slide show of the seventy-six pairs of shoes [Figure 12.3] that had participated in the former event, *A Shoe-In*. If I chose a pair of shoes that I would like to interact with, the computer would give me an interactive reading of my individual shoe-psyche pattern. I picked a pair of bright green high-topped women's rain boots. On the way back to the computer oracle I stopped by a "gossip" column. I was eager to find out what the shoes had said about each other in another performance. Back at the computer, the oracle demanded to know not only my own number but also the number of the shoe that I chose from the slide show. I punched in number fifteen. I began to think about my own shoes and that I might never see them again. Then the printer rolled out two patterns that looked like footprints. The pattern from my original input had been altered by a computer computation with the charge number of the sole-mate I had selected from the slide show.

Figure 12.3   Shoes from Mini Bag. Shoes from which reader selects shoes with which to interact. Photographer: Tom Bates.

JEW-PSYCHE READING: *AROYSGEVORFEN*/ENTERPRISE LURKS WITHIN THE FRAMEWORK OF ARTISTIC ENDEAVOR

At the first interactive event, *A Shoe-In,* the participants' thoughtful and playful responses as to why they wore their shoes on that April rainy evening and the pictures of their exotic shoe poses were inducements to create an artists' book for the market. On thirty-two continuous pages of personalized computer order forms I pasted a Polaroid reproduction of the poised shoes with the shoe wearer's responses to "Why I Wear These Shoes." The question became the title of the book and served as an index for future *Shoe-Field* phases. None sold but one was stolen. I discovered that my marketing skills did not measure up to my aesthetic expertise. I received suggestions that the reward of receiving an attractive graphical image was not sufficiently gratifying. I later proffered another entrepreneurial attempt, a T-shirt imprinted with the participants' own charge value. I had no orders.

After the Media Gallery Installation I endeavored to make my next product more marketable. Included in a seven-inch square clear plastic package was an interactive diskette[12] and a seven-page foldout. Directions for the computer procedure, similar to the experience at the Media Gallery, comprised the introductory text:

> *Shoe-Field* is an interactive artwork. It measures people's feelings about their shoes. By answering the shoe questions on the diskette you will get from the printer one of five plot patterns. The pattern that you receive represents your shoe-psyche charge. This charge is a measure of how different your feelings are about your shoes from those of the average person who has participated in previous *Shoe-Field* installations. After receiving the printout of your charge plot you are invited to select from the mini-shoe bag attached to the back page, a pair of shoes that you would like to interact with. By typing in the number of your selection you will receive a second plot, an interactive plot. This pattern looks like two foot prints which can be considered a podiatric Rorschach blot. You will notice a change in the pattern of your first shoe-psyche plot. This change is due to the influence of your shoe "sole-mate," the shoe that you selected from the mini shoe bag. The computer can now give you a shoe-psyche reading. If you want to take this step just type "y" for "yes."

To enhance this enterprise the shoe-psyche graphic pattern was extended to include a shoe psyche-reading text with personal advice. Unknown to the participants, the readings were derived from color tests[13] and were determined by the color of the shoes they selected from the mini shoe bag. An example of the text in a shoe-psyche reading is: "Suffering from pent-up over-stimulation threatens impulsive and impassioned behavior. To gain independence play down 'victimized' role."[14]

Each of the optional five charges was printed on a paper square in the color appropriate to the intensity of the charge: magenta for plus two, red for plus one, yellow for zero, green for minus one, and pale blue for minus two. When the reader answered the questions asked on the diskette the program calculated a shoe energy charge and its corresponding pattern was printed. For the second printing, the shoe charge of the shoes selected from the mini-shoe bag was considered in the calculation. Its influence is seen when the reader's first printed graphic configuration is altered into an interactive configuration in the next printing.

JEW-PSYCHE READING: *TZEDAKA*/GRATIFICATION FROM SHARING BRINGS PEACEFUL FULFILLMENT

My contribution to *Jews and Shoes* is a response to reviewing the work in terms of my Jewishness. I find this an essential factor in creating the artwork. The underlying structure of the artwork is the concept of a social field, derived metaphorically from a computer program that generates field forces or "vectors." The interpretation of the output is oriented toward evaluating sociability according to positive (attracting) or negative (repelling) quality or "valence." The attitudes that people have toward their own shoes is the key to determining the shoe wearers' sociability.

Force fields are seen in many areas of science. For instance, ocean tides are caused principally by the gravitational fields of the moon and sun pulling on the waters of the earth's oceans. The ocean waters are being affected by these attractive gravitational force fields. In the area of social science is found the concept of interpersonal "field." The field, field force, or vector allows the assignment of a numeric value with entities not usually considered quantitative in nature.[15]

Assigning a numeric value to quantitative feelings about shoes engages a spectrum of social dimensions such as being Jewish.

NOTES

1. Dr Dorothy Washburn, Miller Fellow at the University of California at Berkeley, traced the migration of Native American tribes for her research project (1977). Her methodology involved evaluating the changes in design patterns that she found on pottery shards from ancient archaeological sites. When the Indian tribes had been forced to move and settle with other American Indian tribes, their pottery designs reflected the merger. At first they were complex, but eventually they became more simplified. As the Native American population migrated throughout the United States, the cycle of changing painted design inscription was continually repeated.

2. The artistically enriched computer output was exhibited in 1979 at the Donnell Library Center of the New York Public Library and at the Truman Gallery, New York City.

3. *The Berkeley Gazette* is a daily newspaper published in Berkeley, California.

4. The crew of helpers consisted of Tom Bates, photographer, Eric Wickner, database consultant, and David Rapoport and Scott Morris, computer programmers.

5. Inter-media editor Stephen Moore selected and published the examples of shoe comments in *Boxcar—A Magazine of the Arts* (1983).

6. For example, if a tilde carries a charge value of +1 it will be surrounded by more space and contain more negative characters if its neighbor carries a −2 charge than if another +1 charge tilde has a +2 neighbor. The resultant characters surrounding the latter tilde will contain more positive intensity and the characters will be clustered more closely to each other.

7. Exhibition for CADRE Institute (Computers for Art, Design, Research and Education), San Jose State University (1982). The plot was also exhibited in *Future Histories: The Impact of Changing Technologies* at the Anderson Gallery, Virginia Commonwealth University, Richmond, Virginia (1984) and in *Revealing Conversations* at the Richmond Art Center, Richmond, California (1989).

8. The tiles were exhibited at the Whitney Biennial 2006. At Media Gallery the tiles covered an area of 28 × 16 feet.

9. The quote is from Christine Tamblyn's review of the exhibition for *ARTWEEK* (1986, October 25).

10. A brand of a permanent pencil color crayon.

11. The story is from excerpts of the documentary video of the interactive installation.

12. A diskette was available for participants to answer shoe questions on a computer. According to the shoe answers, the participant was given a printout of one of five graphic plots that represented their charge value, an indication of their attitude about shoes.

13. The Luscher Color Test that reveals your personality through color choice, based on the original German text by Dr. Max Luscher, translated by Ian Scott. Published by Pocket Psych.

14. Ibid., p. 14.

15. This is Scott Morris's explanation of force fields.

BIBLIOGRAPHY

ARTWEEK, West Coast Newsletter. 1986, October 25.

Boxcar—A Magazine of the Arts. 1983. Los Angeles.

Luscher, Max. 1948. *The Luscher Color Test,* trans. Ian Scott. New York: Pocket Books.

Washburn, Dorothy Koster. 1977. *A symmetry analysis of Upper Gila area ceramic design.* Papers of the Peabody Museum of Archeology and Ethnology. Vol. 68. Cambridge, MA: Harvard University.

13 THE THEATRICAL SHOE

THE UTTERANCE OF SHOEMAKING: COBBLERS ON THE ISRAELI STAGE

DORIT YERUSHALMI

Sammy Gronemann's comedy, *King Solomon and Shalmai the Cobbler*, titled in the original German *Der Weise und der Narr; Köenig Salomo und der Schuster*, premiered at the Ohel Theatre in Tel Aviv in 1943. Elegantly translated into Hebrew by poet Nathan Alterman and directed by Moshe Halevy, the theater's founder and artistic director, it was one of Ohel's record successes, running to 300 performances, impressive considering that the total Jewish population in Palestine at the time was below half a million.[1] In 1964 director Shmuel Bunim revived the play at the Tel Aviv Cameri Theatre, restaging it as a musical containing a dozen songs with lyrics by Alterman and music by Sacha Argov. The production, lauded as the first native Israeli musical, was celebrated by critics, and proved an immense box-office hit. By the end of January 1966 it had been performed more than 500 times, with intermittent revivals in 1971 and 1982.[2] In 2005 the Habima Theatre revived the musical, this time directed by Ilan Ronen. It was the hit of the season and, at the time of this chapter, some two years later, is still playing (in repertory) to packed houses.

King Solomon and Shalmai the Cobbler is a unique phenomenon in Israeli theater, a palimpsest that bears the marks of its transformations from the original German text to its conversion into Hebrew, its adaptation into a musical comedy, and its three landmark stage productions, each focusing on a different artistic element, each reflecting a different historical moment, each constructing a unique theatrical text. The play revolves around the idea of deliberately switched identities between an identical-looking king and cobbler, played by the same actor, who embodies four characters: the real king, the real cobbler, the cobbler as a king, and the king as a cobbler. The play's fictional world thus revolves around the very element that stands at the heart of the performative situation: the actor who uses his body as vessel, medium, and arena where the character's image is imprinted and represented.

Michael Bakhtin reminds us that role-playing positions the actor's body as the site of transformation, and life, to use his term, through the interim chronotope of the theater stage (Bakhtin 1981, 84–254). *King Solomon and Shalmai the Cobbler*, which makes structural and thematic use of the theater itself, necessarily raises questions concerning the processes of changed and reconstructed identity, for here the actor plays four characters and their various nuances, revealing the many voices in the human soul, its flexibility, and its ability to undergo change to ensure survival. The role-playing of cobbler and king, which necessitate the trickery and transgression of fake identities, is the basis for many of the comic aspects of the play. The cobbler's low social status licenses the position of the cobbler as the comic figure. The playfulness of the role focuses our attention on the actor, who needs to find the precise physical and vocal expressions for both king and cobbler and extract the full potential embodied in the flexibility of theatrical signals. The acting modus in comedy, typically, is a methodical study of the everyday, demanding that the actor speak to the audience, involve it, and demonstrate through exaggeration the importance of acting in life (States 1995, 22–42).

King Solomon and Shalmai the Cobbler has become part of the Israeli theatrical canon thanks to the cultural richness of Gronemann's original play, its brilliant translation into Hebrew, and its successful transformation into musical comedy. It is rich in motifs embedded in Jewish tradition, bears the influence of the theater culture of Eastern and Central Europe, and encodes humanistic and universal ideas. The fundamental elements of the script are borrowed from folktales and philosophical texts. Typical dramatic characters and connotations associated with the main figure have shaped each director's stage interpretation. In this essay I wish to offer an interpretive reading of *King Solomon and Shalmai the Cobbler* and its productions within a cultural context. I will discuss the influences of various theater traditions on the shaping of the main character, some of its dramatic-theatrical characteristics, and their influence on the stage interpretations given to the play's fictional world.

SAMMY GRONEMANN: BIOGRAPHICAL CONTEXT

Seen within the context of Hebrew drama in prestate Palestine, and in light of his own life story, I consider Sammy (Samuel) Gronemann (1875–1952) as a "cultural cobbler." At the center of his play stands the "little guy" with all his flaws and aspirations, the flip side of the native Hebrew plays of the 1940s, which focused on national and land myths and often placed the Land of Israel as the hero of the drama, with plots demonstrating how to conquer the wilderness, drain the swampland, and make the desert bloom (Levy 1996). Gronemann, son of a pro-Zionist orthodox rabbi in Hanover, was a modern observant Jew, well versed in Jewish and European cultures. A practicing attorney and active Zionist, he served as legal advisor to the Zionist organization and president of the Zionist Congress court. A writer by avocation, he was known as an acerbic humorist, in part owing to his highly successful 1920 novel *Tohuwabohu* (Chaos), in which he satirized German-Jewish contempt for East European Jews, and *Hawdoloh und Zapfenstreich* (1924), which was inspired by his World War I experience on the Eastern Front. Gronemann was a devotee and student of the theater in Germany.

Thus, for example in his 1946 autobiography, *The Memoirs of a Yekke* (German Jew), he offers a dramaturgical interpretation of *The Merchant of Venice,* which he sees as an important lens for issues connected with the so-called Jewish question in the Weimar Republic.[3] Anchored in European dramaturgy, Gronemann also applied himself to the examination

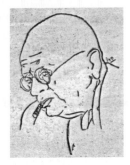

Figure 13.1   Sammy Gronemann, caricature by Hado (*Ma'ariv*, weekend supplement, September 25, 1957, p. 2). Courtesy of the Israeli Documentation Center for the Performing Arts, Tel Aviv University.

of Molière's *The Misanthrope* and Heinrich von Kleist's *The Prince of Hamburg*. He was an enthusiastic fan of Ernst von Wolzogen's *Uberbrettl* cabaret and, on one occasion, even tried his hand at acting. With the rise of Nazism he lost his license to practice law and was expelled from the German writers' union. In 1933 he and his wife moved to Paris, encouraging German Jews to face the gravity of the situation and emigrate to Palestine. They settled in Tel Aviv in 1936. He was 61 years old. Pictures show him as portly, bald, wearing horn-rimmed glasses and a bowtie, and fully armed with cigars (see Figure 13.1).

Gronemann's first encounter with the cultural life of Tel Aviv was at the Matateh, a small satiric theater, where two of his texts were staged, their structural elements (a trial, an examination of identity, actual or virtual doubles) striking a comic-satirical note. The first, *Jacob or Christian,* is about a Jew who hates his Jewish identity.[4] The second, translated into Hebrew by Nathan Alterman, is titled *What's a Gentile Got to Do with Cantoring* and depicts a German Jewish former opera singer, now a cantor, who sings the Yom Kippur liturgy to melodies from the best operas, including Wagner's.[5] Critics enthused about the dramatic structures and the precise molding of characters, eagerly anticipating a Gronemann play written for the big stage. *King Solomon and Shalmai the Cobbler,* originally titled *Der Weise und der Narr* (The Wise Man and the Fool), would be his everlasting gift to the theater of his new homeland.[6]

THE WANDERING TEXT: THE COBBLER AND THE TRADITION OF THE FOOL

Elements of *King Solomon and Shalmai the Cobbler* can be found in two midrashic tales about King Solomon. One, the Talmudic tractate Gittin, recounts that Solomon used the demon Asmodeus to build the Temple, but Asmodeus then overthrew Solomon and put himself on the throne (Gittin 68b). The other source, tractate Kohelet Raba, tells that an angel in the form of Solomon switched places with him and sat on his throne. Solomon then wandered around Jerusalem lamenting that nothing remained of all his wealth and glory but a bowl of groats (Kohelet Raba 2:13). In *King Solomon and Shalmai the Cobbler,* the king is not replaced by either demon or angel, but rather by a proletarian cobbler who shares the lowly status of craftsman in a typical comedy. Gronemann wrote a kind of travesty, which is a comic subgenre whereby a serious work or subject is burlesqued, with grotesque or ludicrous incongruity of style, treatment, or subject matter that reduces the highbrow ideal and abstract, displacing them onto the concreteness of the physical plane.

The plot is suffused with a sense of the carnivalesque, reflecting the European tradition of carnival festivities whose culmination was the mock coronation of a fool as carnival king. It also bears the stamp of the Jewish *Purimshpiel* (Purim play), which was greatly influenced by this tradition and by Gronemann's own Purim play, *Hamans Flucht* (Haman's Curse), written in Germany in 1926.[7] In *Solomon the King and Shalmai the Cobbler,* the cobbler meanders drunkenly through the streets of Jerusalem, pretending to be the king, kindling the ire of the king's men. Learning of the stunning physical resemblance between himself and the cobbler, the king's curiosity is piqued. He commands the cobbler to be brought to the palace and offers to trade places with him. The switch is carried out behind a partition, where the actor exchanges his royal emblems for the cobbler's ragged clothing. In Roman comedic terms Shalmai is a *Bomolocus,* with whom the audience laughs, while Solomon becomes an *Agroyakus,* a serious, humorless character, who speaks in a pretentious manner inviting ridicule. The cobbler manages to take the place of the king and, despite somewhat suspicious faux pas, gains honor as befitting royalty. In contrast, the king finds it difficult to acclimate himself to life among the masses. He tries to convince them that he is indeed Solomon, their king, and becomes a receptacle for the ridicule of the marketplace. In the final scene the cobbler, now tired of his royal role, hides behind a screen, takes out a hammer and an awl from his bag, and briskly fits a shoe with a sole. The clanging of the hammer echoes in the palace, signaling the end of the play.

Some theater critics linked the Gronemann plot to that of Mark Twain's *The Prince and the Pauper,* although Twain's pauper is not a cobbler but a boy reduced to begging for alms. A more relevant equivalent is offered by a fable about a prince and a cobbler told by seventeenth-century English philosopher John Locke (1632–1704) in his milestone essay, *Concerning Human Understanding.* Locke, an empiricist, argued that a human being enters the world as a blank slate, or tabula rasa, and that human knowledge is acquired by experience and interaction. In the fable the prince and the cobbler wake up one day having switched bodies (Locke 1998, 306). The entirety of the memories and impressions imprinted on their consciousness raises such questions as who is the real prince and who is the cobbler? What makes them identical? What defines an individual's identity? Is it what one looks like, or one's consciousness/memory?

The cobbler as an archetype symbolizes more than a craftsman who makes and repairs shoes. In the tales of the Brothers Grimm cobbling is linked to wisdom, understanding, and knowledge.[8] Frequently the cobbler is described as a philosopher, someone who sits in a very small room and mends people's gait, walk, and deportment in life; metaphorically he studies the imprints of life on people's shoes and repairs them as well. Cobbling appears as early as Plato's *Theaetetus,* wherein Socrates directs questions to his pupils regarding knowledge: "Therefore, one who doesn't know won't understand the knowledge of shoes either" (Plato 2004, 21). Somewhat in the same vein there is a famous story about Rabbi Israel Salanter, a leader in the Musar (Ethics) movement. The rabbi noticed a cobbler working late into the night, and when he inquired why he was doing so the industrious cobbler responded, "For as long as the lamp is burning, one must do the repairs" (Jacobs 1984, 232). The rabbi repeated these words throughout his life as a powerful mnemonic to constantly strive for self-improvement. Theological and philosophical interpretations of the cobbler's work stem from the fact that, even though he deals in raw materials and uses crude tools, shoes, the object of his work, intimately intertwine with the wearer's biography, reflecting and radiating the past onto the present. Shoes physically simulate the wearer's movement in space, and his or her life journey. Hidden behind each pair of shoes is the cobbler who made them. Cobbling, then, metaphorically reflects a human being's relationship to the world, and his or her spiritual place therein.

The German title of the play, *The Wise Man and the Fool,* links the cobbler to a long tradition of fools and the confrontation of foolishness and wisdom, as exemplified by Erasmus of Rotterdam's *Moriae Encomium; or, Praise of Folly* (1509/1994). The roots of the conflict between wisdom and foolishness are reflected in the biblical books of Ecclesiastes and Proverbs, both associated with King Solomon. In the Judaeo-Christian tradition foolishness is also an expression of heresy. The intertext of a Jewish cobbler as representing heresy is also found in the medieval legend of Ahasver, the Wandering Jew. He is a man without a country, doomed to wander forever, yet at the same time he symbolizes eternal contact with the physical land, with physical reality, along with a longing for redemption. There is a clear relationship between this figure, whose function, as George Steiner has explained, is to hold a mirror up to the human condition, and the traditional role of the Shakespearean fool.[9] The king's fool, craftsmen, and other characters of inferior status often function in Shakespeare's plays as the rhetorical means for shedding an ironic light on the play's themes. Like them, the cobbler in *King Solomon and Shalmai the Cobbler* holds a mirror up to the king and challenges his traditional supremacy, reminiscent of the opening scene of *Julius Caesar,* wherein shoemaking is described in terms that echo the Socratic idea of the philosopher as healer of the soul, when the cobbler interprets his craft to Flavius: "I am, indeed, sir, a surgeon to old shoes; when they are in great danger, I recover them" (*Julius Caesar,* Act 1).[10]

The cobbler's actions and his props in *King Solomon and Shalmai* strengthen his association with the tradition of the fool. He walks around with a wineskin and, like the king in Falstaff's dreams (*Henry IV*), lowers the price of the wine. More poignantly he commands the ministers to pay homage to the craftsmen, especially to cobblers. A subtle connection can be detected between the jingling of the bells on the traditional fool's costume and the jangling of his tools. The cobbler is a man without a home, who wanders in the town square, where he performs folk theater and stages a parodic "Solomon's trial" wearing a pot on his head. Upon reaching the verdict he swaddles a loaf of bread, cleaves it in two and gives the halves to two members of the king's entourage, who represent the two mothers. When as the cobbler-cum-king he answers the riddles sent by the Queen of Sheba, relating them to body parts, the Queen accepts his answers, not the intellectual solutions offered by the "real" king-cum-cobbler, thus manifesting the paradox of wisdom-within-foolishness.

The king/cobbler juxtaposition provides a network of opposites related to the body and symbolic objects: feet/head, worn-out clothes/purple robes, tools/crown and scepter. As in traditional carnival the cobbler is the trickster; the very fact of his presence reminds us of base and anarchic elements, the subversion that lies within the body.

The wealth and depth of the play lie in its reflexivity of the theater, and in its juxtaposition of a character, that is, the king, who belongs to the classic literary canon and another, the cobbler, who is imported from the town square and popular folk culture. The king and the cobbler complement each other: the cobbler is the motivating force behind the king's playing a new role that touches everyday life, while the king enables the cobbler to experience playing the part in a highly esteemed theatrical space. Crossing the boundary between the palace and the town square, between what is "high" and what is "low," is the arena wherein theater comes into existence. In the "potential space" that the stage provides, institutional legitimacy is granted for being not-yourself, and images and identities can be reexamined.

1943: THE HEBREW TEXT: THE COBBLER AS A FORCE MAJEUR OF THE ACTOR

When Ohel director Moshe Halevy asked poet Nathan Alterman to translate the play, he initiated a series of textual adaptations. Alterman changed the cobbler's name from Shamadai to Shalmai, a shortening of the name Shlomo (Solomon in Hebrew), thereby sharpening both the similarity and the difference between the king and the cobbler. The traditional roots of the character can be seen in the array of expressions that Alterman employed: "Here comes the trickster. Here comes the ruffian cobbler," says the king's minister; the cobbler is called "the shoe-meister," and more than once "fool"; Na'ama, the cobbler's wife, jeeringly calls him "your foolishness." Nufrit, the king's Egyptian wife, says of him, "Yet the Jew is eternal both as riddle and Jew." The cobbler is quick to speak, while King Solomon is skeptical, questioning, considered, and measured, as one in the habit of talking to himself, in contrast to the cobbler, who always needs an audience. The wordplay, the incisive rhyming, the rhythm, the brilliance, and the pithiness of Alterman's Hebrew demanded speaking skills, which in 1943 were beyond the professional abilities of the Ohel actors, according to some critics[11] (see Figure 13.2).

Figure 13.2   Nathan Alterman, caricature by Ze'ev (*Ma'ariv*, weekend supplement, September 25, 1957, p. 2). Courtesy of the Israeli Documentation Center for the Performing Arts, Tel Aviv University.

Halevy's vision was to stage biblical stories, and it appears that this was the reason for his decision to produce the play. Casting Simcha Tsachovel, one of the outstanding actors of the Ohel but not primarily a comic one, in the main role, testified to his desire to emphasize the royal aspect of the tale and the majestic days of the First Temple. The 45-year-old Tsachovel had a bass voice, good diction, chiseled features, and a strong physical presence, yet the critics noted that he was particularly successful at playing the cobbler. They felt that when playing the king he did not project a "classic" image, namely symmetrical and stable, as befitted the image of the "new Jew," who was idealized as muscular, erect, and comely. It seems that the cobbler's grotesque acting style snuck into the king's, thus strengthening the cobbler's presence. Even if not intentional, this subverted the cultural Zionist construct of the "ideal body" and, instead, reflected the body *itself*, its sexuality, its needs, and in particular its lust for life. As can be gleaned from the reviews, Tsachovel succeeded in speaking the comic language of the cobbler, and his acting prompted laughter from the audience. This is significant, for the times offered little to laugh about, as much of the national discourse was devoted to the news of the destruction of European Jewry and debates over rescue efforts. The performance provided a time-out, or safe space, a "theater under fire" that enabled the audience to be entertained and relax within the agonizing historical moment.

1964: THE LOCAL TEXT: THE COBBLER AS PRANKSTER

Director Shmuel Bunim was one of the key forces in the network of cultural agents that shaped Israeli entertainment in the 1950s and 1960s and, before this production, he had already created a popular cultural canon.[12] Bunim chose to stage the play as a musical at the Cameri, a young and highly respected repertory theater, where he served as house director. Although originally written in German, Alterman's much-praised translation and new lyrics earned the play the designation of an original Hebrew Israeli play.[13] The play's adaptation into musical comedy placed the songs at the center of the theatrical experience—in Bunim's words, "It pushed the plot into high gear and thrust the audience from their seats" (Bunim 1994, 142). The musical numbers moved the plot along and reinforced the central love problem involving Na'ama, the cobbler's wife, who is torn between Solomon and Shalmai, who are of course one and the same. The songs also highlighted central motifs, as with the ironic song "The Wise Man and the Fool," sung by the king's courtiers, which reiterated the theme of the difference between wise man and fool, rich and poor. The musical language of Sacha Argov offered a melodic synthesis that fluctuated between West and East, and his imprint on the Hebrew vocal music was immense. Argov was sensitive to words, their significance and innuendo. In composing the melodies he took into consideration the actors' limitations, composing simple, two- to three-minute songs that perfectly suited the words and emphasized the rhyme.

The dances of the chorus drew upon the language of Israeli folk dance. Anna Sokolow, an important American choreographer who had been a student of Martha Graham and had worked with Inbal and other leading Israeli dance companies, did the choreography,

although Bunim stated, "It was I who staged the songs" (Bunim 1994, 146). The choreography, as Bunim recalled, "matched the performance's overall 'intimate' style, which
emphasized the spoken and sung word, rather than visual glamour" (Bunim 1994, 146).
The locality of the text was also manifested in the set, designed by Aryeh Navon. The scenery was purely functional: there were two stationary stages, one on each side, and another
moveable one. Shiny metal props were used to suggest the richness of the palace. The colorful poverty of the marketplace was indicated through torn pieces of fabric, netting, and
scattered props. Critic Yitzchak Avrahami compared this scene to the marketplace in Habima's production of *The Eternal Jew*, writing, "The parallels between the two scenes vividly
elucidate how the Hebrew theatre has come a long way from the pathetic expressionism of
the 1920s to the calculated-yet-rich lightheartedness that it has achieved today" (Avrahami
1964, n.p.). In Bunim's and Navon's artistic modus, the stage itself declared, "I am theater."
(see Figure 13.3).

Bunim cast Illy Gorlitzky, a young graduate of an army entertainment troupe, in the
lead. This decision had far-reaching implications, linking the show to the youth culture
then prevalent in Israel. Gorlitzky was tall, skinny, agile, and light on his feet, with a bob-
bing Adam's apple and smiling, boyish features. In an interview the actor explained how
they worked out the double part: "Our Solomon is only a preparation for Shalmai.... We
concentrated on Shalmai, not because he'll get the laughs and capture the audience, but

Figure 13.3   Illy Gorlitzky in "Solomon's trial." Courtesy of the Cameri
Theatre Archive.

because he's more dangerous.... We wanted to make him folksy yet serious, human, profound" (Natan 1964, n.p.). Character changes were extremely fast, facilitated by the fact that king and cobbler wore the same traditional fool's pointed shoes. The fool's image was enhanced by the cobbler costume: a tunic with a rope tied at the waist and too-short pants. The embodiment of both parts was manifest in voice changes and speech rhythms: Solomon's speech was slow and measured, as befitting dignified restraint, while Shalmai's was rapid-fire, to-the-point, street-smart, yet naive and provincial. Shalmai's, "The Song of the Drunkard" with the repeated line *"vai l'leilì, vai l'yomì"* (Woe to my night, woe to my day) became the musical icon of the show.

What made Gorlitzky's voice unforgettable was its timbre, texture, raspiness, and an evocation of the melodiousness of the words. He caressed every syllable, enunciated every consonant, swayed among the words and relished the rhymes, which occurred not only at the ends of lines, but within them. He created words, chewed and savored them. When he was singing he fully faced the audience, creating an intimacy between the cobbler and his audience. The king, on the other hand, had no songs to sing. Gorlitzky's relationship with his audience intensified as the show progressed, reaching its peak in the final scene, when he became tired of being a king. The final scene was reminiscent of the scenes of Truffaldino in Goldoni's *A Servant to Two Masters,* and Scapin in Molière's *Scapin's Schemings.* At the end, Shalmai/Solomon—cobbler/king movingly pounds a nail into the sole of a shoe, finding the fault line, singing: "An honest cobbler can become a king in an emergency / but kings are automatically disqualified from shoemaking."

The social significance of the Gorlitzky cobbler lies in his natural manifestation of the characteristics of jokester and mischief-maker, which in the context of Israeli culture of the 1960s carried positive associations. The native prankster, singing and dancing Hebrew music so naturally without a hint of a foreign accent, functioned as a cultural metaphor for the new Israeli—one who can get by, who knows that "If I am not for myself who will be?" as Gorlitzky sang in "The Song of the Drunkard," one of the show's highlights. The cobbler/prankster/Israeli engagement in song and dance became a theme of the stage text that externalized the joie de vivre of the collective body. Thus too, fruitful tension exists between Gorlitzky-the-cobbler onstage and Alterman-the-poet off it, the latter's vivacious Hebrew signifying one of Zionism's successes in creating a modern culture in Hebrew (see Figure 13.4).

In the 1960s, reflecting the growing influence of American culture, Israeli theatergoers were exposed to a wave of Broadway musicals, beginning with *Irma La Douce* and *My Fair Lady,* and followed by *Man of La Mancha, The King and I,* and *Fiddler on the Roof,* among others.[14] Vis-à-vis these imports, the musical version of *Solomon the King and Shalmai the Cobbler* provided Israeli audiences with what Roland Barthes calls a text of pleasure: "the text that contents, fills, grants euphoria; the text that comes from the culture, and does not break with it, is linked to a comfortable practice of reading" (Barthes 1975, 14). Gronemann's rich world, filtered into a local text, provided not only pleasure, but also national pride, as it was no less a success than *My Fair Lady,* which ran concurrently on the commercial stage. Culture critics recommended translating the play into English and taking it to

Figure 13.4   Illy Gorlitzky in "The Song of the Drunkard." Courtesy of the Cameri Theatre Archive.

Broadway. When *I'm Solomon,* an American adaptation of the play, opened in April 1968 at the Mark Hellinger Theatre on Broadway, it proved a sensational failure, dryly summarized by Bunim as follows: "went up onstage and came down in one day" (Bunim 1994, 151).

2005: THE GLOBAL TEXT: THE SOUND OF SHOEMAKING

The most recent revival of the play opened at the Habima in 2005. It was directed by Ilan Ronen, the theater's artistic director, who is known for local politico-social interpretations of canonical plays. In his interpretation of *Solomon the King and Shalmai the Cobbler,* Ronen achieved a global aesthetic dimension through theatrical articulation of the components contained in the Cameri canonical production. By "theatrical" I mean exaggerated, enhanced demonstrations of artistic tools, such as the actor's body, the set, the lighting, and musical tempo. The organizing principle of its audio-visual language created a stage spectacle. As the lights went down the set was revealed behind an impressively wrought lithographic screen stretched over the entire breadth of the stage, in the center of which were the upside-down portraits of a king and a cobbler as on Tarot cards. The scenery recalled old-fashioned illustrated biblical storybooks for children and orientalist illustrations of Jerusalem, its naivete imbued with humor and self-irony regarding nostalgia for pre-1967 Israel. The palace was represented by tall, gold-ornamented pillars and giant purple tapestries, with a staircase in the center. The costumes of the courtiers were sky-blue, turquoise, and purple, while the marketplace folk were dressed in warm yellow, orange, and brown. The costumes' texture and cut were an improbable mix of New Age apparel with dreadlocks and headbands, and the traditional Yemenite costumes of the Inbal dance theater. The entire cast wore "Biblical Sandals" that were in fact tap-dancing shoes.

Yoni Rechter, one of Israel's leading popular music composers, adapted Sacha Argov's melodies, with a baroque choral arrangement of the song "The Wise Man and the Fool" opening the show. Rechter also added musical numbers that included blues, rap, rock 'n' roll, and Sephardic and Middle Eastern melodies, with the chorus and orchestra playing a major role in the production. The text was truncated, which added weight to the musical and dance numbers, complemented by the opulence of the set and costumes. All this gave the production the feel and look of a mega-musical.

The lead role of Solomon/Shalmai was played by Avi Kushnir, a popular actor and entertainer. In line with the director's sociopolitical leanings, Kushnir portrayed the cobbler as one who earns a meager livelihood, is dominated by his wife, and for whom the "salvation" he finds in the bottle runs dry too quickly. As king, Kushnir wore a silver cape that obscured the contours of his body, projecting the king less as a sovereign who radiates majesty and more as the chief who has work to do, a position to fill. Kushnir is an actor with frenetic energy, and, unlike Gorlitzky's prankster-cobbler, his Shalmai was an accomplished acrobat, springing and bouncing down the stairs almost at the risk of injury (see Figure 13.5).

The choreography of the production was undertaken by Tzachi Patish and Dani Rachum, founders of Sheketak, a *Stomp*-inspired troupe. The dancing combined percussive gestures, slap dancing, tap, and hip-hop, using various props to produce sounds. They drew inspiration from shoemaking, the rhythms of pounding and hammering. The choreography became a central component, creating an ongoing sense of joyful celebration on-stage. The height of the merging of Sheketak's artistic language and the sound of shoemaking is reached in the scene when the cobbler repairs a sandal in the palace and segues into a sweeping production number. The sound of shoemaking became an aesthetic element, an impressive example of the virtuosity of the cobbler's craft. The acrobatics and

Figure 13.5   Avi Kushnir and the marketplace folks in "The Song of the Drunkard." Courtesy of the Habima Theatre Archive.

mime language transformed shoemaking into a sound-motion entity, which had a sensory and thrilling effect on the audience.

The cultural significance of the 2005 production of the play lies not only in the political-social context but also in its artistic context. The stage interpretation of the fictitious world exaggerated the collapse of civil society, political intrigue, close links between wealth and political power, and the suppression of social protest. As such the material of *King Solomon and Shalmai the Cobbler,* with its artistic kernel and Alterman's brilliant language, stood in stark contrast to concurrent Israeli musicals such as *The Troupe,* with its recycled military entertainment materials from the 1960s and 1970s, or *The One Who Dreamed,* about the life and death of Yitzhak Rabin (Kaynar 2007).

Israeli cultural critic Zohar Shavit argues that today Hebrew has lost its hegemony, noting, "most of the 'higher' needs of our culture are no longer filled by Hebrew, but by English or Russian, and Hebrew is becoming more and more a 'maidservant,' as Yiddish was in Europe until the end of the nineteenth century" (Shavit 2002, 120). *Solomon the King and Shalmai the Cobbler,* like an archaeological dig, exposes the cultural validity of a work whose roots are deep, a work founded on vigorous, playful, and occasionally "dolled-up" Hebrew that lifts the actors and the audience to a sphere of clever and poetic Hebrew the likes of which has not been heard on the Israeli stage for years. In this recent production, the canonical language becomes a dialogical theater language precisely because it is clad in music and dance whose explicit message is more immediate than that of verbal language, part of it being a new utterance of cobbling.

> *Epilogue*
> O words of mirth and suffering,
> That double back on us again and again,
> Some make of them a dirge,
> Others make of them a merry tune. (Gronemann 1975, 151)

The Wise Man and the Fool was written by Gronemann, translated by Alterman, first staged in Palestine at the height of World War II, made into a musical in the 1960s, and imprinted onto the collective memory with the lyric "*vai l'leilì, vai l'yomì / im ein anì li mi?*" (Woe to my night, woe to my day / If I am not for myself, then who will be?) It became a mega-musical featuring an acrobatic cobbler and percussive shoemaking, and it led to this article, which aspires to shed light on cobblers in Israeli theater. The cobbler is a unique figure in the Israeli dramatic corpus, quite unlike the tradesmen who appeared in the immensely popular comedies of Ephraim Kishon in the 1950s, who were clerks, plumbers, shopkeepers, and craftsmen thematically linked to the petite bourgeoisie. The cultural layers and theater traditions to which the cobbler harks back enable actors in different historical-cultural contexts to speak the comic, imperfect language of everyman through him. Through this language Sammy Gronemann's humanistic worldview is reflected, and it places the actor at its center. Johan Huizinga, in his book *Homo Ludens* (1938/1955), wrote that playing is the essence of being a human being and cautioned that under fascism the individual is in danger of losing his playfulness, and thus his essence. There is no doubt that the cobbler, who metaphorically repairs how human beings make their way in the world, is also an actor whose true craft is to get into the shoes of others.

NOTES

1. The Ohel (Tent) Theatre was founded in 1925 in Tel Aviv by Moshe Halevy, who had left the Habima Theatre when it was still in Moscow. Habima settled in Palestine in 1931.

2. The 1971 revival ran for 121 performances. The 1982 revival, performed outdoors in Tel Aviv's Yarkon Park, ran for 15 performances (data from the Cameri Theatre archives).

3. One of the first cultural events in which Sammy Gronemann took part upon his arrival in Palestine was a public trial concerning the 1936 Habima production of *The Merchant of Venice*. Gronemann was among the defense witnesses and emphasized the tragic character of Shylock (Zer-Zion 2003, 73–100). Gronemann's memoirs, along with additional material by him, were recently republished (2002–2004).

4. The skit was translated by poet Avigdor Hameiri, one of leaders of the Matateh.

5. It should be noted that the singer-cobbler Hans Sachs appears as one of the town fathers in a monologue at the end of *The Meistersinger of Nuremberg*, Wagner's only comic opera.

6. Gronemann wrote other plays, among them *The Heine Family*, which was produced by the Habima Theatre in 1947, and *The Queen of Sheba*, produced by the Cameri Theatre in 1951. None enjoyed the success of *King Solomon and Shalmai the Cobbler*.

7. For a discussion of the *Purimshpiel* tradition see Belkin 2002.

8. I am indebted to my teacher, Prof. Shimon Levy, for this insight.

9. On the key status of Shakespeare in German culture see Williams 1990 and Steiner 2001; on the Shakespearean fool see Pyle 1998.

10. See Boulukos 2004, 1083–89.

11. Leah Goldberg in a 1943 review wrote, "Here, when actors start to play with something written in short lines, it appears to us that they are in the same situation as Molière's hero, who coincidentally realizes just now that his entire life, he's been speaking in prose" [translated from Hebrew].

12. *Little Tel Aviv* (1959), a mini-operetta written and edited by Haim Hefer and Dan Ben-Amotz that includes three songs by Alterman.

13. It should be noted that two of Alterman's plays were performed at the Cameri: *Kinneret, Kinneret* (O Sea of Galilee) in 1961, and *Pundák Ha'rukhot* (Ghost Inn) in 1963. Both failed to meet the expectations of audiences and critics. Alterman's musical *Queen Esther*, also produced at the Cameri Theatre in 1966, fell flat on its face.

14. See Almagor 1996 for a survey of the phenomenon.

BIBLIOGRAPHY

Almagor, Dan. 1996. "Musical plays on the Hebrew stage." *The Israel Review of Arts and Letters* 103. Available at http://www.israel-mfa.gov.il/MFA/MFAArchive/1990_1999/1998/7/Musical%20Plays%20on%20the%20Hebrew%20Stage. Accessed February 24, 2008.

Avrahami, Yitzchak. 1964. "*King Solomon and Shalmai the Cobbler* at the Cameri" [in Hebrew]. *Ma'ariv* (September 20). Clipping, n.p. file 57.5.9, The Israeli Center for the Documentation of Theatre Arts at Tel Aviv University.

Bakhtin, Michael. 1981. *The dialogic imagination: Four essays,* trans. Cary Emerson and Michael Holquist. Austin: University of Texas Press.

Barthes, Roland. 1975. *The pleasure of the text,* trans. Richard Miller, with a note on the text by Richard Howard. New York: Hill and Wang.

Belkin, Ahuva. 2002. *The Purimshpiel: Studies in Jewish folk theater.* Jerusalem: Bialik Institute.

Boulukos, Athanasios. 2004. "The cobbler and the tribunes in *Julius Caesar.*" *Modern Language Notes* (comparative literature issue) 119 (5):1083–89.

Bunim, Shmuel. 1994. *Kan Bunim* (Here's Bunim [in Hebrew]). Tel Aviv: Dvir.

Erasmus, Desiderius. 1994. *Praise of folly.* New York: Penguin Classics.

Goldberg, Leah. 1943. "*King Solomon and Shalmai the cobbler* at the Ohel Theatre" [in Hebrew]. *Davar* (January 15). Clipping, n.p. file 18.3.9, The Israeli Center for the Documentation of Theatre Arts at Tel Aviv University.

Gronemann, Sammy. 1920. *Tohuwabohu.* Berlin: Welt-Verlag.

Gronemann, Sammy. 1924. *Hawdoloh und Zapfenstreich; Erinnerungen an die ostjüdische Etappe, 1916–18.* Berlin: Jüdischer Verlag.

Gronemann, Sammy. 1926. *Hamans Flucht; ein Purimspiel in fünf Bildern.* Vienna: Löwit.

Gronemann, Sammy. 1946. *The Memoirs of a Yekke* [in Hebrew]. Tel Aviv: Am Oved.

Gronemann, Sammy. 1975. *King Solomon and Shalmai the Cobbler,* trans. into Hebrew with added lyrics Nathan Alterman. Tel Aviv: Hakibbutz Hameukhad.

Gronemann, Sammy. 2002–2004. *Erinnerungen/Sammy Gronemann; aus dem Nachlass herausgegeben von Joachim Schlör.* Berlin: Philo.

Huizinga, Johan. 1955. *Homo ludens: A study of the play-element in culture.* Boston: Beacon Press.

Jacobs, Louis. 1984. *The book of Jewish belief.* Jersey City, NJ: Behrman House.

Kaynar, Gad. 2007. "Speaking to alienation: Cyclical processes of privatization and ethical accountability in Israeli drama from Rabin's assassination to *mi shechalam* (He dreamed)" [in Hebrew]. *Zmanim* 99: 106–18.

Levy, Shimon. 1996. *Here, there, and everywhere: Space in Canadian and Israeli drama.* Brighton: Sussex Academic Press.

Locke, John. 1998. *An essay concerning human understanding.* New York: Penguin Classics.

Natan, Moshe. 1964. "*The cobbler and the king*" [in Hebrew]. *Davar* (October 9). Clipping, n.p. file 57.5.9, The Israeli Center for the Documentation of Theatre Arts at Tel Aviv University.

Plato. 2004. *Theaetetus,* trans. and with introduction and notes by Joe Sachs. Newburyport, MA: Focus Publishing.

Pyle, Sandra. 1998. *Mirth and morality of Shakespeare's holy fools.* Lewiston, ME: Mellen Press.

Shavit, Zohar. 2002. "Returning to the cultural core" [in Hebrew]. *Panim* [Faces] 20: 133–22.

States, Bert O. 1995. "The actor's presence: Three phenomenal modes." In *Acting (re)considered,* ed. Phillip B. Zarrilli, 22–42. London and New York: Routledge.

Steiner, George. 2001. *Erata, an examined life.* New Haven, CT: Yale University Press.

Williams, Simon. 1990. *Shakespeare on the German stage, 1586–1914.* New York: Cambridge University Press.

Zer-Zion, Shelly. 2003. "Shylock comes to Palestine: *The Merchant of Venice* as directed by Leopold Jessner in 1936" [in Hebrew]. *Cathedra* 110: 73–100.

14   THE CINEMATIC SHOE

ERNST LUBITSCH'S EAST EUROPEAN "TOUCH" IN *PINKUS'S SHOE PALACE*

JEANETTE R. MALKIN

The phrase "the Lubitsch touch" is a synonym for cinematic sophistication. It refers to the romantic comedies-of-manners directed by Ernst Lubitsch after his arrival in Hollywood in 1922, comedies that reinvented the genre via the double vision of a Jewish European/Immigrant American. The Lubitsch we know from *Trouble in Paradise* (1932), *Ninotchka* (1939), *The Shop Around the Corner* (1940), or *To Be or Not To Be* (1942) has style and wit. His touch can be identified in the foregrounding of cinematic inventiveness and in the stimulant of visual ellipsis: editing that leaves the obvious—or not so obvious?—unsaid, unshown, with gaps that assume an urbane, cinematic reader. But it is also, more literally, found in the materiality of his class settings, in the pitch-perfect paraphernalia that define his milieus and encase the bodies of his characters.

Less known is that by the time Lubitsch reached Hollywood at age thirty he had already directed, and acted in, over fifty films in Berlin, many of which were societal comedies of quite a different sort. Those comedies—most of them short one-reelers, almost all of them lost—were made during World War I and were Lubitsch's initiation into film directing. They were a series of films featuring Lubitsch himself in the stock character of a Jewish yokel—often from some small town in the eastern province of Posen—who alights in the big city, finds a job, and ploughs his way to success and the hand of the boss's daughter through havoc, trickery, lascivious humor, and winking wit. These initial films were a huge success and established Lubitsch as a major player in the emerging Berlin film industry. Within two years he moved on to other genres—mainly historical costume dramas and more sophisticated comedies in which he himself rarely appeared. Those dramas—for example *Madame Dubarry* (*Passion* 1919) and *Anna Boleyn* (*Deception* 1920), both great successes in the United States—led to Lubitsch's invitation by the American actress/producer, Mary Pickford, to come to Hollywood, where he would become one of the most important directors of wry, romantic comedies.

This chapter will discuss this recently recovered period of Lubitsch's career by focusing particularly on his first full-length film (approximately 50 minutes), the 1916 *Schuhpalast Pinkus* (Pinkus's Shoe Palace), one of the very few early films still extant. It is a prime example of this genre and combines the Lubitsch persona with themes of business, social climbing, and entertainment in a way that reflects the complex composition of World War I–era

Figure 14.1   Ernst Lubitsch. Berlin. Photo taken in the 1920s.
Courtesy of Deutsche Kinemathek Fotoarchiv, Filmmuseum Berlin.

Berlin Jewry. By focusing on the cultural and historical intertexts of this film, which his contemporary viewers would have easily understood, I will offer a new reading of the material, as well as the symbolic importance of *shoes* in *Schuhpalast Pinkus*. This reading will parallel my discussion of the way Lubitsch, as director, constructs the Jewish bourgeois milieu—the setting of these films and of his own biography—in contrast to the provocative way he himself embodies the central Jewish trickster figure.

LUBITSCH ENTERTAINS WARTIME BERLIN

Ernst Lubitsch's career in the cinema began almost by chance. He had caught the theater bug early on and, despite his father's objection, left school at age sixteen to study and become an actor. In 1910 he convinced Victor Arnold, a German-Jewish comedian, successful in the popular, or "low," folk (*volkstümlich*) tradition—which Lubitsch would adopt in his early films (Eyman 2000, 30)—to take him on as a student. Arnold was a veteran actor in Max Reinhardt's prestigious repertory theater ensemble at the Deutsches Theater, and after a year of training he introduced Lubitsch to this great guru of German theater. As Lubitsch would later quip, "My short stature, black hair, and that 'dark mocking leer' must have impressed him, for he put me to work" (Eyman 2000, 31)—as an apprentice, in mainly minor roles and to little critical acclaim.

Seeking extra work to supplement his small salary, Lubitsch, like other theater actors, looked to the budding film industry. These were the years when the German cinema industry began to find its footing and expand. Movie theaters had been opening by the score in Berlin before World War I, but with the war, and the civilian hunger for entertainment, the leading production companies began to merge and grow and seek new talent. The largest of those companies, the Projektions-AG Union (PAGU), was founded and run by a brilliant German Jew, Paul Davidson, owner of a chain of movie theaters, a leading film distributor, and a major film producer. Davidson would produce all of Lubitsch's German films, in a collaboration that profited them both.

Lubitsch's first real role in the cinema came through Arnold's intervention. Contracted to play Manfred Mayer, the owner of a clothing store, Arnold recommended Lubitsch for the comic secondary role of his ungovernable apprentice, Moritz Abramowsky. The film, *Die Firma heiratet* ("The Firm Marries," released January 1914)—now lost—was set in the *Konfektion* milieu of ready-made clothing, largely a German-Jewish industry at the time. Lubitsch played the bumbling but ambitious newcomer. The film was such a smash that a sequel, *Der Stolz der Firma* (The Pride of the Firm), was produced the same year. This time Lubitsch played the starring role of Siegmund Lachmann, "the first of Lubitsch's lovable schlemiel characters" (Eyman 2000, 42). A bumpkin from Ravitch (Rawicz in the eastern German province of Posen) who loses his sales job after he destroys the shop through his manic clumsiness, Lachmann/Lubitsch sets out for Berlin, lands another job—this time in an upscale clothing store—and wrangles and havocs his way to the directorship, as well as to the hand of the boss's daughter. Arnold was cast in a supporting role. Lubitsch's body language—restless, inventive, relentlessly "Jewish"—had made him a star. But Lubitsch's acting—which until 1918 continued both in Reinhardt's theater and on the screen—seems to have ever consisted of *over*-acting. The theater critic for the *Berliner Tageblatt* wrote of Lubitsch's 1915 role as Lancelot, Shylock's duplicitous servant, in Reinhardt's production of *The Merchant of Venice*, "Ernst Lubitsch as Lancelot, was too much of a good thing" (Eyman 2000, 42). That same "too much" worked hilariously in his favor in these farces, although his brash and broad form of slapstick humor—applied to his Jewish persona—may seem off-putting to us today. Lubitsch had achieved a degree of fame in the cinema that he had yet to achieve in the theater.

Der Stolz der Firma premiered in Berlin on July 30, 1914. Two days later the Great War began. Comedies of this type were no longer forthcoming, and Lubitsch was cast in a series of dramatic roles that were not a success. "I was typed," Lubitsch later wrote, "and no one seemed to write any part which would have fitted me. . . . I found it necessary that I had to create parts for myself. Together with an actor friend of mine, the late Erich Schönfelder, I wrote a series of one-reelers which I sold to the Union Company. I directed and starred in them. And that is how I became a director" (Weinberg 1977, 284).[1] The "type" to which Lubitsch refers, in which he had succeeded, and upon which he draws in his subsequent films, is the prankster or buffoon figure (*Possenfigur*) of the so-called "milieu" or "ethnic" farces (*Possen*). This was an already well-known genre of short silent films, as well as of cabaret and revue (stand-up) sketches, popular at the time. One branch of the genre was set in such German regions as Bavaria, where boorish professors and other figures of oppressive authority were unmasked.[2]

Another branch of the genre was set in the well-known Jewish working-class garment district of East Berlin.[3] The formulaic stories, settings, and stock characters of that genre provided Lubitsch with a ready-made framework.[4] "Even if these small stories"—that is, the narratives common to this Jewish-themed genre—"don't actually take place on Hausvogteiplatz, which was the real center of the mainly Jewish Berlin *Konfektion*—garment—business," writes Michael Hanisch, "the audience's imagination, then as now, would have quickly planted the stories there" (Hanisch 2003, 14–16).[5] Discussing Lubitsch's early films, Herta-Elisabeth Renk suggests that, with his role as Moritz Abramowsky, Lubitsch had created a new, updated version of the old prankster figure. The heart of his interpretation was Moritz's vitality, his Bergsonian *élan vital*. "Lubitsch's farcical heroes conquered a whole phalanx of obsessive Wilhelminian Philistines (*Spiessbürger*) through their cunning and lust for life," she writes (Renk 1992, 22).[6] Lubitsch's dynamism had the same energy that characterized the city in which he worked. This energy might be attributed to Berlin's long eastern border and the outsiders (mainly Jewish) it drew from the eastern provinces. These Jews partook in the expansion, and consumption, of new industries,[7] and in innovative forms of salesmanship, all reflected in the two dozen or so (mainly short) farces that Lubitsch created in Germany.

GEOGRAPHY OF A JEWISH LIFE: BETWEEN EAST AND WEST

The key to understanding Lubitsch's early films is his biography.[8] Not only does it offer clues to his interpretation of the Jewish stock-type he plays, it also reflects the socioeconomic connections among the characters in his films. Born in 1892 in Berlin, Lubitsch grew up on the Schönhauser Allee, the youngest of four siblings, in a two-floor apartment. On the ground floor was the family business, "S. Lubitsch, Betriebwerkstätte für Damenmäntel," a small women's coat factory with eight employees and sales space; on the floor above was the Lubitsch apartment. His mother, Anna Lindenstaedt, came from a town near Berlin and designed coats for the factory. His father, Simon (Simcha) Lubitsch, came to Berlin in the mid-1880s, approximately thirty years old, from Russian Grodno (part of the Jewish Pale of Settlement). This was a time when Berlin was just beginning to expand, and he worked himself up to a comfortable middle-class life. Thus, the Lubitsches belonged to the same strata of Jewish proprietors of *Konfektion* that Ernst Lubitsch uses as the theme of his Jewish films. The family identified itself as assimilated German Jews—more specifically Berliners—although Simon never learned to read or write German. He was, however, verbally fluent and dealt with the marketing side of the business. Simon never became a German citizen; as a result, his children too bore Russian citizenship and the sons were thus barred from military service. Lubitsch attended the prestigious, humanistic Sophien-Gymnasium, situated in close proximity to his home. Out of 550 students in the school, 247 were Jewish, most of them from homes similar to his own (Eyman 2000, 26).

The Schönhauser Allee, which was to remain Lubitsch's home base until his late twenties, was an area populated largely by middle-class Jews. However, it bordered on the Scheunenviertel, which until its partial destruction in 1907 was the teeming living quarters of approximately six thousand *Ostjuden*, East European Jews, poor immigrants who began flooding through Germany's border toward the end of the nineteenth century, and who often used the strategically placed Berlin as a waystation (Hanisch 2003, 10). They spoke mainly Yiddish, ate the kosher dishes they knew from home, dressed in the custom of the East European ghettos, and moved and gesticulated in a manner very unlike the

Germans—or the assimilated German Jews. These fringe figures were a constant target of attack by Germans and German Jews alike, discussed mainly in terms of smell and contagion, and they evoked age-old anti-Semitic fears of the much villainized ghetto Jew. When Alexander Granach (born Yeshaya Gronich), one of Germany's most important actors after World War I, came to Berlin from Galicia in 1906, he joined the mass of *Ostjuden* there. His memoirs recount his first impressions:

> I was told how to go to the Scheunen quarter, and when I got off at Lothringerstrasse, Schoenhauser Tor [at the far corner of Lubitsch's street], suddenly in the middle of Berlin I found myself in a district that looked like Lemberg.... Women with painted faces and big keys in their hands strolled by as they do in the narrow alleys of Stanislau and Lemberg. Dozens of shops, restaurants, egg, butter, and milk stores, bakeries, with signs reading "Kosher." Jews walked about dressed as in Galicia, Rumania, and Russia.... There was a brisk community life too. For the pious there were numerous houses of prayer, named after their sects or their rabbis. There were Zionists of all shades. There were Social Revolutionists, Socialists, and Anarchists. There were [Yiddish] theatres and cabarets [in which Granach would later perform]....My friend and I rented a room in the Lothringerstrasse which we shared with six other boys. I went to work in the bakery to which I had been sent, and soon felt at home in this Berlin. (Granach 1945, 139)

This quarter, only rarely humanized in German or German-Jewish literature as it is here, was reputed to be the home of thieves and whores and would surely have been off limits to the young Lubitsch, who passed the area every day, from the ages of ten to sixteen, on his way to school.[9] There was little interaction between these new immigrants and the assimilated, and wary, German Jews. Indeed, the *Ostjuden* were a source of almost constant tension for Germany's Jews, aggravating the political anti-Semitism that had been growing since Germany's 1871 unification and the granting of full citizenship rights to its Jewish population. It is of crucial importance to note that Jewish emancipation and *embourgeoisement* in Germany since the eighteenth century hinged on the Jews' transformation from "Ghetto Jews" to "Culture Jews"; that is, Jews who adopted the language, comportment, norms, and culture of the German middle class. But that was not all. "Assimilation," writes Steven Aschheim, "was not merely the conscious attempt to *blend* into new social and cultural environments, but was also purposeful, even programmatic, *dissociation* from traditional Jewish cultural and national moorings" (Aschheim 1982, 5). Thus German Jews tended to repudiate their Eastern cousins—often no more than a generation ago, images of themselves—in terms similar to those of the anti-Semites.[10]

Ernst Lubitsch grew up, like many middle-class Jews of the time, surrounded by a largely Jewish population. His choice of theater as a career exposed him to more of the same. Although the Jews (by 1910) constituted less than five percent of the total Berlin population, they were disproportionately prominent in most of the cultural venues.[11] Max Reinhardt's theater ensemble, often attacked as "too Jewish," had a large number of important Jewish actors (including Victor Arnold and later Granach), auxiliary directors, and dramaturges.[12] And the film industry, which Lubitsch would soon join, was in its early years similarly constituted. But aside from the German Jews who were the mainstay of Lubitsch's social network, there were also the marginalized—but fascinating—Eastern Jews who lived a stone's throw away in the Scheunenviertel. Lubitsch would surely see these strange figures on his walks to school—indeed, they could be seen throughout Berlin—and it might have struck him that they were not so different in origin, and probably in body language, from his own father. "In later years," writes Lubitsch's biographer, "Lubitsch would gesture at himself and say, 'My God, no wonder I look like this; my father sat sewing cross-legged all his life.'" The implication was that Simon was a half-step out of the *shtetl*" (Eyman 2000, 27)—and that Lubitsch was a product of that environment. It is an implication that is given flesh in his early Jewish films.

PINKUS'S SHOE PALACE: THE NARRATIVE

Unlike some of his other early films, the hero of Lubitsch's 1916 *Schuhpalast Pinkus,* Sally Pinkus, is a local, a Berliner. We first meet him in bed. He has overslept again and is late for school. "Ich komm noch früh genug zu spät!" (I've got plenty of time to come late) he mumbles to his angry parents. The clothes he puts on over his nightdress, the attempt to flirt with the servant girl replaced by his father's attempt to do the same, the walk to school in knee-high pants through city blocks and public park—all of these mark the setting as petit bourgeois and the genre as an urban farce. In the next scene the twenty-four-year-old Lubitsch ridiculously tries to enter his classroom without attracting the teacher's attention. The teacher—played by Hans Kräly, who cowrote the script, looking stern in a long black Herzl beard—does, of course, catch him. Next we find Sally in a gym class where, alone among the boys, he fails to jump over a gym-horse, but when the teacher isn't looking, crawls under it and pretends to have been successful. He is finally caught cheating on an exam and, despite extensive begging, is thrown out of school. In a scene with his parents, in which he tells of his expulsion, the parents wind up fighting with each other, while Sally escapes.

Now begins the search for work. With only his school report card as a recommendation—which states that he failed to be promoted and failed every subject—Sally is rejected from the first upscale office he enters. Next door he sees a small shoe shop and has an idea: he'll become a salesman. In the run-down shop, owned by a rough-looking man and his pretty daughter, Sally begins his first job by refusing to wait on his first customer—a man with holes in his socks. He kisses the daughter behind a wall of shoe boxes—which all tumble down—and is literally booted out of the shop by the owner. Sally has another idea. He decides to advertise and, in a post office, writes his own recommendation in glowing and arrogant terms, calling his looks "dazzling" and his goal: "Only first-class establishments will be considered; all other offers will be thrown into the trashcan." He gets an answer from Mr. Meyersohn, owner of an important women's shoe-shop, and convinces his mother to buy him a new suit. The next day he arrives at the shop and, before entering, blesses himself

Figure 14.2 Schoolboy Sally flirts with the maid while his father watches. Courtesy of Deutsche Kinemathek Fotoarchiv, Filmmuseum Berlin.

with the words "Hals und Bein bruch" (break a leg)! Again he presents his report card to the cigar-smoking, self-satisfied (and obviously Jewish) boss—and is rejected. But now: "Sally schmusst," the Yiddish and Berlin slang word for talking-up, convincing. With florid body language and the sweetest of smiles he manages to sell himself to the boss. A number of adventures ensue. After work Sally tries to pick up one of the sales girls, only to find that he has carried her bag and walked her all the way to her meeting with her boyfriend. The next day he waits on an attractive woman and after removing her shoe can't resist tickling her delicately arched sole. The woman is outraged, and Sally is again fired.

But before he leaves the shop another woman enters. From the sidelines Sally watches her reject one pair of shoes after another because the size she is being given—her correct size, obviously—offends her vanity. Sally has an idea. Eyes bulging, he rubs his hands and scratches his head, sticks out his tongue, and with a series of quirky faces and nodding head he takes a pair of shoes and replaces her size with a lower one. Her vanity assuaged, the lady, named Melitta Hervé, buys the shoes and flirts with Sally, who promises to deliver them himself. Later, in her wealthy apartment, Melitta, a well-known dancer, offers Sally tea and cookies, and, in a lovely moment of the film, he dunks the cookie into the tea—a practice clearly associated with East European Jews. Melitta bursts out laughing and promptly follows suit. Impressed by him and his wit, Melitta offers to back him in his own business enterprise as a partner. His first act as a wealthy up-and-coming entrepreneur is to return to Meyersohn's shop in tails and top hat, blow cigar smoke in his face, and tell him—now *you're* fired!

The last section of the film shows the transformation not only of Sally, but also of the shoes that have been the main prop of the film. Sally now has a large office and a huge, indeed a majestic, store with double flights of stairs and endless salespeople. Everything is ready—but there are no customers. Sally has an idea. In the next scene we see him give an elegant usher a fancy cushion topped by a pair of fashionable boots surrounded by garlands. Sally enters the theater and takes his place in a front box with a huge bouquet of flowers. We see Melitta dance, a rather silly sort of expressive number that might have been meant to parody the (often Jewish) dancers at the popular Metropol theater in Berlin. The dance shows off her beautiful high-buttoned boots. When she's done, the usher enters the stage with the boots on a cushion, and Sally, from his box, throws the flowers to the dancer and shouts, "Only in Pinkus's Shoe Palace can you find these lovely shoes." In the hall Sally distributes flyers that advertise a shoe fashion show at his shop.

At the triumphant fashion show, stylish shoes of the day are paraded by real models on a long walkway. Sally himself "schmusst," talks up, each pair of shoes as the camera lingers on every heel and buttonhole of the buckled and laced and utterly urban fashions. The next day Sally reads in the trade paper that his "brilliant idea" was a success and will surely mean the blossoming of his shop. In the final shot of the film Sally shows Melitta the article and takes out a checkbook to pay her part of the profits. Then Sally has an idea. Why split the profits? he asks. Instead, why not become my wife and the money will stay in the family! Shyly, she agrees, and the film ends with their embrace and kiss.

PINKUS'S SHOE PALACE: SUCCESS AND SUBVERSION

Schuhpalast was a huge success, Lubitsch's first real hit since *Der Stolz der Firma* (The Pride of the Firm), and "[it] jump-started Lubitsch's stalled career" (Eyman 2000, 48). It opened at two Berlin theaters and, after a week, was seen by 10,872 people; a week later it opened in an additional six theaters. *Schuhpalast* was the first film directed by Lubitsch to really make waves, leading to his first interview in one of the important trade journals. Released in May 1916, in the middle of the war, its success was, however, not unproblematic. The war was going badly and anti-Semitism was seriously on the rise.[13] The atmosphere in Germany was tense and there were protests—from German Jews—that *Schuhpalast* was adding to the hatred by its anti-Semitic portrayal of the Jew. That portrayal (here, as in his other films) shows the Jew as ambitious, lewd, pushy, and smart. And Lubitsch's wildly exaggerated body language seems to be the physical translation of a Yiddish idiom. Lubitsch embodied with knowing self-referentiality what Jackie Mason might call a "too Jewish" persona—and he was under attack. Later commentators would go so far as to call these early films "the most anti-Semitic body of work ever to be produced, if…Ernst Lubitsch had not been Jewish himself!" (Comolli 1968, 31).[14] As with the early Chaplin shorts, this stock figure never changes in essence, only in his situation within a limited range of stories; and while "Jewishness" is never explicitly stated, its coding was unmistakable to its intended audience, and intentionally so.

On August 30, 1916 an article appeared on the first page of the Düsseldorf cinema journal, *Der Kinematograph,* for which the journalist Julius Urgiss had interviewed Lubitsch. Describing him as a "small, lively, still-youthful man" (he was twenty-five!), one of Lubitsch's many famous quips appears in that article. When asked to speak seriously about his cinematic art, Lubitsch interrupted the writer and said, "Oh no, I have enough seriousness (Ernst in German means serious) in my first name" (Hanisch 2003, 7). But the article is in fact a serious source for understanding Lubitsch's anger over the attacks his Jewish persona had generated. The journalist writes that he asked Lubitsch the "most pressing" question—"and it should have been the first question I asked"—concerning his personal opinion of Jewish "milieu" comedies. "Er kam in Erregung"—he was upset, agitated, and answered:

> It is often said that films with a Jewish milieu are offensive. That's a completely implausible standpoint. Should it be the case that such a film arouses disapproval, then it is only and solely due to the performance, which either doesn't suit [or "get"] the essence of Jewish humor—in which case the actor should stay away from such roles; or it is due to excessive exaggeration—which would harm any type of artistic performance and destroy its effect. Wherever Jewish humor appears, it is compassionate and artistic and plays such a great role [in other art forms] that it would be ridiculous to try to do without it in the cinema. (Urgiss 1916, 1)

Lubitsch comes out in defense of Jewish humor, even at the expense of incriminating his own performance. But what *was* it about his performance that evoked so much unhappiness? *Schuhpalast Pinkus* was advertised by PAGU as a "Jewish" film, as became the reputation of its star and the genre of humor he represented. Yet there is nothing "Jewish" about the film. There are no Jewish symbols, no mention of religion, nor does the protagonist come to Berlin from the East. Meyersohn is a Jewish name, and the garment milieu was traditionally considered a Jewish industry, but shoes were not usually included in this definition. The only thing "Jewish" about the film was Lubitsch's character's name, Lubitsch's reputation, and Lubitsch's acting, which Eyman calls "The archetypal Lubitsch performance" (Eyman 2000, 45).

The problem, I contend, was not with the Jewish figure as such, but with the "type" of Jew that Lubitsch was portraying. Lubitsch's early films offer a portrait of his life-world, of the Jewish middle-class business world he knew so well. But they are also a portrait of that "other" Jewish world: the one crowded into a ghetto on the border of his own street; the one that roamed the fringes of Berlin looking for work; the one suppressed in the father who insisted on being German and tried to hide all evidence of his Eastern origins (Eyman tells us that he never spoke Yiddish; 2000, 20). Lubitsch's outsider Sally, from his lithe, animated body, to his quirky faces, rubbing hands, lusty looks, and incapacity to conform, is the very essence of the "other." And it was the presentation of *that* type of

Jewish figure—and *that* type of humor—within a much-advertised, mass-viewed mass media, that, I suggest, evoked most of the protest. It wasn't that Lubitsch had invented this portrayal of the Jewish persona. In fact, it had long been present in many popular venues of Berlin theater and cabaret.[15] But those venues attracted a much smaller and more select audience.

Among those venues we find the Herrnfeld Brothers, whose *Jargontheater* was a middle-class entertainment for Jews, by Jews, and dealing with Jewish themes—but enjoyed by Jews and non-Jews alike. Like all *Jargontheater*—theater using an artificial Yiddish-sounding language that could be easily understood by a German audience—the Herrnfelds' roots lay in the burlesque tradition of the variety theater, as did Lubitsch's performance.[16] They were a much-loved institution in Berlin, so popular that at the turn of the century they built their own theater on Kommandanten Street.[17] Lubitsch was obviously influenced by them. As Peter Jelavich puts it,

> In many ways, Lubitsch's performances were the pantomimic equivalent of *Jargonthe-ater;* indeed, he tipped his hat to the Herrnfelds with a film like *Der Fall Rosentopf* [The Rosentopf Case] (1918), whose title evoked *Der Fall Blumentopf,* a [Herrnfeld] comedy that enjoyed over a thousand performances at their theatre. (Jelavich forthcoming)

Thus, Lubitsch was doing nothing original by presenting an *Ostjude* in the arts. But his was a new mass art, and Lubitsch was going much too public with his *Ostjude* for some people's comfort. Surely he and Davidson, born in the East Prussian town of Lötzen (today Giżycko, Poland), the son of a Jewish businessman, and a shrewd businessman himself, must have known this. I wonder whether their insistence on presenting this film in the middle of the war, in the midst of ominous and growing anti-Semitism—and then decid-ing to create an *additional* series of short films based on the Sally persona—was not a politi-cal statement, a form of knowing, provocative "cookie-dunking." Such cultural activism is rarely found in Lubitsch's American films, except, perhaps, in the courageous *To Be or Not To Be* (1942).

FROM FOOT TO FASHION: THE *OSTJUDE* COMES HOME

Of all of Lubitsch's Jewish "business" films, *Schuhpalast* is the only one (as far as we know) that is not set in the garment industry. This is significant because it takes Lubitsch to a stock of metaphors and implications that go beyond his father's particular branch of busi-ness. Metonymically it places the burden of representation on a small part of the human body, and on a "lowly" part at that. The shoe is an object that, on the one hand, allows for abundant physical and lascivious humor, appropriate to a farce; but, on the other hand, has urban cachet as a fashion object that endows it with savvy and an "insider" position. As Eyman writes, thinking more of his later films, "[Lubitsch] invests a good deal of his screen time in objects: canes, swords, handbags, whatever. It is not the objects themselves that are important, but their relationship to the people who claim them. For Lubitsch, objects are totems of character, physical manifestations of feelings...and desires" (Eyman 2000, 16).

The lowly shoe transforms in this film from common object to near fetish; and with its rise in prestige, Sally too evolves. Shoes have at first the connotation of functionality or necessity. We initially encounter them at Sally's first job, when an obviously lower-class man comes into the shop. Sally removes his shoe and finds a huge hole in his sock. The big toe sticking out of the moth-eaten sock repels the novice salesman and he sidles over to the boss and whispers (with disgust on his face), "I can't serve *him!*"—for which he earns a whack to the head. This preamble to Sally's ambition, and horror at what the sock represents, sets the stage for his self-made transformation. Sally's next development is in his advertisement. There, he describes *himself* as being of "dazzling" appearance and willing to consider only first-class establishments. His second job brings him higher-class customers, and better shoes; but he is still marked as the outsider by his irrepressible urge to tickle a customer's feet. It is only when Sally acquires his own shoe store—his Shoe Palace, bigger and better than even Meyersohn's shop—that the transformation is complete. Both Sally and the shoes are presented in a fully different light.

The long final segment of the film dedicated to the shoe fashion show makes the transformation clear. We recall that when Sally entered Meyersohn's store for his interview, he blessed himself with "Break a leg," like an actor about to give a performance. And indeed he does perform, successfully selling himself to Meyersohn, an upper-class, very German-Jewish business man. In the shoe fashion-show scene, Sally is no longer in need of theatrical

Figure 14.3   Sally prepares to tickle a customer's foot. Courtesy of Deutsche Kinemathek Fotoarchiv, Filmmuseum Berlin.

blessings; he is openly, self-reflexively, master and director of the show. Lubitsch/Sally sets up the sales-entertainment with amazing visual skill. A walkway stretches from the majestic staircases to the length of the store, with spectators sitting on either side of the stage. The models walk the length of the walkway to stage-front, where Lubitsch/Sally receives them—as does the audience sitting in the movie theater. Each model stops at the end of the ramp while Lubitsch/Sally points out the niceties of each fashion product in a body language neither comic nor grotesque. He is the consummate, controlled salesman/director.

Sabine Hake calls the style of this section "documentary" and claims that it "disrupts the flow of the narrative and culminates in a seemingly endless series of close-ups aimed at the prospective buyer/spectator" (Hake 1992, 35). Indeed, the film's diegetic space is opened up for what Peter Jelavich terms "an early example of explicit product placement." But, he continues, "another product being placed . . . is Lubitsch's Jewishness" (Jelavich forthcoming), or, as I claim, the transformation of the *Ostjude*. This brilliant ploy, complete with a final listing of the Berlin stores that donated their fashion shoes for the production, and then listing the credit for the Berlin Jew who directed the film, equates the Jewish persona/director with the shoes. The shoes, previously only part of the story, become independent objects of enticement, signs of being "in" and chic and belonging to the upper crust of the urban circus. With them, Sally too transforms into an object of desire. In the final moments of the show, Lubitsch/Sally himself walks down the ramp, bowing with the loose-armed body language of a professional actor, of *Lubitsch* the actor, to the on- and off-screen audience. It comes then as no surprise that, in the continuing narrative strand, Melitta accepts his proposal of marriage.

CONCLUSION: *SCHUHPALAST* AS HISTORY AND BIOGRAPHY

Shoes, and feet, have always carried a derogatory meaning when associated with Jews. In Sander Gilman's now-classic study of *The Jew's Body*, the Jewish foot—"A Foot-Note to the Jewish Body"—is given pride of place. Gilman's first association is the identification of the Jew's foot with that of "the cloven-footed devil of the middle ages," a foot that, when extracted from the shoe that serves as a mask "of civilization and higher culture," could distinguish the Christian from the . . . holes-in-the-sock Jew (Gilman 1991, 39). Moving on to more urban imagery, Gilman traces the many studies on the connection between Jews and flat feet, which require special shoes. Gustav Muskat, a Berlin orthopedist at the turn of the twentieth century, made the revolutionary observation that the Jew's flat feet were not an inherent pathology, but an acquired one. It is the effect of the city and modern life on the Jew that causes this deformation: "The Jew is both the city dweller par excellence as well as the most evident victim of the city. And the occupation of the Jew in the city, the Jew's role as merchant, is the precipitating factor for the shape of the Jew's feet" (Gilman 1991, 49). Gilman ends the chapter by bringing further evidence, this time from German-Jewish doctors and scientists of the time, that the social factors *leading* to foot deformation were to be found not in Jews as such—but in Russian or East European Jews. Thus the evidence of a larger percentage of flat-footedness among Jews could be accepted, while the factors leading to this deformity could be projected "on to a group labeled as inherently 'different,' the Eastern Jews" (Gilman 1991, 58–59).

While in no way directly indicated in Lubitsch's film, Sally's trajectory from poor shoe salesman who has to suffer tattered socks, to the "merchant" who sells shoes in the city but is not in charge of his fate, to the owner of a hugely successful *Schuhpalast* in which the shoe becomes the very icon of the urbane and fashionable, is the same trajectory followed in Gilman's discussion of the Jew's foot: from outcast to insider German-Jew. More than most of Lubitsch's early films, this film feels autobiographical: the story of a young ambitious Berlin Jew striving to succeed. Yet although the world of the film is familiar, it is given in a register significantly different from the register in which Lubitsch *acts*. There is the sense of a superimposition of two genres, similar to the absurd juxtapositions found in some of the Marx Brothers' films, where a reasonably sane environment is invaded by the anarchistic force of a group of child-hoodlums. And as with the Marx Brothers, Lubitsch's anarchic force is subversive. *Schuhpalast* evokes, on the one hand, the milieu of urban, assimilated German Jews who had "made it"; and on the other hand the outsider figure of the *Ostjude*, from whom German Jews had tried so hard to distance themselves. Set in the world of Jewish Berlin, written, produced, and acted by mainly Jewish artists, these early films can be seen as an autobiography of their inner geography and (especially in *Schuhpalast*), of their outer history. It also reflects an urban generational transformation—reversed. The father who was yesterday a stranger is today the insider who looks askance at the new stranger, here personified by the son. Thus, *Schuhpalast* is both the story of German-Jewish assimilation, and a confrontation between the assimilationist and his own past and present. Lubitsch/Sally is both the outsider *Ostjude* and the insider assimilated Jew, both the story of his own father, and the story of the contemporary outsiders upon whom his father had turned his back.

NOTES

1. This quote appears in a letter Lubitsch wrote to Weinberg dated July 10, 1947, apparently in not very good English.
2. This theme of authority and hierarchy reflected the stifling patriarchal social structure of pre–Weimar Republic Germany—and is best captured in Heinrich Mann's novel *Professor Unrath* (1905), which was later filmed by Joseph von Sternberg as *The Blue Angel* (1930).
3. This is a setting whose popularity (not only among Jews) might be explained through its encapsulation of capitalist anxieties in Wilhelminian Germany.
4. Lubitsch was working within a comic groove that had already been popularized during the early years of the German film industry by actors such as Leo Peukert, Guido Herzfeld, Ernst Matray, and Anna Müller-Lincke. See Bergfelder Carter, and Göktürk 2002, 30–31.
5. All translations from the German, unless otherwise noted, are my own.

6. These qualities were so obvious that PAGU advertised Lubitsch as representing "Exuberance, wit, and humor"; and as being a "never-tiring creator and actor" (Eyman 2000, 49).

7. At the turn of the twentieth century no other large European city counted as great a percentage of immigrants among its citizens. As Walther Rathenau (the German-Jewish industrialist, writer, and later foreign minister of the newly formed Weimar Republic) quipped: "Most Berliners are from Posen; the rest are from Breslau," implying that an (over-) large segment of the population was from the east, and was Jewish (Richie 1998, 860). For a more detailed discussion of German Jews and Berlin, especially in theater, see my "Break a Leg!," the introductory chapter of Malkin and Rokem forthcoming.

8. The following facts are taken from Eyman (2000) and Hanisch (2003).

9. This is Michael Hanisch's conjecture (2003, 10).

10. For a full and fascinating discussion of the German-Jewish animus against the *Ostjuden,* see Aschheim 1982, especially Chapter 3: "Caftan and Cravat: 'Old' Jews, 'New' Jews, and Pre–World War I Anti-Semitism," 58–79.

11. See Lowenstein, Mendes-Flohr, Pulzer, and Richarz 2000, 33. The exact numbers given are 144,043 Jews, which comes to 4.35 percent of the total population.

12. For a detailed discussion of the importance of Jewish Germans in the creation of German modern theater see Malkin and Rokem forthcoming.

13. According to the *Leo Baeck Institute Yearbook* (1974, 143), rumor had it that the Jews were shirking their military responsibility, were underrepresented in the army, and were fighting in the rear. A few months after the release of *Schuhpalast* the German Military High Command ordered its infamous *Judenzählung* (a Jewish census); the census, however, proved the opposite: eighty percent of the *over*-represented German Jews served on the front lines, almost three thousand Jews had already died on the battlefield, and more than seven thousand had been decorated. The findings were promptly suppressed.

14. See Hake 1992, 30–31 for other examples of derogatory views of Lubitsch's portrayal of the Jew.

15. See Otte 2007.

16. On the Herrnfeld Theater, see Sprengel 1997, 55–117 and Otte 2007, 145–59.

17. This building was later used as the theater and base of the Jüdische Kulturbund, the Nazi-created Jewish Cultural League where Jews were allowed—and forced—to perform theater for other Jews only.

BIBLIOGRAPHY

Aschheim, Steven E. 1982. *Brothers and strangers: The East European Jew in German and German Jewish consciousness, 1800–1923.* Madison: University of Wisconsin Press.

Bergfelder, Tim, Erica Carter, and Deniz Göktürk, eds. 2002. *The German cinema book.* London: BFI.

Comolli, Jean-Louis. 1968. "Der Stolz der Firma." *Cahiers du Cinéma* 198 (February): 30–31.

Eyman, Scott. 2000. *Ernst Lubitsch: Laughter in paradise.* Baltimore, MD: Johns Hopkins University Press.

Gilman, Sander. 1991. *The Jew's body.* New York: Routledge.

Granach, Alexander. 1945. *There goes an actor,* trans. Willard Trask. New York: Doubleday, Doran and Co. Originally published (1945) as *Da geht ein Mensch: Roman eines Lebens.*

Hake, Sabine. 1992. *Passions and deceptions: The early films of Ernst Lubitsch.* Princeton, NJ: Princeton University Press.

Hanisch, Michael. 2003. *Ernst Lubitsch: Von der Berliner Schönhauser Allee nach Hollywood.* Berlin: Hentrich & Hentrich and Centrum Judaicum Berlin.

Jelavich, Peter. Forthcoming. "How 'Jewish' was theatre in imperial Berlin?" In *Going Public: Jews and the making of modern German theatre,* ed. Jeanette R. Malkin and Freddie Rokem. Iowa City: University of Iowa Press.

Lowenstein, Steven M., Paul Mendes-Flohr, Peter Pulzer, and Monika Richarz, eds. 2000. *Deutsch-jüdische Geschichte in der Neuzeit.* Vol. 3, *1871–1918.* Munich: Beck.

Malkin, Jeanette R., and Freddie Rokem, eds. Forthcoming. *Going Public: Jews and the Making of Modern German theatre.* Iowa City: University of Iowa Press, Forthcoming.

Otte, Marline. 2007. *Jewish identities in German popular entertainment, 1890–1933.* New York: Cambridge University Press.

Renk, Herta-Elisabeth. 1992. *Ernst Lubitsch.* Hamburg: Rowohlt/Monographie.

Richie, Alexandra. 1998. *Faust's metropolis: A history of Berlin.* New York: Carrol and Graf.

Secker & Warburg. *Leo Baeck Institute Yearbook.* 1974. London. Leo Baeck Institute.

Sprengel, Peter. 1997. *Populäres jüdisches Theater in Berlin von 1877 bis 1933.* Berlin: Haude & Spener.

Urgiss, Julius. 1916. "Künstlerprofile: Ernst Lubitsch." *Der Kinematograph* (August 30).

Weinberg, Herman G. 1977. *The Lubitsch touch: A critical study,* 3rd rev. ed. New York: Dover.

CONTRIBUTORS

Edna Nahshon is associate professor of Hebrew at the Jewish Theological Seminary in New York and senior associate of Oxford University's Centre for Hebrew and Jewish Studies. She has written extensively on Jews, performance, and theater. Nahshon is the author of *Yiddish Proletarian Theatre: The Art and Politics of the Artef, 1925–1940* (1998), and *From the Ghetto to the Melting Pot: Israel Zangwill's Jewish Plays* (2006), and editor of *Jewish Theatre,* a collection of essays (forthcoming, 2008). She is currently working (with Professor Michael Shapiro) on a collection of essays that map out Jewish responses to *The Merchant of Venice,* and on a book titled *Spectacular Justice: Mock Trials and Public Jewish Discourse.*

Ora Horn Prouser is executive vice president and dean of the Academy for Jewish Religion, a pluralistic rabbinical and cantorial school. She received her Ph.D. from the Department of Bible at JTS, where she was adjunct faculty for nearly 20 years.

Catherine Hezser is professor of Jewish Studies at the School of Oriental and African Studies of the University of London. Her area of specialization is the social history of Jews in Roman Palestine. She has published numerous books and articles; among them are: *The Social Structure of the Rabbinic Movement in Roman Palestine* (Zübingen, 1997), *Jewish Literacy in Roman Palestine* (Zübingen, 2001), and *Jewish Slavery in Antiquity* (Oxford, 2005).

Rivka Parciack holds a Ph.D. from the Hebrew University in Jerusalem, where she now teaches at the Jewish folklore program. She has contributed essays on East European Jewish life to books and periodicals in Hebrew, English, and Polish and is the author of *Here and There, Now and in Other Days* [in Hebrew] (Hebrew University: Magnes Press, 2007) a study of Jewish cemeteries and memorial sites in Poland and Israel.

Orna Ben-Meir is a fashion and costume designer and museum curator. She holds a Ph.D. in theatre studies from Tel-Aviv University and teaches at the Shenkar College for Engineering and Design and the Kibbutzim College of Education. Her most recent exhibition (December 2007) was devoted to the scenographic work of Buki Shiff. Her research focuses on Israeli and Jewish theater, scenography and its links to the plastic arts, and fashion in its cultural context. She is currently working on a book on theatrical costumes.

Mayer Kirshenblatt is a self-taught artist living and working in Toronto. An exhibition of his work organized by the Judah L. Magnes Museum in 2007 will travel to the Jewish Museum (New York) and Jewish Historical Museum (Amsterdam), among others. *They Called Me Mayer July: Painted Memories of a Jewish Childhood in Poland before the Holocaust* was a finalist for the 2007 National Jewish Book Award. *Shtetl,* a video documentary about his work, premiered in 1995.

Barbara Kirshenblatt-Gimblett is university professor and professor of performance studies at New York University. Her books include *Image before My Eyes: A Photographic History of Jewish Life in Poland, 1864–1939* (with Lucjan Dobroszycki), *Destination Culture: Tourism, Museums, and Heritage,* and *The Art of Being Jewish in Modern Times* (edited with Jonathan Karp). Her edited volume *Writing a Modern Jewish History: Essays in Honor of Salo W. Baron* recently won a 2006 National Jewish Book Award. She was honored in 2008 with the foundation for Jewish Culture Achievement Award in Scholarship and with the Mlotek Prize for Yiddish Culture. She is currently leading the core exhibition development team for the Museum of the History of Polish Jews on the site of the former Warsaw Ghetto.

Robert A. Rothstein is professor of Slavic and Judaic studies and of comparative literature, and adjunct professor of linguistics at the University of Massachusetts Amherst, where he also holds the Amesbury Professorship in Polish Language, Literature, and Culture. Among his publications in the area of Yiddish studies are the entry on Ashkenazic folklore for the *Greenwood Encyclopedia of World Folklore and Folklife,* articles on Yiddish verbal aspect, Yiddish songs of drunkenness, Yiddish mixed-language songs, klezmer slang, Odessa at the intersection of Yiddish and Russian folk culture, language play in Yiddish folklore, and the translation of Moshe Beregovski's *Jewish Instrumental Folk Music,* which he co-edited.

Jeffrey Feldman is a cultural anthropologist and adjunct assistant professor at New York University, where he teaches in the Graduate Program in Museum Studies. He has examined the role of museums in modern Jewish culture and social life with a particular focus on art exhibitions and cultural projects in Europe. His recent publications include "Contact Points: Museums and the Lost Body Problem," (in *Sensible Objects,* edited by E. Edwards, Berg, 2007) and "The X-Ray and the Relic: Anthropology, Bones, and Bodies in Modern Italy" (in *In Corpore: Bodies in Post-Unification Italy,* edited by L. Polezzi, Fairleigh Dickenson, 2007). Feldman is also an expert on the framing of communication in American politics. His analyses of American politics can be read on *The Huffington Post* and his own Web site, *Frameshop.* He has published two books on politics and language, *Framing the Debate* (Ig Publishing, 2007) and *Outright Barbarous* (2008).

Shelly Zer-Zion earned her Ph.D. in theater studies from the Hebrew University of Jerusalem. She was a Fulbright post-doctorate fellow at the Department of Hebrew and Judaic Studies, New York University, and is currently a post-doctorate fellow at Tel Aviv University. She teaches at the Hebrew University of Jerusalem, Schechter Institute for Jewish Studies, and the University of California Santa Cruz. Her research focuses on the interconnections between Hebrew, Yiddish, and German theaters, a topic on which she has published several articles in English, Hebrew, and German.

Ayala Raz is senior lecturer at the Fashion Design Department, Shenkar College of Engineering and Design, and served as head of the Fashion Design Department in the years 1985–1992. Raz focuses her research on twentieth-century Israeli fashion and has contributed numerous articles to local and international periodicals on this topic. She is the author of *Changing Styles: A Hundred Years of Fashion in Israel* (in Hebrew, Yediot Acharonot, 1996). She is the author of the interactive multimedia knowledge base "Fashion's Lines: Designers and Styles in the 20th Century" (Tel-Aviv, Ort Israel, 1998). Ayala Raz has worked as a fashion designer and consultant and curated the exhibition, "First Settlers' Clothing," at the Rishon-Le'Zion Museum in Israel.

Andrew Ingall is an assistant curator at the Jewish Museum, New York. His essay, "Making a *Tsimes,* Distilling a Performance: Vodka and Jewish Culture in Poland Today," appeared in *Gastronomica—The Journal of Food and Culture* (University of California Press, 2003).

Sonya Rapoport, new media artist, is recognized as a pioneer in computer-based art, producing cross-cultural, interdisciplinary artworks and interactive installations since the mid-1970s. Her exhibitions venues include: Documenta; Ars Electronica; ISEA; Art Biennial-Buenos Aires; Museo Nacional Centro de Arte Reina Sofia, Madrid, BIOS 4, Centro Andaluz de Arte Contemporáneo, Seville; and the Whitney Biennial 2006, New York. She has contributed chapters or chapters are about her work in the publications *Art/Religion/Spirituality* (Sao Paulo, Brazil: Pronex/CNPq), *Art and Biotechnologie* (Montreal: University of Montreal Press), *Women Art and Technology* (MIT Press), *From Technological to Virtual Art* (MIT Press), and *Information Arts* (Cambridge, MA: MIT Press). Rapoport's writings and critiques appear in the MIT publication *Leonardo/ISAST,* where she serves on the Governing Board of Directors.

Dorit Yerushalmi holds a Ph.D. in Theatre Studies from Tel Aviv University and is a lecturer in the Theatre Departments at Haifa University. Her essays appeared in *Assaph: Studies in Theatre;* in *T.D.R.: The Drama Review* (in English); in *Motar, Teatron—An Israeli Quarterly for Contemporary Theatre;* and in *Mikan: Journal for Hebrew and Israeli Literature and Culture Studies* (in Hebrew). She recently served as guest co-editor of a special issue of *Zmanim* that was devoted to Israeli theater (Summer 2007). She is co-editor of a book of articles on the play *The Dybbuk* and its various productions.

Jeanette R. Malkin is senior lecturer and former chair of the Theatre Studies Department at the Hebrew University of Jerusalem. She is the author of *Memory-Theater and Post-modern Drama* (University of Michigan Press, 1999); of *Verbal Violence in Contemporary Drama: From Handke to Shepard* (Cambridge University Press, 1992); and co-editor of the forthcoming *Jews and the Making of Modern German Theater* (University of Iowa Press). Her articles on contemporary theater, on Heiner Müller, Thomas Bernhard, Samuel Beckett, and Robert Wilson, and on Jews in pre-1933 German theater have appeared in many academic journals and edited books.

INDEX